Ripley's Believe It or Not!®

Executive Vice President, Intellectual Property Norm Deska
Vice President, Exhibits and Archives Edward Meyer
Senior Director of Publishing Amanda Joiner

Editorial Manager Carrie Bolin
Editor Jessica Firpi
Junior Editor Jordie R. Orlando
Researcher Sabrina Sieck
Text Geoff Tibballs
Feature Contributors Jessica Firpi, Jordie R. Orlando, Sabrina Sieck
Factchecker James Proud
Indexer Yvette Chin
Proofreader Rachel Paul
Special Thanks to Ripley's Social Media Team

Designers Luis Fuentes, Penny Stamp
Production Coordinator Amy Webb
Reprographics *POST LLC
Cover Artwork Jordie R. Orlando, Sam South, Penny Stamp

Ripley's Believe It or Not!

SHATTER YOUR SENSES!

PUBLISHING

a Jim Pattison Company

www.ripleys.com/books

CONTENTS

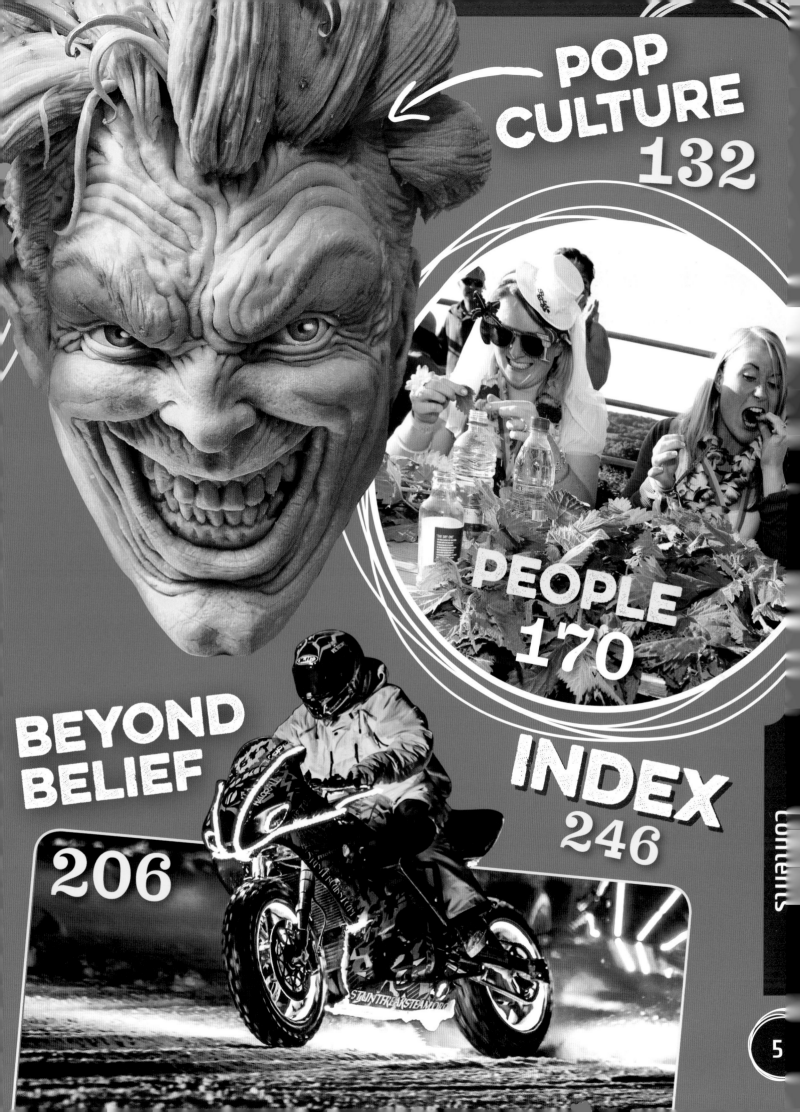

SEARCHING South America

Robert Ripley was the most traveled man of his time, always on the hunt for unusual items to add to his collection, and his "Ramble Around South America" may have been one of his most prolific trips.

In 1925, Robert Ripley set sail on his first and most extensive trip to South America. There, he would report back to the world on the wonderful things he saw in a syndicated feature column called Ripley's "Rambles Around South America," promising readers they'd "learn things about the continent that are not found in books."

Traveling along the border of the continent for 72 days, he did it all, from sailing through the Panama Canal to visiting the corpse of Saint Rosa in Lima (Ripley's hometown, Santa Rosa, was named for the pious Peruvian). Ripley even purchased his collection's very first shrunken head while in Peru!

Intrigued, Robert Ripley returned to South America in 1939, spending a good bit of time in Colombia, where some of his favorite stories were found.

ATTA-BOY

6½ INCHES TALL

REDUCED & MUMMIFIED HUMAN FIGURE

JIVARO — PERU

Ripley with Atta-Boy, a human from the Jivaro tribe in Peru, reduced to just six-and-a-half inches tall and mummified.

'ROUND THE WORLD WITH ROBERT RIPLEY

Following in Robert Ripley's footsteps, Ripley's Believe It or Not! Vice President of Exhibits and Archives Edward Meyer returned to Colombia in 2016 and made some unbelievable finds!

Colombian artist Ernesto Aviles Zambrano painted these tiny portraits, landscapes, and national symbols of his country in the early 1950s, shortly before going insane.

PAINTED ON A PIN HEAD THIS SIZE:

Werregue baskets are said to be so tightly woven that they will hold liquids without leaking! The werregue is a type of palm tree, and handcrafts made from its fibers come from a small community in the rainy jungles of the Colombian pacific, in the delta of the San Juan River. It can take up to several months to make just one basket!

Ripley's ——— Believe It or Not!

DOOLITTLE AND DALLEY ARE BUSINESS PARTNERS in Kidderminster, England

THE HAG FISH HAS 3 HEARTS

THE OLDEST LIVING MAN AND **JAVIER PEREIRA** BELIEVED TO BE 166 YEARS OLD —AND STILL IN GOOD HEALTH DISCOVERED IN THE ANDES MOUNTAINS, COLOMBIA BY A BELIEVE IT OR NOT EXPEDITION 1955

THE OLDEST WORKING MAN IN THE WORLD **CHARLES SMITH** of Auburndale, Fla. IS STILL EMPLOYED AT THE AGE OF 113 AND HAS WORKED REGULARLY FOR 100 YEARS! Submitted by DR. LEO L. SPEARS Denver, Colo.

RIPLEY VISITING WITH AN ANDES-INCA NATIVE

After his death, Believe It or Not! returned to Colombia on Ripley's behalf to discover Javier Pereira, the oldest man in the world. Believed to be 167 years old, Pereira was a Zenú Indian who claimed to have been born in 1789.

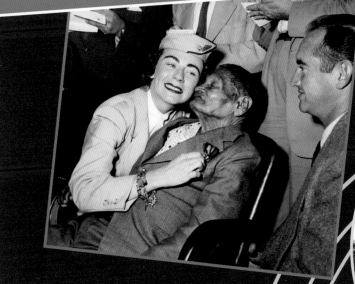

AMAZING ARTIST

Believe it or not, Zuly Sanguino of Bogota, Colombia, paints by holding the brush with her mouth. Zuly was born with tetra-amelia syndrome, a very rare disorder characterized by the absence of all four limbs.

→ **Robert Ripley was many things throughout his lifetime: traveler, writer, and cartoonist, to name a few, but one of his greatest loves was baseball.**

In 1913, he injured his arm while trying out for the New York Giants, leading him to pursue a career as a full-time artist. Despite this, Ripley retained his love for America's pastime, and in 1939, he formed a celebrity charity team that included the legendary Babe Ruth. In 2016, Ripley's Believe It or Not! and the Louisville Slugger Museum & Factory in Kentucky teamed up to create the Oddball exhibition, which featured over 100 baseball oddities, rare Ripley drawings, and exhibits made from typical ballpark snacks!

BEFORE BECOMING A CARTOONIST, RIPLEY PURSUED A BASEBALL CAREER!

BATTER UP!

BABE RUTH!

The Believe It or Not! baseball team at Madison Square Garden, May 5, 1939.

WAX ON!

➔ It was a busy year for the Ripley's F/X team! They were the first to create a wax figure of then-presidential candidate Donald Trump—and not just one figure, but three! Using photographs as a reference, it took about six weeks to hand-sculpt and create each likeness. On another presidential note, Ripley's recently acquired the famous dress Marilyn Monroe wore while singing "Happy Birthday" to John F. Kennedy. Our F/X team worked quickly to recreate the movie star's figure for display.

The Monroe F/X team casting the model's legs.

TRAVELING SHOWS ➔ Ripley's interactive Traveling Shows bring one-of-a-kind experiences to a global audience, including South Africa! The South Africa Traveling Show was a popular and successful exhibition from October 2016 to April 2017.

AMSTERDAM ATTRACTION

➔ In July 2016, Ripley's Believe It or Not! opened its newest attraction—in Amsterdam, the Netherlands! Located in Dam Square, the museum features five floors filled with 600 curiosities from around the world!

SHATTER YOUR SENSES!

➔ The Ripley's writers, researchers, and editors have spent the last year tracking down stories and photos so incredible you won't believe your eyes . . . or ears or nose!

But whether you believe it or not, every word in this book is true. Let Ripley's overwhelm your senses with more than a thousand stories that might make your skin crawl, but don't turn your nose up at it—you may find it's an acquired taste.

TOUCH

HEAR

SMELL

SEE

TASTE

TELL US WHAT SHATTERS YOUR SENSES!

KEEP IN TOUCH—if you have an amazing ability or see something extraordinary, let us know! Send us your photos or videos and you may be featured in the next book.

RIPLEYS.COM/SHATTERYOURSENSES

BRAIN INFESTATION → Yadira Rostro, of Garland, Texas, suffered terrible headaches for nine months—until a scan revealed that parasitic tapeworms were growing at the base of her brain. Doctors removed a piece of her skull and took eight larval sacs from her brain.

SNAIL MAIL → A postcard sent from London, England, to Llandudno, Wales, in 1960 was finally delivered in 2016. It had taken 56 years to travel just 240 mi (384 km).

LATE PAYMENT → In 2015, Kent Broyhill sent $100 to the University of Nebraska-Lincoln as payment for parking tickets that he had been handed more than 40 years earlier. He had tried to pay the fines before his 1974 graduation at the campus police station but was told that the school accepted only cash. As his pockets were empty, he was allowed to pay as soon as he could. He forgot all about the tickets for decades until a conversation with an old college friend made him realize he had not kept his promise.

COCKROACH FAMILY → When Mr. Li, 19, complained of an earache, doctors in Dongguan, China, found a family of 26 cockroaches—one adult and 25 babies—living in his ear canal.

INVERTED STAMP → A rare 24-cent Inverted Jenny U.S. postage stamp sold at auction in New York in 2016 for $1.3 million. A hundred stamps depicting a Curtiss Jenny biplane were accidentally printed upside down and circulated in 1918 until someone noticed the error, making them highly collectible.

SLEEP DISORDER → Those who suffer from the rare mysterious genetic condition Fatal Familial Insomnia are never able to sleep. Fewer than 40 families worldwide have been diagnosed with the disease, which begins in middle age and denies the body and brain the chance to rejuvenate, eventually leading to death.

BIRD SMUGGLER → In April 2016, a man was arrested at Tan Son Nhat International Airport in Ho Chi Minh City, Vietnam, after trying to smuggle 18 live songbirds stuffed down his pants. The birds were hidden in special pouches strapped to his legs.

TRAPPED HAND → Four-year-old Leo Shorthouse spent six hours with his hand trapped in a vending machine in Melbourne, Australia. Fire crews eventually freed the boy, who had managed to push his hand through three anti-theft mechanisms before it became stuck.

SELF-TYING SHOELACES → A German company has invented shoelaces that tie themselves. When you put on the smart shoe, pressure sensors reveal that your foot is in position and trigger a tiny motor in the heel that pulls the laces tight. To remove the shoes, you click your heels together twice and the motor releases a spring in the shoe's tongue, which loosens the laces.

HOMEMADE PANCREAS → When Andrew Calabrese's pancreas gave out at age three, leaving him facing Type 1 diabetes for the rest of his life, his father Jason, from San Diego, California, built an artificial pancreas system using a free online project, OpenAPS.

TRIBAL KING → In 2015, Eric Manu, a landscape gardener from Langley, British Columbia, Canada, learned that he was to be crowned king of a 6,000-person tribe in southern Ghana. His uncle was king of the Akan tribe until his death in 2013, and Eric was eventually chosen as his successor.

SNAIL HAZARD → A driver lost control of his car near Paderborn, Germany, after it skidded on the slimy trail left by a line of snails as they crawled across the highway. The car flipped over and was wrecked, but the driver was unhurt.

FIRE
Fishing

⊕ **With an average age of 60, only 30 fishermen in Jinshan, Taiwan, still fish for sardines using fire—a traditional method dating back hundreds of years.**

From May to July, these remaining fishermen use just three boats—of which there were originally 300—to net hundreds of sardines as they leap out of the water, attracted by the light. At night, the fishermen light a bamboo stick using chemicals and then wave the fire over the side of the boat. On a good night, the men can haul in 3–4 tons of sardines, earning them more than $4,500. Although the government provides the fishermen with a subsidy, their fascinating tradition is still at risk of becoming history.

UNWRAPPED & UNBELIEVABLE

SWALLOWED TOOTHBRUSH → Five-year-old Keshav Sahu, from Chhattisgarh, India, lived for almost a year with a 6-in-long (15-cm) toothbrush in his stomach before it was eventually removed in an operation. He had not told his parents that he had swallowed the toothbrush, so at first they kept giving him medicine for his stomach pains.

SLEEP DISORDER → Due to a rare neurological disorder, Jody Robson, from Birmingham, England, falls asleep for up to three weeks at a time. She is believed to have Kleine Levin Syndrome (also known as Sleeping Beauty Syndrome), which even caused her to sleep through the birth of her first child. She relies on her husband, Steven, to fill her in on the events of her lost weeks.

SHOE RIDDLE → If you take your shoe size, multiply it by 5, then add 50, multiply that number by 20, add 1016, and then subtract the year in which you were born, the answer will give your shoe size followed by your age (provided you have not yet had your birthday this year).

LEG BREAK → A four-year-old from Michigan had her leg broken more than 300 times to save it from being amputated. She was born with a rare disability called proximal femoral focal deficiency, which caused her left leg to be deformed and much shorter than her right leg. Her parents were initially presented with two treatment choices—amputation and prosthesis—before deciding that a better option was to have the girl's leg lengthened, a complex procedure that required her mother to break her daughter's leg three times a day for four months. By the end of the treatment, the girl's leg had grown by over 4 in (10 cm), enabling her to lead a more normal life.

It is estimated that the **ANCIENT EGYPTIANS CREATED** at least **70 MILLION** human mummies!

Some corpses have been found **MUMMIFIED WITH HONEY**—a process called mellification.

As late as 1970, New York City drug stores sold **POWDERED MUMMY** at $40 an ounce for medicinal purposes!

Per his request, British philosopher **JEREMY BENTHAM** was preserved upon his death in 1832. His clothed skeleton and mummified head are on display at the University College of London, where his body has at times **ATTENDED MEETINGS AND SPECIAL EVENTS!**

Tribes in West Papua, Indonesia, preserve the corpses of their relatives by **SMOKING THEM OVER A FIRE!**

In Victorian England, the Royal College of Surgeons once **SOLD TICKETS** to the public to watch an Egyptian mummy being fully unwrapped.

Due to a linen shortage, Egyptian mummies were imported to the U.S. during the **CIVIL WAR** so that their wrappings could be **MADE INTO PAPER!**

DISNEY TREAT → Chelsea Herline, from San Francisco, California, enjoyed a day out at Disney World in 2016 using a ticket from 1994. As a four-year-old she had visited the Orlando, Florida, attraction with her family on a four-day pass but was too ill to go on the last day. As the unused ticket had no expiration date, she was allowed back in for free 22 years later.

SEEING DOUBLE → Identical twin sisters Leah Rodgers and Sarah Mariuz gave birth on the same day in different cities, at the same time in their respective time zones. On June 30, 2016, Rodgers gave birth to a son, Reid Joseph, at 1:18 a.m. mountain standard time in Denver, Colorado, and exactly one hour later, Mariuz delivered a daughter, Samantha Lynne, at 1:18 a.m. Pacific daylight time in La Jolla, California.

STOLEN SIGN → A large blue metal antidrugs sign that was stolen from New Smyrna Beach, Florida, in the late 1980s during "a fit of youthful exuberance" was returned anonymously to the city police department in 2016 along with a $50 money order and a request for forgiveness.

AGE GAP → Janet Horrocks, age 57 from Lancashire, England, has worn blonde hair extensions and undergone $60,000 worth of cosmetic surgery so that she can look exactly like her 35-year-old daughter, Jane Cunliffe. The two women now look so similar that they are often mistaken for sisters.

SCHOOL HYSTERIA → After four children suddenly fainted in a "warm" classroom in North Yorkshire, England, it created a ripple effect that made dozens of their classmates feel ill, too. Investigating medics found that 40 students and one teacher had succumbed to nothing more than mass hysteria.

NAMESAKE TECHNIQUE → Forty-two years after the Heimlich maneuver was named after him, 96-year-old Ohio surgeon Dr. Henry Heimlich used the technique for the first time in an emergency situation to save the life of a woman who was choking on a hamburger. Noticing 87-year-old Patty Ris in distress at the dinner table, he jumped up from his seat, put his arms around her, and pressed on her abdomen to dislodge the food.

over 2,500 years old!

Ripley's Exhibit
Cat. No. 168047
Mummified Hand
Taken from a tomb
in the 1820s
Origin: Egypt

Believe it or not, in the 16th century, powder from ground-up mummy parts was used to make a color of paint—called "mummy brown"!

GOLDEN Monk

→ **The body of a monk was preserved in a giant pottery jar and removed three years later to be turned into a golden statue for worship.**

Buddhist monk Fu Hou died in 2012 at the age of 94 after practicing Buddhism for nearly 80 years in Quanzhou, China. As a way to honor his devotion and inspire others, mummification experts sealed his body in a large pot. After three years in the jar, the body was removed, cleaned, and covered in gold leaf. The body of Fu Hou now resides in a glass case on a mountain, where people can visit and worship.

Other than dried out skin, the body showed very few signs of deterioration. Monks whose bodies remain intact after mummification are said to be truly virtuous.

17

Skate Park Church

A 100-year-old derelict church in Llanera, Spain, has been transformed into a magical indoor skate park called Kaos Temple.

Built in 1912, the private church of Santa Barbara was abandoned in the 1930s and remained unused until the skating ramp was installed in 2012. Artist Okuda San Miguel covered the walls and vaulted ceilings with colorful geometric figures.

DYNASPHERE

Invented in 1930 by Englishman Dr. J. A. Purves, the Dynasphere was a single, giant motorized wheel meant to revolutionize transportation. Also nicknamed "Jumbo," the Dynasphere was just one of many "monowheels" designed in the early 1900s that never took off due to their inherent danger and impracticality. The Dynasphere was reported to reach speeds of 30 mph (48 kmph), however, it was nearly impossible to steer and braking too fast put the passengers at risk of "gerbiling." Gerbiling happens when the outer wheel stops but the inner wheel continues to spin, sending the driver into uncontrollable loops inside the Dynasphere—just like a gerbil going too fast on a hamster wheel!

HONEST DUTCH → A recent fall in the crime rate in the Netherlands means there are more empty cells than criminals in the prisons. So convicted felons from Belgium and Norway are sometimes sent to be kept in Dutch jails.

OVERDUE BOOK → A book borrowed from a library in Whitehorse, Yukon, in 1965 was returned 51 years later from New Zealand. *The Story of Madame Curie* was recently discovered and sent back to Whitehorse by Roslyn Selby, whose family had accidentally taken the book with them when they moved from Canada in 1967.

NIGHT VISION → Although he has just 10 percent of most people's vision during the day, legally blind Tim Doucette, of Quinan, Nova Scotia, Canada, can see much more than the average person at night—and has become a respected astronomer. Born with congenital cataracts, as a teenager he underwent an operation that removed the lenses from his eyes and widened his pupils. Since his pupils now let in a lot of light, by day everything he sees is too bright and overexposed, but by night, he has amazing vision and can pick out tiny objects in the dark sky that are invisible to people with regular sight.

MODEL MONSTER → When a 2016 scientific survey of Loch Ness, Scotland, identified a 30-ft-long (9-m) body on the floor of the lake, hopes were high that the legendary monster had finally been found. Instead, the remains turned out to be a model of the monster, which had been made for the 1970 movie *The Private Life of Sherlock Holmes* and had sunk during filming.

CEMENTED RELATIONSHIP → Nathan Atkinson proposed to Yasmin Pearce by using bricks and mortar to spell out the words MARRY ME YAZ on the internal walls of the house they were building together near Perth, Western Australia.

BALL HUNTER → Glenn Berger makes a living by retrieving up to 1.7 million lost golf balls every year from lakes on Florida golf courses. Selling them, he claims to have earned around $15 million from his unusual career. One hole alone—the "Island Hole" at TPC Sawgrass in Jacksonville—sucks down about 100,000 balls a year, but his diving missions are not without risk, as he once discovered when he felt his arm in an alligator's mouth.

SAME NAME → When Billy Wright, from Bournemouth, England, discovered a transatlantic doppelgänger on Facebook—with the same ginger hair, beard, mustache, and almost identical nose and eyes—he was stunned to learn that he and the stranger also share the same name! The other Billy Wright, from Athens, Pennsylvania, even has a similar job. U.K. Billy is a construction worker, and U.S. Billy is a metal worker.

PENNY DEPOSIT → Seventy-three-year-old Otha Anders, of Ruston, Louisiana, went to the bank and cashed in $5,136.14—all in pennies. The senior citizen transported his haul of over half a million pennies, which he had been collecting for more than 45 years, in fifteen 5-gal (19-l) plastic water jugs. It took bank staff five hours to count the coins.

LEAP DAY → On February 29, 2016, Chad and Melissa Croff, from Columbus, Michigan, welcomed their second leap-year day daughter. Baby Evelyn shares a birthday with older sister Eliana, who was born on February 29, 2012, the previous leap day.

SELFIE PERIL → In the first nine months of 2015, more people died while taking selfies than were killed by sharks. There were at least 12 selfie-related deaths across the world, compared to only eight deaths from shark attacks.

About 85 million years

About 65 million years

TIME

➲ Believe it or not, you live closer to when the Tyrannosaurus rex walked the Earth than when the Stegosaurus did! According to fossil records, the Stegosaurus lived more than 150 million years ago, while T. rex lived only 65 million years ago. Despite so many depictions of the T. rex and Stegosaurus fighting each other, it's impossible based on when they lived! Just like this mind-boggling fact, some parallel events in history seem so unlikely that they will warp your mind!

Frontiersman Daniel Boone begins to explore modern-day Kentucky.
Meanwhile . . .
The world's first car was invented by Nicolas Joseph Cugnot!

REPLICA OF THE FIRST CAR!

Plymouth Colony drafted its first law on October 4, 1636.
24 days later . . .
On October 28th, Harvard University was founded!

One thousand settlers set off down the Oregon Trail from Independence, Missouri, on May 22, 1843.

5 days later . . .
Scottish inventor Alexander Bain patented the fax machine, on May 27, 1843.

The Eiffel Tower was presented at the 1889 World's Fair.
That same year . . .
Nintendo was founded as a card company.

1636

1769

1843

1889

WARP

George Lucas's *Star Wars* was released on May 25, 1977.

Meanwhile . . .

France was still using the guillotine! The country's last beheading by the medieval device took place on September 10, 1977.

Time For Pizza?

Cleopatra lived closer in time to the building of **the first Pizza Hut** than the building of **the Egyptian pyramids!**

In 1959, Hawaii became the 50th state in the United States.

That same year . . .

The Daytona International Speedway, where the Daytona 500 takes place, officially opened.

Pixar's *Toy Story 3* is released on June 18, 2010.

That same day . . .

The last execution by firing squad in the United States occurred.

6 — 7 8 9 10 10 9 8 7 —

1959 1977 2010

FEELING BLUE

➔ At the edge of the Thar Desert in India lies a sea of blue—the city of Jodhpur. It is believed that the vibrant hue was originally used to identify the homes of Hindu priests, known as Brahmin. Over the years, others began following suit, and now almost the entire city is a stunning shade of sapphire. The blue pigment is also said to protect the houses from termites.

DOUBLE YOLKS ➔ Nikki Corbishley, from Wellington, New Zealand, discovered that every single egg in a carton she opened had two yolks. The odds of finding 12 double-yolk eggs from the same box are estimated to be one in a quintillion—that's 18 zeros!

OLYMPIC TRIPLETS ➔ The lineup for the women's marathon at the 2016 Rio de Janeiro Olympics included identical triplets from Estonia—the 30-year-old Luik sisters, Liina, Lily, and Leila. They were the first triplets ever to compete in the Olympic Games, let alone in the same event. Lily finished 97th, Leila was 114th, but Liina dropped out before the 22-mi (35-km) mark.

UNEXPLODED SHELL ➔ Kathryn Rawlins, from Warwickshire, England, was shocked to discover that the object she had used as a flower vase for 30 years was really an unexploded World War I bombshell, which could have killed anybody within 66 ft (20 m) and blown up her entire house. She had found it buried in the playing fields of her old school and had filled it with water and her favorite flowers for decades, until in 2015 when she saw a TV war documentary and realized that it was a live shell.

Sliced Noodles

➔ In August 2016, at the annual Shanxi wheaten food festival, more than 100 cooks sliced noodles into a massive boiling cauldron with a diameter of 22 ft (6.7 m)!

The feat was an awesome sight to behold as each chef stood in front of the huge pot and shaved off bits of dough into the water. Knife-shaved noodles are a kind of traditional dish for locals of Shanxi Province, China, so the event attracted hundreds of spectators hoping to get a taste.

Here a cook uses a 3.5-ft-long (1.07-m) broadsword to slice noodles.

SHEEP GAS → In November 2015, a Singapore Airlines flight from Sydney, Australia, to Kuala Lumpur, Malaysia, was forced to make an emergency landing because the gas passed by the airplane's cargo of 2,186 sheep had set off smoke alarms.

FOREIGN ACCENT → When Lisa Alamia, of Rosenburg, Texas, woke from the anesthetic after undergoing jaw surgery, she found herself speaking with an upper-class English accent—despite the fact that the only time she has ever been outside the United States was to visit Mexico. She has been diagnosed as suffering from the rare neurological disorder known as Foreign Accent syndrome.

EGG SMASH → After a truck carrying 120,000 eggs crashed on a highway in Jiangsu Province, China, the mass of yolk from the broken eggs caused traffic to be delayed for several hours.

MARRIAGE PROPOSAL → Ben Kemp, of Roseworthy, South Australia, spelled out "Will you marry me" in bales of hay across a bushfire-ravaged field and then took girlfriend Jadine Mold up in a helicopter so that she could read—and say "yes" to—the proposal.

GOOD DEED → Norwegian real estate broker Vemund Thorkildsen found $55,000 hidden underneath the fireplace of his new Oslo apartment—and donated it all to charity.

CALORIE COUNTER → Wenyao Xu, a computer scientist at the State University of New York in Buffalo, has created a hi-tech necklace that counts the calories you consume by listening to the sounds you make when chewing different foods.

FIRST DRINK → At the 2016 Bridgewater Country Fair, volunteer firefighter Jim Lillis downed the first alcoholic drink served in the small Connecticut town for 81 years. Bridgewater had been the last dry town in the state until residents recently approved alcohol sales.

HUGE DIAMOND → A diamond nearly the size of a tennis ball was found at the Karowe mine, Botswana, in 2015. The 1,109-carat stone is the second largest diamond ever discovered, behind the Cullinan Diamond, which is featured in the U.K. royal family's crown jewels.

MARRIED PHONE → Los Angeles artist Aaron Chervenak loves his smartphone so much that he married it in a special ceremony at a chapel in Las Vegas, Nevada, on May 20, 2016. He wore a tuxedo for the occasion and even placed a ring on the phone.

DOUBLE DECKER → Paul Caspers, a plumber from Edmonton, Alberta, Canada, spent four months building a street legal, hybrid vehicle consisting of an old yellow school bus with a 1973 Bay Window Volkswagen welded to its roof. The strange double decker is called the Bustache because of the small mustache painted on the front of the VW. It has sleeping space for 13 people, with an internal trap door allowing access to the top deck, and its own outdoor shower.

ABSENT WORKER → Joaquin Garcia, a supervisor for a water company in Cadiz, Spain, failed to show up for work for six years—and nobody noticed. Managers only realized he was missing when he was to be presented with a long-service award.

BOY DRIVER → Police in Jinan, China, stopped a car in a routine check and found a 10-year-old boy driving himself to school with his grandma in the passenger seat.

MEDICAL MIRACLE → Born with his heart outside his rib cage, Arpit Gohil, of Gujarat, India, was not expected to survive, but in 2015, the "medical miracle" celebrated his 18th birthday. He has a rare condition called Pentalogy of Cantrell, which means that his heart beats just millimeters below his skin and the slightest bump or fall could kill him instantly. Nevertheless, he works as a farm laborer and is able to drive a tractor and till the land.

CONSTANT SNEEZING → Twelve-year-old Katelyn Thornley, of Angleton, Texas, contracted a mystery condition that caused her to sneeze 12,000 times a day—sometimes sneezing 20 times per minute.

RING LOCATED → When Jay Bradford, of Belmar, New Jersey, lost his wedding ring after it fell off his finger and sank to the bottom of the ocean while he was fishing, his hopes of ever finding it seemed nil. Four days later, however, boat captain Nick Barsa defied 35 mph (56 kmph) winds and used GPS coordinates to locate the exact spot where the ring was lost; then salvage diver Mark Thompson took just 10 minutes to find the band resting on a rock.

BOTTLED PUTIN → Shoppers in Moscow, Russia, can buy a new cologne said to smell like President Vladimir Putin. Created by perfumer Vladislav Rekunov, who says it captures Putin's personality in a bottle, Leaders Number One sells for $130 and contains hints of lemon, blackcurrant, and fir cones.

ROOSTER OUSTED → Early cuckoo clocks featured the sound of a rooster, but its multi-note call was difficult for the clock's mechanism to replicate, so the simple two-note call of a cuckoo became popular.

CLEAN GETAWAY → After escaping custody in Jasper County, East Texas, fugitive Wesley Evans was found hiding in the dishwasher in his girlfriend's apartment, having first removed the racks.

> People suffering from Alice in Wonderland Syndrome see objects as much smaller or larger than they really are.

PRESIDENT'S HAIR → A lock of hair from Thomas Jefferson sold at auction in Dallas, Texas, in 2016 for $6,875—nearly 190 years after the former president died.

MONEY TRAIL → For more than three years, a mystery benefactor has been hiding over $50,000 worth of $100 bills in various locations around Salem, Oregon, for strangers to find and keep.

FLUKE SHOT → Off-duty sheriff's deputy Jose Marquez produced a shot in a billion when he fired a bullet straight down the barrel of a suspect's gun, thereby disabling it. Marquez was visiting his girlfriend's apartment in Aurora, Colorado, when two suspects approached him in the parking lot with their guns drawn. One was wounded in the leg and arrested, while the other got away.

RARE BIRTH → In January 2016, the first baby born in the Italian town of Ostana in 28 years was delivered. The small Alpine town boasted more than 1,000 residents a century ago, but many moved out and now there are only 85 residents, only about half of whom live there all year-round.

RING SEARCH → When Bernie Squitieri, from St. Louis, Missouri, realized he had accidentally thrown his wife Carla's $400,000 wedding ring out with the garbage, the couple were allowed to search the truck on its way to the landfill site—and found the ring after sifting through 3,000 sq ft (279 sq m) of trash.

CHEESE AVALANCHE → Tomasz Wisniewski, of Shropshire, England, was rescued after spending eight hours trapped under a mountain of cheese. The forklift truck driver was buried beneath an avalanche of cheddar and Red Leicester when giant 44-lb (20-kg) blocks of cheese collapsed at a warehouse. Fire crews eventually pulled him out, unharmed.

NO TWO ALIKE!

⊙ Photographer Michelle Lynn Fritz was able to capture these delicate, snowflake-like patterns on bubbles as they froze over during a frigid Pennsylvania winter. Fritz typically photographs flowers, but the chilly air left no blossoms for her to shoot. Instead, she took to her backyard with a mixture of children's bubble solution and glycerin, blew some bubbles, and began taking pictures of the beautiful, flower-like patterns that bloomed during the freezing process.

SPECIMEN
STUFFED SHELVES

⊕ **Hundreds of thousands of dead birds, mammals, fish, plants, minerals, historical artifacts, and more are stored at the Smithsonian National Museum of Natural History in Washington, D.C.**

Believe it or not, less than 1 percent of the museum's collections are on public display at any given time. The rest are carefully labeled and sorted into drawers, jars, and shelves, where they can be easily found for display or scientific research. Multiple versions are kept of every specimen so scientists have a more complete picture of what a species, area, or culture was like at specific times throughout history.

Clown CORPSE

⊙ **Carl Crew is the proud owner of the body of a 105-year-old clown named Achile Chatouilleu!**

Crew runs the California Institute of Abnormalarts, or CIA, located in North Hollywood, California. It's part-museum, part-sideshow, and all weird! The embalmed body of a man who died in 1912 and asked for his body to be displayed forever in his favorite clown costume is now one of its most popular attractions.

Q *How did you come to possess the body of a dead clown?*

A A family came through, and they were talking about their circus ranch, which houses all these crazy things—one of them was a relative on display. Since they were always away from the ranch and their relative never really got to be shown, I told them, "Bring him down!" and they did, 21 years ago. Now they come back every year, and we do a memorial service for Achile Chatouilleu.

What does "Achile Chatouilleu" mean?

The translation is "The French Tickler."

How was the body of Chatouilleu preserved?

His family had him hermetically sealed in clown makeup,

Shriners parade in 1906 in Detroit. He was one of the last bodies to be gravity embalmed. They used to strap the body down to a table and then turn it upside down, letting gravity pull the chemicals into the body while it bled out.

Do you perform any upkeep on the body, such as touching up makeup?

No way, I'd have to call hazmat! He's embalmed with mercury and arsenic—very toxic.

Are there any other preserved bodies at the CIA?

We have two other bodies. One of them is Madame Wong, and she is a midget magician jewel thief. Fot Choy was a magician from underground opium dens in San Francisco.

Fot Choy with his golden teeth.

ACCORDING TO CREW, THE CROSS IN MADAME WONG'S HAND WAS THE LAST THING SHE STOLE BEFORE BEING CAUGHT!

SPECIAL DAY → Jodie and Mark Ballingall and their daughter Libbie all share the same birthday—August 1—beating odds of 48 million to one. Libbie arrived nine days late at a hospital in Worcestershire, England, having been due on July 23, 2016.

APT NAME → A freight train car that derailed in Charles City, Iowa, caused $10,000 worth of damage to a trackside bar called DeRailed!

HIDDEN TREASURE → Angela and Angus Milner-Brown, from Biggar, Scotland, bought an old chair for $7.50 at an auction, but kept it in the attic for nearly 10 years because they could not afford to have it upholstered. When they finally had the chair restored, they discovered diamond jewelry worth $7,500 hidden inside.

FRUIT STOPS

→ Comparing typical bus stops to those in Japan is like comparing apples and oranges—literally. Originally designed and built for a 1990 expo in Osaka, Japan, these cute fruit-shaped bus stops are scattered all over the town of Konagai, and they've been a peachy feature for 25 years. Tourists and locals can visit shelters shaped like giant melons, strawberries, oranges, or tomatoes. How do you like them apples?

SMILE PLEASE → A man who robbed a photo booth in Batavia, Illinois, of $75 made it easy for police by triggering the camera, which promptly reeled off a series of images. The photo machine is designed to take pictures automatically when it senses someone tampering with the cash drawer.

REPLACEMENT FINGERS → When Frank Barreda lost the fingers on his right hand after they were crushed in a workplace accident, doctors in Sydney, Australia, replaced them with his toes. He thought he had lost the use of his hand forever, but by rebuilding his blood vessels and nerves and transplanting his toes, surgeons have given the hand a new lease on life.

Ripley's Exhibit
Cat. No. 171876

Taxidermy Foosball
Taxidermy hamster and squirrel play foosball
Origin: Hungary

STILL WORKING → Three years after British scuba diver Adele Devonshire lost her camera in the sea off the coast of Berwickshire, Scotland, it washed up 600 mi (966 km) away in Sweden—in full working order.

FEW CLUES → A letter was delivered safely to Rebecca Cathrine Kaadu Ostenfeld's house in Búðardalur, Iceland, even though it had no name and address on the front—just a sketched map. The instructions on the letter told the postman to take it to "a horse farm with an Icelandic/Danish couple and three kids and a lot of sheep," adding that "the Danish woman works in a supermarket in Búðardalur." The letter was sent by a tourist who had stayed on the farm but could not remember the owner's name or address.

SWOLLEN NECK →
Hong Shu, from Guangzhou, China, developed a rare condition where huge, fatty deposits accumulated on his neck and throat and led him to be known locally as "the man with the horse's neck." A fatty tumor on his throat measured more than 6 in (15 cm) wide, while on his neck he had two lumps, both more than 7 in (17.5 cm) wide. The liquor-related condition—Madelung disease—left him struggling to eat, sleep, or breathe until doctors removed the growths in multiple surgeries.

STICKY WALLS → A bee infestation at Rookwood Hospital in Cardiff, Wales, caused honey to drip down the walls. When beekeepers investigated, they found a colony of more than 100,000 bees in the roof above one of the hospital wards.

TREE BED → The pilot of a microlight airplane spent a night stuck up a tree near Degenfeld, Germany, while waiting to be rescued. After crash-landing in the tree, he was left 100 ft (30 m) above ground for more than 12 hours because rescuers were unable to bring him down in the dark, for fear of dislodging the plane.

OPERATION TOOTHPICK →
When Horacio Rodriguez complained of "stabbing heart pains," doctors in Buenos Aires, Argentina, discovered the cause was a whole toothpick, which he had apparently swallowed a year earlier and had lodged in his heart. The toothpick was removed in a seven-hour operation.

VOMITING DISORDER → Sherrie Duggan, of Birmingham, England, was diagnosed with cyclical vomiting syndrome—a disorder that caused her to vomit up to 15 times an hour. To combat it, she has to eat a strict diet of white meat and boiled vegetables.

⊙ In May 2016, a pizzeria in Naples, Italy, gathered 250 pizza makers in a successful attempt at making the longest pizza in the world.

The event was held along the Naples waterfront, where chefs labored for 6 hours 11 minutes, creating a massive 1.15-mi-long (1.9-km) margherita-style pizza. Five traditional wood-burning pizza stoves were used to cook the creation. Amazingly, the team used more than 4,400 lb (1,996 kg) of flour, more than 3,500 lb (1,588 kg) of tomatoes, 4,400 lb (1,996 kg) of mozzarella cheese, 53 gal (200 l) of oil, and 66 lb (30 kg) of basil.

Nice SLICE

OVER 20 FOOTBALL FIELDS LONG!

BELATED DIPLOMA → On March 9, 2016, on her 93rd birthday, Dorothy Liggett finally received the high school diploma that she had been denied in 1942 because she was married. She had been just a few weeks from graduation from North High School in Akron, Ohio, when she was expelled after it was discovered that she had a husband. She was presented with the diploma 74 years later after her daughter wrote to the Akron Public Schools superintendent.

SISTERS REUNITED → Over 40 years after orphaned sisters Holly Hoyle O'Brien and Meagan Hughes were separated in South Korea, they found themselves working on the same floor at a hospital in Sarasota, Florida. The two women were both hired as nurse's aides at the Doctors Hospital within two months of each other in 2015—in the same department and working the same shift. As they became friends and started taking about their family histories, they learned that they shared the same Korean last name. It then dawned on them that they could be sisters, and a DNA test confirmed it.

SHARED PAST → In 2015, two men in their 90s who live in the same apartment block in Somerset, England, discovered that they had both taken part in the same World War II bombing mission over Graz, Austria, 70 years earlier. In June 1945, before George Rhodes and his fellow Allied soldiers entered a railway yard, RAF pilots including his neighbor Graham Brown dropped bombs on the city to clear the way for the ground troops.

ROAD BLOCK → A 90-minute car chase in Queenstown, New Zealand, ended when a 150-strong flock of sheep blocked the road and stopped the suspects' getaway. The car, which had been spotted speeding without license plates, was brought to a halt by a farm worker herding the flock along a rural road. Ironically, it later emerged that the sheep were owned by a local police officer.

TWO DARRELLS → Frustrated at not being able to vent their anger online at manager Darrell Clarke, who shuns social media, fans of English soccer club Bristol Rovers instead settled for bombarding the Twitter account of the Philadelphia City Council president, also named Darrell Clarke. They sent the U.S. politician numerous messages over a period of months, but he ignored all the tweets until he finally "liked" a fan's photo.

PROLONGED EXPERIMENT → An experiment on seed germination at Michigan State University has been running for almost 140 years and will not end until at least the year 2100. It began in 1879 when botanist Dr. William James Beal set out to discover how many times weeds need to be pulled out before they stop growing back entirely. He placed 50 seeds from 23 different plant types in 20 sand-filled bottles and buried them on the university campus to establish how long they can remain dormant without water or sunlight. Beal opened six of the bottles before he retired, and the experiment has been passed on to other scientists down through the decades.

SNOW DISGUISE → Wearing white camouflage against the snow, a 21-year-old man from Quebec, Canada, was arrested in Vermont in January 2016 while pulling a sled loaded with more than 180 lb (82 kg) of prescription pills across the border into the United States. Border agents were only alerted to his presence after he tripped a sensor on the railroad tracks.

ELECTION CONFUSION → Three candidates for the post of mayor at a 2016 election in the town of Draguseni, Romania, were named Vasile Cepoi. The victorious Vasile Cepoi was reelected for a fourth term, beating off the challenge of the other two Vasile Cepois. None of the three men are related.

ICING THE PUCK

In Kärnten, Austria, fearless free divers go beneath the ice and brave water temperatures as low as 35.6°F (2°C) to compete in a game of underwater hockey! Using the underside of the ice on a frozen lake as their hockey rink, two players hold their breath in 30 to 60 second bursts and attempt to score in their opponent's net before switching off with a teammate. An underwater ice hockey game lasts for three 10-minute periods—a long time to spend in frigid water! Above the ice, hot saunas are available to help warm up the chilly competitors.

www.magiclife.com

MAGICLIFE

Cracked Up

➡ Tourists smashed sledgehammers into the glass panels of the world's longest and tallest glass-bottomed bridge to demonstrate its safety!

The bridge spans 1,411 ft (430 m) across the Zhangjiajie Grand Canyon in China and hangs 984 ft (300 m) aboveground. It is lined with large panels of glass that tourists can walk across to reach the opposite side of the canyon. Every panel is made up of three layers of glass, each 0.6 in (15.2 mm) thick. Even with sledgehammers, no one was able to break through more than just the top layer!

A 4,409-lb (2,000-kg) car with 11 passengers was driven over the fractured glass to prove that the bridge is stable even when cracked!

Thirty people tried and failed to bust through an entire panel.

AUTO REBUILT → Experts rebuilt a 1928 vintage Bentley automobile whose parts were found scattered around the home and garden of its former owner—and put it up for sale for over $1 million. The 4.5-liter, art deco-styled car, one of only eight ever made, had been owned by Stuart Wallace, but following his death, the dismantled auto pieces were discovered all over his three-story home in London, England. A clutch was found on the stairs, the dashboard was in a spare bedroom, and the original headlights were hidden under a bed.

DOUBLE DELIGHT → Brothers Chris and Matt Hicks became fathers and uncles on the same day in 2015—and both their partners' babies were born at the same hospital in Kenosha, Wisconsin, and were delivered by the same doctor.

SKELETON BURIAL → After being kept in a cupboard at a school in Merseyside, England, for over half a century, "Arthur" the skeleton was given a proper burial in 2015 when teachers discovered that his bones were real and not plastic. He had been used for decades in science lessons until a laboratory technician decided to have his bones tested, and the results showed that they were those of a man from India who had died around 1900.

METEORITE GUNS → American company Cabot Guns created a pair of handguns almost entirely from a piece of a Gibeon meteorite that crashed on Earth about 4.5 billion years ago. The slides, frames, triggers, grips, and magazine releases are all made from the meteorite, which was discovered in Namibia, Africa, in the 1830s.

BOTTLE VOYAGE → In 2013, Terra Gallo put a message in a bottle and tossed it into the ocean off Monhegan Island, Maine. Three years later, she received a handwritten letter from a fisherman saying that the bottle had turned up 3,000 mi (4,800 km) away in Spain.

SNAP DECISION → Jessie Kinsinger tried to escape from police officers in Lakeland, Florida, by running into a lake, only to have his hand and forearm bitten off by a lurking alligator. When he crawled out of the water, three-quarters of his left arm were missing.

ANCIENT COIN → While hiking in eastern Galilee, Israel, Laurie Rimon noticed a shiny object in the grass and discovered a 2,000-year-old coin. The coin, dating back to 107 AD, shows the face of Emperor Augustus and is only the second of its kind to be found in the world.

NO SALES → In the six months that he worked as a car salesman in Texas after his return from the moon, Buzz Aldrin did not sell a single car.

DAILY HICCUPS → Lisa Graves, of Lincoln, England, has had hiccups every day for over eight years. She has hiccuped up to 100 times a day ever since she was four months pregnant with her first child, Emily.

STRANGE STRIKES

During a soccer match in the Democratic Republic of the Congo, all 11 members of the opposing team were killed by a bolt of lightning—the home team **CURIOUSLY CAME OUT UNHARMED.**

Aptly named **ROD WOLFE** of Chebanse, Illinois, has been struck by lightning **TWICE!**

Baseball pitcher Ray Caldwell of the Cleveland Indians was hit by lightning during a game in 1919—and **CONTINUED TO PLAY!**

U.S. Park Ranger Roy C. Sullivan **SURVIVED** being struck by lightning **SEVEN TIMES** between 1942 and 1977!

A typical lightning bolt is about the same circumference as a **U.S. QUARTER!**

The rod at the top of the Empire State Building takes about **100 STRIKES** of lightning per year!

PUMPING BLOOD → The human heart pumps blood around the body with such force that it could squirt it 30 ft (9 m) across a room.

BLUE DIAMOND → A single diamond was bought for $48.5 million by a Hong Kong businessman at an auction in Geneva, Switzerland. The rare and flawless Blue Moon Diamond sold for over $4 million per carat.

STILL ALIVE → A Spanish doctor who had been missing for 14 years before being declared dead in 2010 was found living as a hermit in Italy in 2015. Carlos Sanchez Ortiz de Salazar had disappeared from his home in Seville in 1996, and nothing had been heard from him until two villagers foraging for mushrooms stumbled across his camp in a Tuscany forest.

DOG IMPERSONATION → Chasing four suspects in the dark in Wiltshire, England, police officer Steve Hutton barked like a dog so convincingly that one of the men froze and gave himself up.

↑ YOUR UPLOADS

Deformed Plant

Barbara Norwick of Kinmount, Ontario, Canada, submitted this amazing photo of a blueweed plant exhibiting fasciation, or cresting, which is a rare condition of abnormal growth. Scientists aren't sure what causes the deformity, but they believe it is probably caused by a hormonal imbalance. This imbalance may be the result of a random genetic mutation, or it can be caused by insects or bacteria.

ROYAL DENTIST → Peter the Great (1672–1725), tsar of Russia, was an enthusiastic amateur dentist and would perform on the spot extractions on anyone he encountered who appeared to have a diseased tooth.

STURDY BAG → Martin McCaskie, of Mold, North Wales, has been reusing the same plastic shopping bag for over 35 years. He got the bag from a supermarket in 1981 and has used it for his groceries more than 2,000 times.

BIONIC ARM → James Young, from London, England, has a battery-operated, custom-built bionic arm that incorporates a phone charger, a flashlight, a smartwatch, and even a drone. He lost his left arm after falling under a train in 2012, and the design of the keen gamer's new metal arm is loosely based on Venom Snake's bionic limb in *Metal Gear Solid V*. It is also fitted with a plastic hand that is worked by the muscles in his back. The muscle signals are detected by sensors and enable him to pick up tiny objects such as coins.

PINEAPPLE LEATHER → Developed by Dr. Carmen Hijosa in the Philippines, piñatex—or vegan leather—is an eco-friendly material that looks like leather but is made from pineapple leaves.

People with porphyrophobia have a deep, persistent fear of the color purple. Just seeing a purple car or house door can induce a panic attack.

MIRACLE BABY → Delarine Saisi, a seven-month-old baby girl, was pulled out alive from the rubble of a six-story building in Nairobi, Kenya, four days after the block collapsed in May 2016.

GATECRASHERS WELCOME → Shelly Osterhout and Paul Johnson invited gate-crashers to attend their wedding reception at a shopping mall in Fort Myers, Florida—and around 200 total strangers showed up.

OLD STUDENT → With his bushy white beard and walking stick, 68-year-old grandfather Durga Kami attends school in the same class as 14 and 15 year olds. He was unable to finish his studies as a child, so now he goes to the Shree Kala Bhairab higher secondary school in Phedikhola, Nepal, six days a week to complete his education.

REPORTED DAD → When Michael Richardson ran a red light in Quincy, Massachusetts, his six-year-old son Robbie, sitting in the back seat, immediately called 911 to report it. After speaking to the operator, he handed the phone to his father, who apologized for the violation. Robbie wants to be a police officer when he grows up.

RUN RUN REINDEER

→ A single strike of lightning killed 323 reindeer near Hardangervidda, Norway—possibly the deadliest lightning strike in history.

Reindeer herds typically stay close to one another, but during a heavy thunderstorm on August 26, 2016, it is speculated that they may have gathered even closer out of fear, making them an easy target for Mother Nature.

believe it!

33

CAPTAIN

and **MAYBELLE**

ELECTRICITY FLOWS THROUGH CAPTAIN'S BODY AND OUT OF THE SWORD TO LIGHT MAYBELLE'S TORCH!

HIGH VOLTAGE

SWALLOWING A BLADE ATTACHED TO A BAR WEIGHED DOWN BY CINDER BLOCKS!

⊙ **Chris and Elaine Steele, of Atlanta, Georgia, have been performing classic sideshow stunts as vaudeville couple Captain and Maybelle for over 17 years, setting world records along the way and capturing the world's attention on *America's Got Talent*, season 6.**

Their show includes a variety of feats, including eye-socket weight lifting, glass eating, fire breathing, human suspension, and of course, sword swallowing. A fixture during Ripley's yearly World Sword Swallower's Day festivities, Captain became the new record holder for "weighted sword swallowing" when he downed a 17-in (43-cm) blade with 84 lb (38 kg) of weights attached! Captain also blew over 500 fire balls while filming a fire breathing sequence for *The Hunger Games: Catching Fire* movie.

Ripley's EXCLUSIVE

Q *How long have you guys been performing?*

A CAPTAIN: I've been weird my whole life, but I started entertaining about 17 years ago. Maybelle and I got together in 2008 and started performing as a couple. Of course, that's when we got our momentum, once we started performing together.

Why did you start sword swallowing and doing other classic sideshow acts?

C: Fascination. When I was young, I would go to the carnival, and I was fascinated with the entertainers, from fire breathers to sword swallowers. But I was more fascinated once I knew it was real, that it wasn't an illusion. In my mind, if they could do it, I could do it.

Captain performs a human blockhead routine with a running power drill!

Q Were you each into sideshow acts before you guys met?

A **MAYBELLE:** When we met, we both had an interest in sideshow acts and in extraordinary things. After we'd been together for a couple years, he decided he was going to learn how to sword swallow.

Which stunt was the most difficult to learn?

CAPTAIN: Sword swallowing was by far the hardest to learn, but it was also the most gratifying to get. It took about 4 ½ years before I was honestly able to take that sword, and I was even injured in the process. It scared me, because I realized it is very life threatening.

What is your favorite stunt to perform?

M: It really depends on the crowd. One of the things that is so easy but gets the biggest reaction is when he does the blockhead trick [hammers a nail into his nose], and I pull the nail out and then lick it. People will leave the show. They gag. They don't want to watch anymore. But I think my favorite part is the interaction and the comedy that we incorporate between us.

C: The hardest thing we do is talk on the microphone, carry a crowd. A stunt is always better if you're building it up and you've got them on the edge of their seat.

M: If I can get a laugh out of somebody, that's what I want, and if he can make them cringe, then that's what he wants.

Have you had any accidents?

C: I was practicing swallowing swords, and you have an esophageal sphincter that's inside of your body that you're pushing and forcing through in the beginning. Every muscle in my esophagus was restricted and squeezing that sword, then I pulled it out, and literally bruised and busted blood vessels all the way from my throat to my stomach. It didn't involve large amounts of bleeding, but it took well over a week for me to even swallow my own saliva.

M: He faced dehydration, so we had to get fluids in him. He lost 17 lb (7.7 kg) in one week because he could not even eat food.

Interesting stories you'd like to share?

M: The Bahamas! We got hired a couple years ago to go to the Bahamas. A former member of Parliament would bring anywhere from 8 to 20 circus entertainers to the Bahamas, and he would have us perform in two or three different primary schools a day all across the islands. These kids had never seen a circus, never seen a magician pull a rabbit out of a hat.

C: Those kids went nuts 'cause they'd never seen a rabbit other than on TV. We performed for 15,000 kids in 16 days. It was amazing.

M: I think it was the feeling of giving these kids something that they'd never seen before and making that connection with them. Traveling from school to school and seeing their living conditions: not one had a cell phone, not one had an electronic. It's something that's stuck with me for so long.

C: We took more away than they honestly did. When I left there, it made me look at the world completely different.

13 SWORDS!

SHE SWALLOWS & DIGESTS THE WHOLE BALLOON!

Q Which one of you has more tattoos?

A Me, I have about 450 hours' worth of tattoo work on me. Pretty much my entire body is covered. I made a promise to my wife I would never do a tattoo on my face until I was 50 years old.

Captain uses his eye sockets to lift a bucket holding a 10-lb (4.5-kg) brick!

Ripley's
Believe It or Not!
www.ripleys.com/books

Once one of the most popular roadside attractions in the United States, the Weeki Wachee mermaids have been performing underwater since 1947.

Weeki Wachee
MERMAIDS

People from far and wide traveled to the secluded town of Weeki Wachee Springs, Florida, to marvel at the mermaids—even the "King of Rock and Roll" himself, Elvis Presley! The original 18-seat theater was built 6 ft (1.8 m) deep into the limestone of a spring and featured large glass panels to watch the performances through. As the show's popularity grew, so did the venue, and in 1959, a new theater able to hold 500 spectators was built 16 ft (4.9 m) underwater.

The attraction was the creation of dive instructor Newton Perry, who developed a method of breathing underwater without using an unwieldy tank strapped to the back. Instead, the mermaids he trained breathed from free-flowing air hoses that were far less noticeable and allowed the swimmers to participate in stunts that would be awkward to perform in scuba gear. The shows are still performed to this day, using many of the same techniques mastered 70 years ago.

SURPRISE DISCOVERY → When Dave Cook, of Chesterfield County, Virginia, bit into a McDonald's cheeseburger, he found a $20 bill sandwiched between two pieces of meat under the bun.

TOO SIMILAR → After identical twin brothers married identical twin sisters, all four decided to undergo minor cosmetic surgery so that they could tell each other apart. Zhao Xin and his twin brother Zhao Xuan from Shanxi Province, China, married twin sisters Yun Fei and Yun Yang from a nearby village in February 2016, but friends and family constantly complained that they could not distinguish them. The surgery decision was taken after one brother found himself holding the hand of his sister-in-law one night after dinner. The couples even drive identical white Volkswagen cars, with just a one letter difference on the license plate.

INVENTED LANGUAGE → Forty percent of twins speak to one another in an invented language that only they can understand, a phenomenon called idioglossia.

The talented mermaids perform in 16 to 20 ft (4.9 to 6 m) depths and sometimes have to swim against a 5 mph (8 kmph) current!

AIR HOSE FOR BREATHING!

LEMON SMUGGLER → A woman on a flight from Hong Kong was barred from entering New Zealand after border officials at Auckland Airport discovered that she was hiding six lemons in her underpants. It is illegal to bring any food into New Zealand that could harbor pests or diseases.

HOSPITAL PROPOSAL → When Kristopher Jones, of Merseyside, England, woke from a three-week-long coma, the first thing he did was propose to his girlfriend Charlotte Pilling from his hospital bed. He had undergone emergency bowel surgery and at one stage had been so ill his family was told he would not survive.

FRIED SNAKES → Workers sent to disconnect the power at a home slated for demolition in Morganton, North Carolina, found two dead snakes in the electrical box. One snake had slithered across two hot terminals and was electrocuted, and the second snake received a lethal jolt when it tried to eat the first.

USEFUL BOOK → In 2016, Dr. Michael Kelly, a leading plastic surgeon in Miami, Florida, returned a 40 years overdue library book, along with a $500 donation. He had borrowed the book from the Kanawha County Library, West Virginia, in the mid-1970s but had forgotten all about it until he recently found it on a bookshelf at his home. Its title? *So You Want To Be a Doctor*.

TOILET BEDS → In 2016, New York City placed 50,000 oysters in Jamaica Bay—on beds made with the porcelain from 5,000 recycled toilets.

RARE CONDITION → Ollie Trezise, of Maesteg, Wales, was born with encephalocele, a rare condition which caused his brain to grow through a crack in his skull and into his nose. The protruding sac it created gave him a bulbous nose, prompting his mom, Amy Poole, to call him her "real-life Pinocchio."

CEREAL BAT → Sehr Rafique, of Glasgow, Scotland, found a fur-covered, decomposing bat at the bottom of a box of breakfast cereal.

JACK

GREEN PARADE

→ If you're ever in the town of Hastings, England, at the beginning of May, you might want to paint yourself green and join the Jack in the Green Festival! The seaside town hosts a four-day event that attracts thousands who come to revel in the folk dancing and merriment, all to celebrate the start of summer. The main event is the parade, which sees costumed individuals (known as "bogies") covered in green paint and garlands make their way to Hastings Castle, where they symbolically slay "Jack" to free the spirit of summer.

CRAZY CROCHET

➔ This house isn't painted pink—it's covered in yarn! A team led by New York artist Olek crocheted yards upon yards of the vibrant material in order to cover two houses—one in Avesta, Sweden, and another in Kerava, Finland. The women worked in pieces, crocheting large squares and then connecting them together like an oversized quilt.

WRONG NUMBER ➔ Trying to call home from the International Space Station on Christmas Eve 2015, British astronaut Tim Peake accidentally phoned the wrong number. Instead he asked a total stranger, "Hello, is this planet Earth?" prompting her to think it was a prank call.

CHEESE MISSION ➔ Eighty-two-year-old Anthony LoFrisco, of Wilton, Connecticut, drove seven hours to Ottawa, Ontario, Canada, just so that he could be the first person to cut into a 1,000-lb (454-kg), 12-ft-long (3.6-m) chunk of Italian provolone cheese.

PRESCHOOL CRUSH ➔ It was not until a year after their first date that Amy Giberson and Justin Pounders, of St. Petersburg, Florida, discovered that they had a crush on each other as three-year-olds—30 years earlier. They met as adults through an online dating service, and when they learned that they had both been at the same preschool at the same time, their parents produced a photo of them together as little children.

TWIN BIRTHS ➔ Twin brothers Stefan and Gareth Kershaw live on opposite sides of the world—but their wives Katie and Kate gave birth on the same day. On October 13, 2015, Stefan and Katie became parents in Cheshire, England, as did Gareth and Kate 10,000 mi (16,000 km) away in Australia—even though the two mothers had different due dates.

LOTTERY LUCK ➔ Construction worker Bruce Magistro, from New York, won a $1 million lottery prize twice in four years, beating odds of two billion-to-one.

MUG SHOT ➔ Unhappy with the mug shot that police officers in Lima, Ohio, had posted of him on their Facebook page, drunk driving suspect Donald "Chip" Pugh sent them another photo that he felt was more flattering.

SHAME SIGN ➔ Convicted of stealing from a store, Gregory Davenport, of Youngstown, Ohio, chose to wear a sign reading "I AM A THIEF. I STOLE FROM WALMART" instead of spending 30 days in jail. Judge Jeffrey Adler gave Davenport the choice, which required him to wear the sign in front of the store for eight hours a day over a period of 10 days.

INSTAGRAM COUPLE ➔ Erica Harris, from Murietta, California, and New Yorker Arte Vann got married at Ontario International Airport, California, in January 2016 just minutes after meeting in person for the first time. They had first made contact 10 months earlier on Instagram, where she had been attracted by his avatar.

GOAT YOGA ➔
Lainey Morse of Albany, Oregon, knows how to get zen in the goat pen—by offering goat yoga classes at No Regrets Farm! The goats roam freely during these outdoor sessions, interacting with patrons between poses!

MISSION: INSTALL

➡️ **In May 2016, the 66,000-lb (30,000-kg) ET-94 space shuttle fuel tank made its way slowly through the streets of Los Angeles, California, surprising crowds of onlookers and spawning the hashtag #ETcomeshome.**

The rust-colored 15-story-tall tank crawled along at about 5 mph (8 kmph) on route to its new home at the California Science Center, where it is now displayed with the retired space shuttle *Endeavour*. A team of 30 engineers worked out the elaborate logistics, which required crews trimming trees and removing utility lines, street lines, and even traffic lights as it made its way through town. The California Science Center is now the only place in the world visitors can see a complete space shuttle stack in launch configuration.

WARTIME SWEETHEART ➔ In 2016, 93-year-old widower Norwood Thomas, of Virginia Beach, Virginia, flew 9,770 mi (15,730 km) to Adelaide, Australia, to be reunited with his wartime girlfriend, 88-year-old Joyce Morris, more than 70 years after they first met. The pair originally met in London, England, in 1945 but lost contact after a misunderstanding and went on to marry other people. However, in 2015, Morris, by then a divorcee, asked one of her sons to search for Thomas online and was able to locate him and arrange a meeting.

WEIGHTY PROBLEM ➔ Before being put on a crash diet, Arya Permana, age 10, from Cipurwasari, Indonesia, weighed a whopping 422 lb (192 kg). Always hungry, he ate five oversized meals a day and ballooned so much that he could not walk without assistance and wore a sarong because his parents could no longer find clothes that fit him. He also had breathing problems because of his weight and had to sleep with his head leaning against a wall, which left him with a permanently bruised forehead.

MISSING SHIPWRECK ➔ Nearly 100 years after disappearing on its voyage from California to American Samoa, the wreck of the USS *Conestoga* was found 185 ft (56 m) deep in the ocean about 20 mi (32 km) west of San Francisco. The Navy tugboat with its 56 officers and crew went missing after departing the Golden Gate strait on March 25, 1921—16 years before the Golden Gate Bridge opened—and a three-month-long search found no trace of the vessel.

THREE TORNADOS → The town of Codell, Kansas, was hit by a tornado on the same date, May 20, for three consecutive years—1916, 1917, and 1918.

CRAB DRESSING → Scientists at the University of Bolton in England have invented a bandage made from crab shells that is supposed to heal wounds faster than conventional dressings. They spent 10 years developing the new technique, which uses chitosan, a mineral found in crustacean shells that kills bacteria and speeds up the healing process.

SELECTIVE EATER → Jodie Brown, from Wolverhampton, England, had a selective eating disorder for more than 10 years, causing her to eat only lemon curd sandwiches and feel sick if she tried anything else. After a hypnotherapist finally cured her, she started tasting new foods and can no longer bear to look at lemon curd sandwiches!

GREAT SURVIVOR → Over the course of four years, Kyle Cook of Lakeland, Florida, survived a lightning strike, a bite from a venomous spider, and a bite from a rattlesnake. In 2012, a bolt of lightning knocked him back 6 ft (1.8 m), rendered him unconscious for a minute, and caused him to have a mild heart attack; in April 2016, a recluse spider bit his left hand, requiring him to undergo surgery to drain the toxins; and in August 2016, a rattlesnake attacked him in his backyard, resulting in another trip to hospital, although luckily the venom did not get into his bloodstream. Before these recent misadventures, he had also survived bites from an alligator and a Burmese python.

BIRTHDAY ODDS → In a room of 23 people, there is a 50 percent chance of two people sharing a birthday. With a group of 75 people, there is a 99.9 percent chance.

MIRACLE CURE → Colin Seaman of Norfolk, England, suffered excruciating migraines almost every day for 50 years until they suddenly stopped after he had an ear pierced. The 70-year-old grandfather had tried all manner of drugs and injections without success and once even clipped clothes pins onto his face, but it was only the piercing that miraculously cured the headaches.

NO NOSE → Baby Angelito Zavaleta was born in Chimbote, Peru, without a nose. Instead of a nose, he was born with two tubes growing out of his face—the result of a rare genetic disorder called Patau syndrome. In time he will have an operation to treat the malformation and give him a normal nose.

NEWFOUND SKILL → Roy Calloway, age 78, from Swansea, Wales, had never been able to play a musical instrument, but after suffering a stroke, he suddenly found he could play the piano.

TRAGIC COINCIDENCE → In July 1974, 17-year-old Neville Ebbin was riding his moped in Hamilton, Bermuda, when he was hit by a taxi and killed. Almost exactly one year later, his younger brother Erskine, then 17 himself, was killed riding the same moped on the same road by the same taxi driven by the same man—and carrying the same taxi passenger.

BRONCOS SWEATERS → In the buildup to Super Bowl 50, Rebecca Herberg knitted Denver Broncos sweaters for the 150 baby goats that were expected to be born in the spring of 2016 on her farm at Montrose, Colorado. She knitted orange sweaters for the female goats and blue ones for the males.

NIGHTTIME MYSTERY → Young brothers Shoaib Ahmed and Abdul Rasheed, from Pakistan's Balochistan Province, lead normal active lives by day, but at night they are left paralyzed, unable to open their eyes, move, eat, or talk. Local people have dubbed them the "solar kids" because they believe the boys get energy from the sun, but puzzled doctors dismissed the theory after observing that the brothers remain active when it is cloudy or when they are kept in a darkened room during the day.

NINJA DOG ⊙ IKEA Japan introduced the Ninja Dog in 2016—an all-black hot dog on a black bun! The frank's pitch-black color comes from the use of edible bamboo charcoal.

NEARLY A FOOT LONG!

ICE Tires

→ **With the help of a team of sculptors, Lexus spent three months crafting a working set of wheels made of ice.**

Each ice wheel took 36 hours to make, and the sculptors replicated every detail—even the tires' tread patterns. The wheels, which were strong enough to support the 2-ton vehicle, also had LED lights added to give them a watery glow. Before completing an icy ride, the Lexus NX car itself was put in a freezing chamber for five full days at −22°F (−30°C), which left the SUV covered in ice and cold enough to keep the ice tires and rims frozen when installed.

GB GY65 HBN

STONE TEARS → Ding Aihua, from Lufang village in Shandong Province, China, has cried tears of stone for more than seven years. Whenever she has a headache, she produces hard, silvery white, soybean-size pebbles under her eyelids. Her husband, Liang Xinchun, has removed dozens of the stones using an iron wire, but doctors are struggling to find a way of treating the mysterious condition.

LONG WAIT → The average wait for new Green Bay Packers season tickets is approximately 30 years.

LUCKY TREE → Phra Prawit Techapalo, a Buddhist monk living at the Cheepakhao Temple in Thailand, won almost $175,000 on the lottery thanks to a lucky number revealed to him by a tree. He said he chose 84 as the last number on his winning ticket while examining the texture of a teak tree in the monastery grounds.

SHOULDER AD → American middle-distance runner Nick Symmonds sold 9 sq in (58 sq cm) of advertising space on his right shoulder to T-Mobile for $21,800. The two-time Olympian put the flesh up for auction on eBay, stipulating that it would be a temporary tattoo.

SOFT LANDING → A woman who plunged 60 ft (18 m) from a department store balcony in England had a lucky escape when she happened to land on a bed that had only recently been placed there as part of a seasonal display.

STAR SAND

→ You don't have to look to the sky to see stars in Okinawa, Japan—just visit the islands of Taketomi, Hatoma, and Iriomote, where star-shaped sand sprinkles the beaches! The stars are actually the exoskeletons of tiny organisms known as Foraminifera. When Foraminifera die, their shells remain in the sea and are washed ashore by the tides.

43

MARILYN

THE FIVE MILLION DOLLAR DRESS

THE MOST EXPENSIVE DRESS EVER SOLD AT AUCTION!

On November 17, 2016, Ripley's placed the winning bid for Marilyn Monroe's "Happy Birthday, Mr. President" dress. Including all taxes and fees, the gown cost more than $5 million—making it the most expensive dress ever purchased at auction according to Guinness World Records!

The iconic dress was famously worn by Marilyn Monroe on May 19, 1962, when she sang "Happy Birthday" to President John F. Kennedy at Madison Square Garden. Making quite the entrance—late to the stage—she wowed the crowd with her breathy version of the song, wearing the stunning, skintight, sheer dress.

Believe it or not, this pricey piece of pop culture history also racked up quite the bill in 1962. The fabric alone for the dress originally cost $12,000. That would be over $95,000 today!

MORE THAN 6,000 HAND-SEWN RHINESTONES!

MARILYN MONROE

President Kennedy's Birthday Party
MAY 19, 1962
MADISON SQUARE GARDEN
GALA ALL STAR SHOW
END ARENA
SEC. 112 ROW SEAT
CONTRIBUTION $25. PER PERSON
New York's Birthday Salute To The President, Inc.
SPONSORED BY THE STATE AND NATIONAL DEMOCRATIC
COMMITTEES AND CITIZENS FOR KENNEDY

PRESIDENT KENNEDY'S
BIRTHDAY PARTY
SATURDAY EVENING
MAY 19, 1962
MADISON SQUARE GARDEN
8:30 P. M.
END ARENA
SEC. 112 ROW SEAT
CONTRIBUTION $25. PER PERSON

BLONDE BOMBSHELL ➡ A bottle of peroxide and a movie contract turned Norma Jeane Mortenson into the witty and beautiful icon the world now knows as Marilyn Monroe. On August 5, 1962, at the young age 36, Monroe's life came to a tragic end—just months after her now-famous performance for President John F. Kennedy.

Auction Blockbusters

➡ Monroe's dress sold for an unprecedented $4.81 million, outselling countless other well-known costumes, some of which you may recognize . . .

Julie Andrews Sound of Music dresses	$1,300,000
Kate Winslet Titanic red chiffon dress	$330,000
Daniel Radcliffe Harry Potter and the Sorcerer's Stone glasses	$20,000
Harrison Ford signed Indiana Jones fedora	$9,600

THE DRESS WAS SO TIGHT FITTING, IT'S SAID THAT MONROE HAD TO BE SEWN INTO THE DRESS!

YOUNG and OLD

⊙ **Siblings Keshav Kumar and Anjali Kumari of India appear elderly, but they're actually quite young.**

Anjali is seven years old and her little brother Keshav is just 18 months old. Doctors believe the brother and sister are cases of either the genetic disease progeria or the connective tissue disorder cutis laxa. They have an 11-year-old older sister, Shilpi, who appears normal for her age and hopes a cure will be found for her younger siblings.

RIPLEY'S EXPLAINS

Progeria is a genetic disease that causes rapid aging in children, resulting in sagging skin, painful joints, and poor eyesight, among other symptoms. It is extremely rare, affecting just one in 4 million newborns worldwide—making it incredibly difficult for doctors and scientists to search for a cure. The disease doesn't affect learning or motor-skill development, but it does cause children to grow and gain weight slower than normal. Sadly, the genetic mutation also causes hardening of the arteries, which causes most people with progeria to die of heart attack or stroke at a young age.

LOVE IN THE AIR

➔ Zhou Wenlong and Jiang Huizhu tied the knot while hanging from a glass bridge in China's Shiniuzhai National Geopark! The lovebirds said "I do" in a hammock that dangled a precarious 590 ft (180 m) above the ground. The ceremony was held on the seventh day of the seventh month of the Chinese lunar calendar—also known as Chinese Valentine's Day.

PENNIES ➔ Eight million blank [pennies] spilled across Interstate 95 in New [Castle,] Delaware, in September 2016, when [a trac]tor-trailer carrying them to the [Philadel]phia Mint overturned and caught [fire. Had] they been stamped, the coins would [have bee]n worth about $81,600.

TWINS ➔ A pair of twins in Vietnam [have diff]erent fathers—one of fewer than 10 [such ca]ses in the world. The family decided [to have t]he two-year-olds tested when they [noticed t]hat one child had thick, wavy hair [and the] other had thin, straight hair. The [phenomen]on, known as heteropaternal [super]fundation, occurs when a woman's [eggs are f]ertilized by two different men in a [short peri]od of time.

SENATOR ➔ Eighteen-year-old [boy ha]s pleaded guilty to impersonating [an of]ficer after posing as a state [senator o]n a tour of Mohawk High School [in Marion,] Ohio, during which time he [taught] a politics class for an hour. Telling [offi]cials he had replaced real-life [senator Da]vid Burke because of an illness, he [convin]ced a car dealership to give him [a car and] a driver for the day. His deception [was u]ncovered when Senator Burke [visited t]he school a month later.

HUNGRY MICE ➔ A scheme to rebuild essential road tunnels in Brussels, Belgium, was delayed because it was discovered that the original construction plans had been eaten by mice. For decades, the plans had been stored in the pillars under a highway bridge, but when engineers consulted them in a bid to ease the city's increasing traffic chaos, they found that the documents had been gnawed by rodents.

FALLEN LEAVES ➔ We reported in *Ripley's Believe It or Not! Unlock the Weird!* how Kyle Waring, of Manchester-by-the-Sea, Massachusetts, shipped Boston snow to people in warm climates. In the fall of 2015, he came up with another enterprising scheme by sending bundles of preserved, colorful, handpicked New England leaves to customers around the world for $19.99.

PRESERVED TWINKIE ➔ A Twinkie has been preserved in a glass box at a private school in Blue Hill, Maine, for more than 40 years—and is still in good condition. The experiment started in 1976 when Roger Bennatti was teaching a chemistry lesson at George Stevens Academy on food additives and shelf life. Bennatti has since retired, so the snack now resides in the office of the Dean of Students.

WEEPING WALL ➔ In January 2016, more than 1,000 worshippers—at a rate of around 60 a day—flocked to an apartment block in Surrey, British Columbia, Canada, after an oily substance mysteriously started seeping from a bedroom wall and from small statues of Jesus and Mary. According to tenant Sanaan Alyais, the weeping wall was a manifestation of the Virgin Mary.

URINE SOCKS ➔ Scientists at the University of the West of England have designed urine-powered socks that can send messages when the wearer takes a pee. The hi-tech socks are embedded with 24 microbial fuel cells that are activated by fresh urine. The urine enters the socks through a tube in the heel and is circulated around the cells as the wearer walks, charging the tiny batteries and producing enough power to send a message. The inventors say the socks could be used to transmit a person's exact location in an emergency.

CHRISTMAS TREE ➔ An artificial Christmas tree owned by Kaye Ashton, from Sheffield, England, has been put up every year for almost a century. The tree was bought by her grandmother in 1920 and has been passed down through two generations of the family, even surviving German bombs during World War II.

believe it!

47

In the past, the faces of the performers were also painted, but today they wear intricate masks.

MUMMIFIED SAILOR → The mummified body of German adventurer Manfred Fritz Bajorat was found off the coast of the Philippines in 2016, hunched over a table on the yacht in which he had been sailing around the world for the past 20 years. Although he had suffered the fatal heart attack only a week earlier, the salt water in the ocean air had mummified his corpse in just a few days.

ANONYMITY BID → Police officers in Tallmadge, Ohio, said that to avoid being identified by his fingerprints after a traffic stop, Kirk Kelly, a fugitive from Tampa, Florida, chewed off his fingertips. He was eventually identified by his tattoos.

LUXURY CHAMBER → Japan's Mizuguchi Hospital offers expectant mothers a magnificent birthing chamber styled after the opulence enjoyed by the 19th-century Empress Elisabeth of Austria. The room has regal chandeliers and silverware, silk towels, and a king-sized bed complete with satin sheets and velvet pillows. Patients are even served afternoon tea.

CARTOON LOOKALIKE → Krystina Butel, of Wakefield, West Yorkshire, England, has had $200,000 worth of cosmetic surgery in her quest to look exactly like a cartoon drawing of her that was done on the Spanish island of Ibiza in 2001 when she was 15.

KINDLE SURPRISE → When James Potten, of Bristol, England, received a package from a courier company, he assumed it was the Kindle he had ordered—but instead he opened it to find a box containing a human tumor specimen that was intended for delivery to a hospital in London.

ONE TOUGH FISH

→ New Jersey fisherman Edward Grant caught this oddly shaped flounder in Raritan Bay! The fish appears to have miraculously healed from an encounter that would have meant the end for most, leaving it with a bite-shaped chunk missing from its body. Grant released the flounder back into the water, saying, "I figured if he survived whatever had happened to it, [he] deserved to go back."

PLAY OF THE TIGERS

⊕ In southern India, troupes of painted men perform a mesmerizing and colorful folk art parade during the annual harvest festival—Pulikali, the play of the tigers.

This 200-year-old event takes place mainly in the Thrissur district of Kerala, where artists take hours to paint and decorate performers with oil paints, turning them into tigers and leopards. The theme of the performance is playing hide-and-seek with a hunter. Dance troupes, each made up of about 40 to 50 members, play out the elaborate dance to the beat of traditional Indian percussion instruments while thousands of spectators cheer them on.

MALE IMPERSONATOR → Surwati, a 40-year-old Indonesian woman, posed so successfully as a man for six months that she even managed to trick another woman into marrying "him." She took the name Muhamad Efendi Saputra and claimed to be a male police officer. After a whirlwind romance, Muhamad married 25-year-old Heniyati on Java Island, but the union remained unconsummated, and a few months later, the increasingly suspicious bride found a card that revealed her husband's true identity and gender.

PEACE PROTESTER → Connie Picciotto camped outside the White House to protest for peace for 35 years. She joined the antinuclear White House Peace Vigil in 1981 and remained there almost constantly for three-and-a-half decades, right up until her death in 2016.

FAKE PASSENGER → A woman was ticketed by police in Dix Hills, New York, for driving in a carpool lane with a dummy passenger that even had its own briefcase. She was pulled over on the Long Island Expressway for driving in a lane that can only be used at busy times by vehicles with passengers—but her companion was just a pile of clothes topped with a baseball cap.

DEADLY GAME → Kristy Edgelow's children played catch with a split tennis ball for 20 minutes in North Fremantle, Western Australia, unaware that a deadly blue-ringed octopus was hiding inside it. Her children had found the cracked ball in the Swan River and only stopped their game when her son noticed something moving inside it. A blue-ringed octopus carries enough venom to kill 10 adults.

ANT COLONY → Shreya Darji, a 12-year-old girl from Banaskantha, India, has had more than 1,000 ants removed from her ears. Since the colony first formed inside her ear canal, at least 10 large ants have crawled out of her ears every day. Baffled doctors have tried drowning them with antiseptic and pulling them out using an endoscopic camera, but the ants keep returning.

WRESTLER ABE → Abraham Lincoln was inducted into the Wrestling Hall of Fame in 1992 in the category "Outstanding American." He proved an accomplished wrestler in his youth, losing only once in around 300 matches, and pioneered a move later known as the chokeslam, where he lifted his opponent clear off the ground by the throat and then slammed him down again.

believe it!

49

MARATHON WEDDING → Lynnette Beedle and Stephen Klejka, from Hudson, Ohio, married on the starting line for the 2016 Pro Football Hall of Fame Half-Marathon in Canton—and then ran the 13.1-mi (21-km) race. The couple wore full running gear for the wedding ceremony, with the bride adding a veil and the groom strapping on a bow tie.

MYSTERIOUS BLEEDING → Marnie-Rae Harvey, a teen from Stoke-on-Trent, England, suffers from a mystery condition that causes blood to seep from her nose, ears, fingertips, scalp, and tongue up to five times a day.

APPROPRIATE NAME → In June 2016, a man from Matteson, Illinois, won the state lottery for the second time, using the exact same numbers, winning over $1 million total. His name? Larry Gambles.

CROCODILE TEARS → Crocodile tears syndrome is a rare condition where people start to cry uncontrollably when they eat.

VENDING MACHINE → In Nashville, Tennessee, in 2015, used-car website Carvana opened the world's first fully automated, coin-operated car vending machine. The five-story glass structure can store up to 20 cars at a time.

SPIDER BATTLES

➔ Arachnophobes beware. Every June, the people of Kajiki, Kagoshima, Japan, partake in Kumo Gassen, or spider battles, a tradition going back 400 years.

Townspeople young and old buy or capture female *Argiope amoena* spiders, affectionately called samurai spiders, rearing and training them in their homes. The large purple and yellow spiders fight two at a time in a tournament, and the last spider standing is the winner. Not to worry! The spiders don't kill each other, and sharp-eyed referees stop aggressive fights—with their bare hands—before the spiders can hurt each other.

There are three ways to win: bite an opponent on the abdomen, wrap the rival's abdomen in thread, or cut the opponent's thread.

SWIMMING LESSON

→ Most people recall taking swimming lessons in their youth, but in 1906, it looks like swimming lessons were downright unforgettable. Curiously, these two children were given a swimming lesson in the River Thames at Wallingford, Oxfordshire, England, while kept afloat by ropes attached to poles!

Here a swimming instructor teaches a young child to swim in November 1926.

THREE YOLKS → Cooking breakfast in her sister's restaurant in Norfolk, England, Megan Watkins cracked open an egg that had three yolks—a 25 million-to-one occurrence.

PRECIOUS SEWERS → An estimated $20 million worth of precious metals are flushed into U.K. sewers every year—chiefly through gold teeth falling out while brushing or wedding rings falling off while people are washing their hands.

TROUBLEBREWING → In December 2015, 19-year-old Bud Weisser was arrested on a charge of trespassing at the Budweiser brewery in St. Louis, Missouri.

HEALED SKIN

M.S. 050880
GRUPO B - (T) V6
01

FISH SKIN GRAFTS

→ Doctors in Brazil successfully treated severe burns by covering them with dressings made of fish skin! The skin comes from the abundant and disease-resistant tilapia fish. The skin goes through a process that removes the scales, muscle tissue, possible toxins, and the fishy smell before it is stretched, laminated, and cut into strips. These strips can then be placed on damaged skin, such as burn victim Maria Ines Candido da Silva, who was the first patient to receive this treatment.

↑ The flexible and moist nature of the fish skin makes it the perfect material for dressing burns.

M.S. 050880
GRUPO B (T) - V3
01

➔ **Brittany Walsh of Las Vegas, Nevada, can shoot an arrow from a bow—with her feet!**

Brittany's unique skill comes from decades of dedication, practice, and patience—she has been a professional gymnast and acrobat for over 20 years. One of her specialties is hand balancing, during which she'll place her hands onto small blocks attached to beams called "canes," and then, with incredible strength and grace, hoist her body over her head. From there she can accomplish a multitude of impressive stunts, including archery!

Q **What do you love most about hand balancing?**

A I love that hand balancing makes me feel strong and centered all at the same time. It is definitely a sort of escape for me; it is a place I can go to where things make sense and I feel powerful, but I also have the freedom to be creative in its art form. And this is my job!

What inspired you to perform archery with your feet and how did you learn?

When I was first getting into circus and acrobatics in 2006, a friend pointed out a photograph in an old circus book of a woman performing the bow and arrow stunt that I now perform. My friend suggested that I attempt to replicate the stunt. I thought he was just making a joke and laughed it off, but he insisted that I give it a try, so we made a trip to the local sporting goods store and picked up a youth bow and arrow set. I gave myself a couple weeks to try to learn the trick and realized that my friend's idea was not so far-fetched after all. While it only took a few weeks to figure out the trick, it took at least one year to master the aim. Even now I am constantly finding ways to make the trick new, exciting, and challenging, such as wearing a blindfold, having an audience member hold the target, or shooting at greater distances. Funny enough, I rarely do any kind of archery with my hands—I have to say, my aim is much better with my feet!

What are some safety measures you take during your performances?

It is crucial that I am able to do a proper warm up prior to a performance. If I don't, I don't feel like I can perform at my optimum ability and I run the risk of injuring myself. Now that I frequently perform with a person holding the target for my bow and arrow finale trick, it is important that I check in with that person beforehand to make sure that they understand the way in which I need them to hold the target so that they remain safe during the stunt.

What new stunts are you currently working on?

In terms of hand balancing, I am always striving to improve my flexibility and to work on new and challenging one-arm balances. I am also working on exploring more movement with the rest of my body while maintaining a one-arm handstand hold. There may also be a one-finger balance in the near future.

What do you like to do in your spare time?

Traveling! I love to get out and explore new and different places and cultures and meet new people and try different food. I also enjoy going out dancing, hiking, watching documentaries, learning new languages, painting, and cuddling with my two cats, Nuktuk and Houdini.

Acrobritt

Brittany calls herself a "well-balanced" performer, incorporating elements of contortion, balance, and danger into her acts.

"MY AIM IS MUCH BETTER WITH MY FEET!"

Q What's your most difficult move?

A The most challenging moves that I do are one-arm balances. They require strength, focus, and impeccable technique.

SING SING SKELETONS

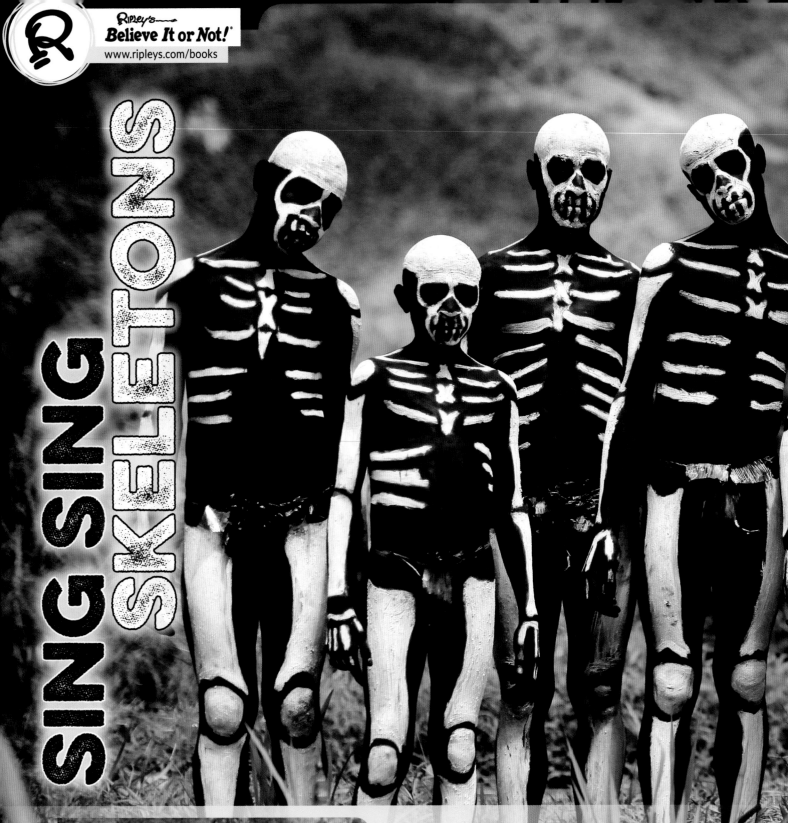

➔ **Members of the Chimbu tribe of Papua New Guinea paint themselves as skeletons using clay and ash!**

The paint jobs are combined with spooky dances that were originally intended to intimidate enemies. They are now part of an event called a "Sing Sing," where nearby clans gather to celebrate their culture.

ACROSS THE POND

→ The original London Bridge that once spanned the River Thames no longer resides in London— it's in Arizona! The founder of Lake Havasu City, Robert P. McCulloch, bought the bridge for nearly $2.5 million in 1968, when it was put up for sale because it had begun to slowly sink into the Thames. Each brick was numbered as the 850-ton bridge was disassembled and then put back together in the exact same order after traveling 5,300 mi (8,530 km) to America. Three years of construction later, the London Bridge officially reopened in Lake Havasu City, Arizona, on October 10, 1971.

The channel beneath the bridge was dug and flooded AFTER it was rebuilt!

CHESS VILLAGE → The small Indian community of Marottichal in Kerala is known as the "Chess Village" because almost every villager plays the game. An estimated 90 percent of the residents— from young children to old men—are chess enthusiasts, often meeting for a game at a local restaurant. They originally took it up as a distraction to stop them from drinking the local liquor that they produced for a living.

LUNCH BOXES → The Lunch Box Museum in Columbus, Georgia, houses Allen Woodall's collection of more than 3,500 metal lunch boxes and their matching thermos flasks, featuring such popular childhood icons as Flipper, Hopalong Cassidy, Superman, and Scooby-Doo. Woodall began collecting them in the 1940s, and some of the boxes are worth as much as $10,000 each. Among the rarer items is a 1930s electric lunch box, designed to keep a child's meal warm.

BOLT FROM THE BLUE → People can be struck by lightning even when the center of a thunderstorm is 10 mi (16 km) away and there are blue skies overhead.

WORM LINE → Following heavy rain, dozens of clumps of writhing earthworms suddenly appeared in an almost perfectly straight line down the middle of a road in Eisenhower State Park, Texas, on May 29, 2015. They stayed there for two days before vanishing underground, but their arrival and alignment remains a mystery.

TUK-TUK POLO

→ In Galle, Sri Lanka, they play polo with tuk-tuks instead of horses. While a driver steers the three-wheeled vehicle, players in the back seat hit the ball with their polo sticks. The rules of the game are similar to horse polo. No team may have more than two tuk-tuks in one half at any given time, and only one tuk-tuk from each team can enter the goalmouth. No tuk-tuk can stop in front of the goals. In Galle, the event has replaced the elephant polo championships, which were cancelled after the 2007 contest when one elephant went rogue and smashed into several spectators' cars.

SUNKEN SHIPS → Between 1936 and 1961, 15 decommissioned ships were deliberately sunk to create an artificial breakwater and calm the seas of Comox Harbor at Royston, British Columbia, Canada.

WITCH WATCH → All brooms are hidden away in Norway on Christmas Eve in case they are stolen by witches or evil spirits.

ANIMAL CURRENCY → The Croatian national currency, the kuna, is the Croatian word for a marten, a small, ferret-like animal. In Roman times, taxes in the region were collected in the form of marten skins, which were highly valued.

FIRST FLIGHT → On September 15, 2015, an airplane landed on the remote South Atlantic island of St. Helena for the very first time, finally making it accessible to the outside world. There is now a weekly flight service from Johannesburg, South Africa, to St. Helena, whereas previously the island could only be reached by a five-day boat trip.

MUMMIFIED DOG

STUCK SiNCE 1960!

⊙ **In Waycross, Georgia, visitors to the Southern Forest World museum can feast their eyes on Stuckie the mummified dog!**

Found in 1980 by a logging contractor, Stuckie is a preserved four-year-old hound, and while no one is sure how he managed to get stuck in the hollow tree, experts think he has been stuck since 1960! Due to environmental conditions in the chestnut oak, the dog never attracted the usual organisms that feed on carcasses, which allowed the acids in the tree to harden the dog's skin.

SALT CATHEDRAL

⊕ An hour away from Bogota, Colombia, deep into Zipaquirá Mountain, sits a Catholic cathedral carved entirely out of salt.

Located 590 ft (180 m) belowground, the cathedral is built in the heart of an abandoned salt mine and features salt sculptures and a cross 16 ft (5 m) high. Despite the countless number of salt mines throughout the world, the Zipaquirá Salt Cathedral is only the second of its kind.

CHOCOLATE BAR → A pop-up bar in London, England, was made entirely out of chocolate, serving beer from edible glasses. Designed by food artist Prudence Staite for Easter 2016, the 16-ft-wide (5-m), 6.5-ft-high (2-m) bar required nearly half a ton of chocolate and featured a chocolate dartboard, chocolate bar stools, and even a chocolate TV screen.

LIGHTNING ESCAPE → A powerful lightning strike flung 65-year-old Brian Phillips across the kitchen of his home in Bedfordshire, England, but his life was saved because he was wearing a pair of rubber-soled slippers that his daughter had bought him for Christmas.

BLACKFLY FESTIVAL → The village of Adamant, Vermont, stages an annual festival to mark one of the region's great spring pests: the blackfly. Events include the Blackfly Parade, a fashion show featuring bug-related hats, a blackfly poetry competition, and a blackfly pie contest, where cooks prepare dishes that look like blackflies.

NEON NOODLES → Japanese food writer and scientist Kurare Raku created neon pink noodles that glow in the dark, and no one is sure how.

BIG BAGUETTE → Sixty French and Italian bakers worked for seven hours to create a 400-ft-long (122-m) baguette for an exhibition in Milan. The baguette weighed 412 lb (187 kg) and, to avoid the risk of breakage, had to be cooked in a special self-propelled oven, which moved the dough along, baking it in 66-ft (20-m) segments.

SUPERHERO RESTAURANT → Two DC Comics–themed restaurants in Malaysia are decorated with superhero memorabilia, and every item on the menu has a superhero tag. These include Batman branded waffles, lattes with Superman symbols, Wonder Woman turkey rolls, and the Dark Knight Mini Wagyu Beef Burger.

UNUSUAL VILLAGE → La Colonia Tovar is a picturesque, quintessential German village—in the middle of Venezuela. Known as the "Germany of the Caribbean," the mountain village boasts white-walled, red-roofed, chalet-style Alpine houses while the residents feast on sausages and sauerkraut, washed down by cold beer. It was founded in 1843 by a group of immigrants from the Black Forest, and with no paved road connecting to Caracas, the Venezuelan capital, until the 1960s, the community was largely left alone to adopt a Germanic way of life.

26 GENERATIONS → R. J. Balson & Son, a butcher store in Dorset, England, has been in business for more than 500 years, having started out when Henry VIII was king of England. During that time, it has passed through 26 generations and survived floods, fires, plagues, wars, and 23 monarchs.

There are more than 3,000 stallholders at the Ima Market in Imphal, India—and they are all women.

FAMILY WELL → After his wife was refused access to a local well, laborer Bapurao Tajne spent six hours a day for 40 days single-handedly digging his own 15-ft (4.6-m) deep well in Kalambeshwar village, Maharashtra, India, so that his family could have drinking water.

BURRITO CHALLENGE → Any customer who can finish the 30-lb (13.6-kg) Gran Chingon burrito in an hour at the Don Chingon restaurant in Brooklyn, New York, is rewarded with a 10 percent share of the restaurant's profits. The $150 handmade tortilla measures about 3.5 ft (1.1 m) in diameter and is filled with chicken, steak, chorizo, cheese, rice, beans, and salsa and has to be washed down with a red-hot ghost pepper margarita. Only one Gran Chingon burrito is made per day because it takes two hours to prepare.

DANGER BRIDGE → The Kuandinsky Bridge in the Siberia region of Russia stretches 1,870 ft (570 m) over the Vitim River but is only 6.5 ft (2 m) wide, and there is no barrier to prevent cars and trucks from plunging into the frozen water below. The decaying metal structure is covered with old wooden railway sleepers that become very slippery in icy conditions and often have to be replaced by the drivers themselves in order to complete the perilous crossing. Drivers also have to cross the bridge with all their windows down to prevent the fierce wind from blowing them off.

DUAL PURPOSE → Hot Spot, a café on the Greek island of Lesbos, serves as a coffee house during the day and a shelter for stray dogs at night.

There are over 71,000 mi (114,260 km) of train tracks in India!

ALL ABOARD!

⊕ An astounding 23 million people ride the train every day in India—but some brave passengers must cram themselves inside, latch onto the sides, or balance on the roofs of locomotives to get to their destinations. Despite having the second largest rail network by passengers in the world and 12,000 passenger trains in operation within the country, overcrowding is still a huge problem for Indian railways.

DEMU 11106

COMMODITY CITY

Aisles are labeled so shoppers don't lose their way within the hundreds of hallways.

➡ **Yiwu International Trade City has over 60,000 vendor booths inside of a massive 46 million sq ft (4.3 million sq m) shopping center!**

Yiwu, China, also known as China Commodity City, is the world's largest small commodity wholesale market. It's basically a gigantic mall for people looking to buy large quantities of products. With over 400,000 different products on display, shoppers can find almost anything imaginable—for instance, clocks, toys, fake plants, jewelry, and holiday decorations.

Snake-Covered STATUE

SNAKES AROUND THE HEAD ARE SAID TO PREDICT A GOOD HARVEST.

⊙ **Every May, hundreds gather in the Italian town of Cocullo to drape snakes onto a statue in a festival known as *Processione dei Serpari*.**

The festival celebrates the town's patron saint, St. Dominic, who is said to have cleared an invasion of snakes from the town's fields and cured snakebites during the 11th century. For hundreds of years, the townspeople and tourists have been thanking St. Dominic by parading his statue through the town and draping it with dozens of non-venomous snakes—an act believed to protect attendees from snakebites for the year. Months before the festival, snake handlers known as *serpari* gather the reptiles from the wild, remove their fangs, and care for them until it is time to celebrate. The snakes are released after the festival, and their fangs grow back.

T-SHIRT BAG → Nearly 1,500 volunteers in Ipoh, Malaysia, spent six months sewing together a huge bag made from 2,984 old T-shirts. The finished bag is 25 ft (7.6 m) long, 10 ft (3 m) wide, and 18 ft (5.4 m) high.

MINIATURE EXHIBITION → A 2016 art exhibition in Nottinghamshire, England, featured 32,283 miniature paintings—each on a card the size of a business card, so that if laid out in a line, they would stretch for nearly 2 mi (3.2 km).

WRONG MAN → A statue that was erected in 1977 in Stockton-on-Tees, England, to commemorate John Walker, the 19th-century inventor of the friction match, was discovered nearly 40 years later to be of the wrong man. It is of another John Walker—an actor from the same period who only looked like the inventor.

LONG LIVES → One in three people on the Greek island of Ikaria lives well into their nineties, and many go on to become centenarians. The islanders attribute their longevity to a diet low in meat but rich in vegetables and their tradition of taking afternoon naps.

CD FAÇADE → For a 2015 international craft exhibition, three walls of an old tobacco processing plant in Cheongju, South Korea, were covered in 489,440 CDs. The glittering façade was made up of compact discs collected from nine different countries, including Japan, China, and the United States. It holds the world record for the largest display of compact discs ever.

CUP TOWER → Artist Mark Poulier, of Melbourne, Australia, created a perfectly detailed model of Italy's famous Leaning Tower of Pisa using eight paper coffee cups and drawing in the architectural features with pen and ink.

UNDERGROUND ENTERTAINMENT → A theme park in Turda, Romania, is located 400 ft (122 m) underground in an old salt mine. Attractions at subterranean Salina Turda include a Ferris wheel, a boating lake, and a bowling alley.

SOLE CITY → Over 76 percent of the total 37,000 population of Canada's Yukon Territory lives in its only city—Whitehorse. The nearest big city to Whitehorse is Edmonton, Alberta—1,239 mi (1,994 km) away.

BORING SPEAKERS → At the annual one-day Boring Conference in London, England, speakers discuss such mundane topics as sneezing, toast, similarities between 198 of the world's national anthems, the font Comic Sans, barcodes, ice cream truck jingles, desktop inkjet printers of 1999, and the sounds made by vending machines.

STAG CALLS → At the annual Jagd and Hund show in Germany, competitors try to imitate the sounds of stags, using a variety of aids including glass cylinders and the hollow stalks of the cow parsley plant.

BOILING RIVER → A 4-mi-long (6.4-km) stretch of river deep in the Amazon rainforest in Mayantuyacu, Peru, is so hot that the water in it boils. Dipping a hand into the 80-ft-wide (24-m) river would give a person third-degree burns in less than half a second, while any small animals such as frogs that fall in would fry to death instantly. The boiling water is thought to be caused by hot springs that are fed by a geological fault line.

KISSED APPLES → There are online stores in China selling apples at higher prices because the fruit has been kissed by female flight attendants. Some sellers charge up to $20 per apple, claiming that it has been kissed by as many as 500 attendants.

SILKWORM SNACK

➔ In a country esteemed for its delicious BBQ and its side dish staples like kimchi, South Korea might have trouble convincing you to eat beondegi—boiled silkworm pupae. Sold in street markets and served in a cup, these insects give off a pungent aroma as they are boiled with sugar and soy sauce in a giant pot.

SIGN LANGUAGE ➔ Every one of the 3,000 residents in the remote Balinese village of Bengkala knows sign language. Since the number of hearing and speech impaired people in Bengkala is at least 15 times higher than the world average, villagers developed their own unique sign language, kata kolok or "deaf talk," to communicate with each other through gestures.

THANKFUL VILLAGES ➔ There are just 14 villages in the whole of the United Kingdom that did not lose a soldier fighting in either World War I or World War II.

SECRET FOREST ➔ A fierce storm that hit the beach at Portreath, Cornwall, England, in January 2016 uncovered the remains of a submerged petrified forest, believed to be around 5,000 years old.

BURNING TREE ➔ On June 12, 2016, a tree near Springdale, Arkansas, burst into flames from the inside after a huge lightning bolt had split it in half. The fire consumed so much of the tree that it eventually fell.

SALMON BUNKERED ➔ After heavy rainfall caused local flooding in December 2015, a live salmon was found swimming in a bunker at Peterculter Golf Club, Aberdeen, Scotland.

COMPACT NIGHTCLUBS ➔ In Berlin, Germany, two Deutsche Telekom phone booths were turned into nightclubs that are so small they can only accommodate up to nine people at a time. Each "Teledisko" contains a smoke machine, strobe lights, light effects, dry ice, a disco ball, and a touchscreen that allows clubbers to choose their favorite music.

MORBID LOCATION ➔ Petros Mirisis opened an ice cream store in a former funeral parlor in Chicopee, Massachusetts—and claimed that his ice cream was "a taste to die for."

SLIPPING AWAY ➔ The village of Ropoto, Greece, is slowly slipping away! Once famous for their apple trees, the hilltop settlement was abandoned after a major landslide in 2012 displaced the community of around 300 families, turning the once thriving village into a ghost town. Today, Ropoto continues to slide downhill, and since the landslide in 2012, the ground has sunk an incredible 4 to 6 in (10 to 15 cm).

Selling AIR

覆盖率
%的空气 广东鱼家

花钱买

工业的污染 等于买健康

→ **Villagers in Guangdong Province, China, have capitalized on clean mountain air, selling bags of it to city-dwelling visitors.**

In a country where smog and pollution close down schools, roads, and airports, tourists looking for a breath of fresh air can purchase bags of it for 10–30 yuan ($1.50–$4.50) each. These pop-up shops at Lianshan Mountain display signs that say, "Buying air equals buying health" and "Air without industrial pollution." Some patrons consider it a joke, while others actually bargain with the retailers and haul the air back to the city.

FOOD BLOGGER → James McGowan, a food blogger from Amherstburg, Ontario, Canada, has eaten at McDonald's restaurants in more than 50 different countries, including Russia, Malaysia, Germany, Japan, Greece, and Qatar.

HOT ROCKS → Elderly women in Xi'an, China, press their bodies against hot rocks on summer days to improve their health. They can be seen lying on, leaning on, or even hugging large sun-heated boulders in order to treat stiff muscles.

THE WiNGS MOVE, iT LiGHTS UP & ROARS!

ROUGHLY A 10-FT WiNG SPAN

Ripley's Exhibit
Cat. No. 171277
Matchstick Dragon
Over 273,000 matchsticks!
Two-headed dragon by
Patrick Acton
Origin: Gladbrook, Iowa

DIVERSE CITY →
More than 120 different languages are spoken in Calgary, Alberta. The city's population is so diverse that 25 percent of Calgarians are born outside Canada.

RECYCLED CROCKERY → German designer Julian Lechner makes solid coffee cups and saucers from dried coffee grounds. He creates the eco-friendly dishes by combining coffee grounds with wood chips and biopolymers, and the product is so durable it can even be put in a dishwasher.

PHONE-FREE BAR → The Gin Tub cocktail bar in Brighton, England, has installed a cell blocker in its ceiling so that none of its customers can use their cell phones. Instead, old-style rotary phones are placed on tables, and these can be used to dial patrons at neighboring tables or to call the bar for more drinks. The idea behind the scheme is to encourage people to talk to each other rather than stare at their phone.

TOOTHACHE PLANT → The shrub *Acmella oleracea* is also known as the toothache plant because if you chew or rub a leaf on the gum area of a sore tooth, it makes your mouth numb within just a few seconds.

SLOW PROGRESS → From the time Pluto was officially discovered in 1930 to the time its status as a planet was rescinded in 2006, it had not completed a full orbit around the sun.

PINK WATERFALL → Cameron Falls in Alberta, Canada, turns pink after heavy rainfall. The rain washes a red sediment called argillite from the rock and into the water.

INDOOR POOL → To cool down in a summer heat wave, Hasim Kilicoglu built a 10 ft × 6 ft (3 m × 2 m) swimming pool in the living room of his home in Hilvan, Turkey. First he built a wall; then he lined it with plastic sheeting before finally filling it with water.

AMAZON TREES → There are so many different tree species growing in the Amazon rainforest—up to 16,000—that it will take another 300 years to discover them all. Scientists estimate that another 4,000 tree species there have yet to be identified.

BUDDHIST HEARSE

→ Mixing Western tradition with Buddhist culture, some hearses in Japan certainly stand out! Sitting on a standard American chassis, these cars have been extensively modified to look like an ornate Buddhist temple. Carved out of wood, they are covered in gold leaf, decorated with brass, and covered with a copper roof!

NUCLEAR NIGHTMARE

Releasing at least 100 times more radiation than the atom bombs dropped on Nagasaki and Hiroshima, the Chernobyl nuclear power plant is the site of history's worst man-made disaster.

February 1986

Ukraine's Minister of Power and Electrification states that the odds of a meltdown at Chernobyl's nuclear power plant are "one in 10,000 years."

April 26, 1986

1:23 a.m. Routine testing begins.

April 26, 1986

1:24 a.m. Pressure builds in reactor Number 4, causing an explosion that immediately releases deadly radiation into the air. Thirty separate fires ignite.

THE DISTORTIONS IN THIS PHOTO ARE CAUSED BY EXTREME LEVELS OF RADIATION!

ELEPHANT'S FOOT Today, there is still a structure at the heart of the plant, known as the Elephant's Foot, that is incredibly radioactive. A melted lava-like mixture, it is so deadly that 30 seconds of exposure will cause severe dizziness. Within two minutes, cells begin to hemorrhage. An exposure of five minutes is fatal. As it continues to melt through the concrete base of the power plant, the city will remain uninhabitable for at least the next 100 years.

ABANDONED AMUSEMENT

↪ Ukraine's Pripyat Amusement Park was slated to open on May 1, 1986, but things did not go according to plan. Instead, it operated for just a few hours following the fallout, while the town was being evacuated. Today, with radiation levels in some parts of the park still dangerously high, the rides remain unridden and rusty.

April 26, 1986
1:45 a.m. Firefighters arrive, unaware of the risk of radiation.

April 27, 1986
Evacuations begin for all residents within 6 mi (10 km) of the plant.

April 27, 1986
Ahead of schedule, the Pripyat Amusement Park opened briefly during the evacuation, in an attempt to keep residents positive.

May 1, 1986
May Day parades to honor plant workers proceed, despite radiation being released. Nuclear rain fell as far away as Ireland.

GAME OF DRONES ➔ Drone enthusiasts in Melbourne, Australia, stage special races for their custom-built quadcopters, flying the lightweight machines around a course for an hour at speeds of over 40 mph (64 kmph). Races often take place in large abandoned warehouses where the flyers have to react quickly to ensure their drones do not crash into walls, pillars, or each other.

IDEAL NAME ➔ For the first time in its 36-year history, the 2016 Ernest "Papa" Hemingway Look-Alike Contest in Key West, Florida, was won by a man named Hemingway. White-bearded Dave Hemingway, from Raleigh, North Carolina, who is not related to the late author, beat 140 other entrants to take the prize.

EXPENSIVE TEA ➔ A single gram of Da Hong Pao tea from an original tree costs $1,400, making it worth over 30 times its weight in gold. Its value is due to its rarity, as there are only a few original Da Hong Pao trees left in China's Fujian Province. The tea has been said to possess outstanding medicinal properties ever since it apparently cured the sick mother of a Ming dynasty emperor hundreds of years ago.

INSTANT ACCOMMODATION ➔
Following a ferocious blizzard in January 2016, Patrick Horton spent three hours building an igloo by hand in the backyard of his home in Brooklyn, New York, and then listed it on Airbnb for $200 a night.

MARTIANS WELCOME ➔ St. Paul, Alberta, Canada, has a UFO landing pad, built in 1967 in an attempt to attract Martians to the town.

TOWN SALE ➔ The ghost town of Swett, South Dakota, was put up for sale in 2015 at a price of $250,000, reduced from $400,000. The 6-acre plot includes a tavern, a three-bedroom house, and a former tire shop. The town's heyday was in the 1940s when it had 40 residents as well as a post office and grocery store. Swett's previous owner, Lance Benson, once gave the town up as part of a divorce settlement before buying it back in 2012, only to lose it to a bank three years later.

world

69

ONBASHIRA
FESTIVAL

➔ Once every six years, thousands of people gather in the Suwa region to chop, ride, and raise massive 50-ft (15-m) logs during Japan's Onbashira Festival—an ancient Shinto tradition that's been taking place for more than 1,200 years.

Onbashira, or Sacred Pillars, is a two-month-long event to replace the sacred pillars at four shrines, thereby purifying the shrines. The pageantry unfolds in stages: the first being Yamadashi, the locating and felling of 16 massive 150-year-old fir trees weighing more than 10 tons each.

After the branches and bark are removed, ropes are attached for the second and most dangerous stage: Satobiki, where hundreds of men drag and ride each log 6 mi (10 km) down steep hills to a Shinto shrine. It's an honor to ride the logs and stand atop the attached wooden beams covered in streamers. The danger becomes very real at the steepest hill, where the beams are removed and the loggers hold on for dear life as they tear down the hill at top speed.

The last portion of the festival is the ceremonial raising of the logs in front of the shrine and is called Onbashira, the namesake of the entire festival. Unbelievably, the new pillars are raised with the riders still clinging tightly as they ascend. The log riding and raising often result in serious injuries—sometimes even fatal. However, according to Shinto beliefs, any Onbashira Festival participant's death is considered honorable and worthy of historical remembrance.

73

CHAIR-IOTS OF FIRE

➔ The Isu-1 Grand Prix is a keenly contested Japanese sport in which riders race office chairs! Each team has three members who, wearing helmets and knee and elbow pads, take turns to sit on and steer office chairs and complete as many laps of the 590-ft-long (180-m) course as possible in two hours. The contest originated in Kyotanabe but has become so popular that there are now races in 12 different Japanese prefectures, as well as one in Taiwan.

FLESH SOUP ➔ The classic Mexican soup pozole was originally made with human flesh by the Aztecs. Pork was substituted once cannibalism was banned.

CONTAINER VILLAGE ➔ Appalled by rent prices in San Francisco, Luke Iseman and Heather Stewart set up Containertopia, a village in Oakland, California, where all the residents live in shipping containers. The 160-sq-ft (15-sq-m) metal containers serve as small apartments and can be modified to incorporate glass windows, electricity, and a private shower and toilet. They rent for just $600 a month, compared to $3,500 for a one-bedroom apartment in San Francisco.

SUNDAE BEST ➔ Around 1,500 volunteers in Ludington, Michigan, prepared an ice cream sundae that stretched for more than 2,970 ft (905 m), extending over eight blocks.

SHOE CHURCH ➔ A new church in Budai, Taiwan, is built in the shape of a giant high-heeled shoe, consisting of a metal framework fitted with 320 blue glass panes.

BOG BUTTER ➔ In 2016, a turf cutter discovered a 2,000-year-old lump of butter buried 12 ft (3.6 m) below the surface in Emlagh bog, County Meath, Ireland—and it was still edible. The chunk of butter weighed 22 lb (10 kg) and was described as smelling like cheese. Often wrapped in animal hide, butter was buried in Irish bogs to preserve it and was sometimes used as an offering to the Celtic gods.

POPULATION STAMPEDE ➔ The 193-acre area that houses the annual Calgary Stampede holds an average of 120,000 people per day, making the grounds the third largest city in Alberta every July, behind only Calgary itself and Edmonton.

CHEESE POWER ➔ A power station in Albertville, France, generates enough electricity from locally produced cheese to supply power to a community of 1,500 people. Skimmed whey, a by-product of Beaufort cheese, is mixed with bacteria to convert it into biogas, a mixture of methane and carbon dioxide. The gas is then fed through a machine, which heats water to 194°F (90°C) and generates electricity.

LINT BEER ➔ The 7 Cent Brewery, based near Melbourne, Australia, has created a beer made from belly button lint. Belly Button Beer was produced with yeast grown from the lint that had collected in the brewer's own navel and is described as tasting like a Belgian-style witbier with hints of clove and banana.

PLATFORM CITY ➔ Neft Daşları, a huge oil platform complex in the Caspian Sea off the coast of Azerbaijan, is a functional city with a population of around 2,000 and over 187 mi (300 km) of streets built on piles of dirt and landfill. It was constructed in 1949 after engineers found oil in the region, thousands of feet beneath the seafloor. In its heyday, the man-made island boasted eight-story apartment blocks, a soccer field, a library, a bakery, a laundry, a 300-seat movie theatre, and even a tree-lined park, built with soil shipped from the mainland.

GRUESOME CAKES ➔ Taking her inspiration from her job as a nurse at a hospital in Rochester, New York, Katherine Dey bakes gory cakes that look like real human brains, hearts, and blood-soaked, severed heads. Her anatomically accurate brain cake, which even has the stem attached, is a mix of red preserves, cream, and sponge. She also makes cakes in the shapes of newborn babies, undersea monsters, and pigeons.

DIFFERENT CALENDAR ➔ The remote Shetland island of Foula (with a population of about 30), off the north coast of Scotland, celebrates Christmas and New Year's almost two weeks later than the rest of the United Kingdom. It still operates according to the old Julian calendar, meaning that Christmas Day falls on January 6 and New Year's Day is January 13.

MILLIONAIRE VILLAGE ➔ By harvesting rainwater to produce plentiful crops in what was once a drought-ridden region, the remote farming village of Hiware Bazar in Maharashtra, India, has gone from being impoverished in the mid-1990s to being the country's wealthiest village today. The residents' income has multiplied over 30-fold in just 20 years, and in 2016, 60 of the 235 families living there were listed as millionaires.

RATTLESNAKE ROUNDUP

The live rattlesnakes are kept in a giant pit, where they must be "stirred" to keep them from suffocating.

⊙ **Over 12.5 tons of snakes were caught for a rattlesnake festival in Sweetwater, Texas!**

The Sweetwater rattlesnake roundup is said to be the largest one in the world. Every year, about 25,000 people gather to watch and participate in the capturing and beheading of thousands of diamondback rattlesnakes. No part of the snake goes unused—the skin is turned into leather, the meat is fried up to be eaten, and the venom is collected for research purposes.

Spectators young and old alike take part in skinning the rattlesnakes.

world

75

DARK VORTEX ➔ In 2016, NASA's Hubble Space Telescope discovered a mysterious dark vortex the size of the United States on Neptune.

ONLY MONARCHY ➔ The Kingdom of Tonga is the only monarchy in the South Pacific. The same royal family—the House of Tupou—has ruled the islands since the modern-day constitution was adopted in 1875.

MANURE FIRE ➔ It was so hot in upstate New York on July 5, 2016, that a pile of horse manure at a property in Throop suddenly burst into flames. It took three local fire departments two hours to douse the burning manure.

OIL RESERVES ➔ Texas has 11.76 billion barrels of crude oil reserves—enough to fill more than 1,500 Empire State Buildings.

BELL RINGING ➔ San Francisco stages an annual Cable Car Bell Ringing Competition—and the 2016 champion, Leonard Oats, won with a bell-ringing version of Michael Jackson's "Bad."

WEALTH INDICATOR ➔ The people of Kenya's Pokot tribe measure their wealth by cows, and the number of women a man can marry is determined by the number of cows he owns.

THE POISON GARDEN

⊙ Alnwick Castle in Northumberland, England, plays host to the small but deadly Poison Garden—filled exclusively with around 100 toxic, intoxicating, and narcotic (illegal) plants. Surrounded by the beautiful 12-acre (4.9-hectare) Alnwick Garden, the boundaries of the Poison Garden are kept behind black iron gates, only open on guided tours. Visitors are strictly prohibited from smelling, touching, or tasting any plants, although some people still occasionally faint from inhaling toxic fumes while walking in the garden.

Vinca major

THESE PLANTS CAN KILL

Euphorbia x martini

CORAL
Skeleton

◉ Filipino artist Gregory Raymond Halili created a life-size skeleton out of pieces of washed-up coral.

Coral turns white when it dies, creating an eerie resemblance to bones and making it the perfect medium for Halili to work with. The mock bones in Halili's piece appear to hover a few inches above a 7-ft-long (2.1-m) driftwood table, an illusion he accomplished by drilling the wood and coral pieces, then connecting them all together with steel needles and superglue.

Halili found the perfect coral pieces to fit together like a puzzle.

Q Where did you go to find the coral?

A I gathered all the coral along the beaches of Calatagan, Anilao, and Bolinao here in the Philippines. It is interesting to note that the type of corals I found differs in each area.

How long did it take you to assemble the coral skeleton?

Assembling the entire skeleton took about a year, slowly building them together. It took almost two years, and quite a few beach trips, just to gather the coral. It required patience and determination and a little luck just to find the right shapes. Finding the right driftwood was a challenge as well.

How many pieces of coral are in the entire skeleton?

I tried to be as accurate as possible in terms of scale and skeleton pieces. I honestly did not count how many coral pieces are in the skeleton. My aim was to build structures that will feel like the real thing without cutting the corals. The skull, ribs, femurs, humerus, ulna, and radius bones are built up of fragments of corals.

Which "bone" was the hardest to find?

The hardest "bone" to find was the skull. There are many corals that are shaped like a cranium but are not the right size. I wanted to be honest with the work, so I looked for a long time and finally found it on a Calatagan beach.

Ripley's EXCLUSIVE

world

77

WINE SPA

➔ Soak your worries away in a pool filled with red wine at the Hakone Kowakien Yunessun resort in Japan. Bathers at this spa get to enjoy the rejuvenating power provided by antioxidents in the wine, which are said to help protect the skin. This resort also offers visitors the chance to soak in coffee, green tea, and sake—all of which are believed to have a variety of health benefits.

HAIR DISPLAY ➔ The Hair Museum of Avanos, Turkey, is filled with locks of hair from more than 16,000 women, with each exhibit accompanied by the name and address of its former owner. The museum was created by Chez Galip, who encourages visitors to his pottery shop to cut off a lock of their hair and present it to him for display.

MAP MISTAKE ➔ There is a small piece of the United States located 75 mi (121 km) inside Canada. Minnesota's Northwest Angle in Lake of the Woods can only be accessed by road through the Canadian province of Manitoba, yet it is very much American. It is the result of a mistake on a map in 1783 that has never been corrected. The border between the United States and Canada should have cut through the lake only, but the map was drawn wrong and accidentally included the peninsula. The 100 people who live there have to pass through two border crossings and make a five-hour round trip just to go grocery shopping in the United States.

ZAQISTAN REPUBLIC ➔ New York City resident Zaq Landsberg bought two acres of land in a remote part of Box Elder County, Utah, on eBay and created the republic of Zaqistan. Declaring himself president, he designed a yellow-and-red flag, official-looking passports, and a border control gate guarded by a robot sentry. His unofficial nation is 60 mi (97 km) from the nearest town and 15 mi (24 km) from a paved road.

UNDERSEA MAILBOX ➔ For a month in 2016, a mailbox off Green Island, Taiwan, was located 40 ft (12 m) underwater to collect postcards deposited by tourists at the Shilang Diving Area.

HERE IS THE 2016 WINNER.

CHEESE IT

Believe it or not, an annual cheese-rolling contest is held in Cooper's Hill, Gloucestershire, England! Competitors race, or throw themselves, down a steep hill trying to catch 7-lb (3.2-kg) circular Double Gloucester cheeses, and the winner gets to keep the cheese. Injuries are common, though, with the incline and wet grass producing broken bones every year.

MONSTER MOJITO → A team of 40 people in Punta Cana, Dominican Republic, took more than an hour and a half to make a 930-gal (3,519-l) mojito—so big that it needed to be put in a reinforced glass container that was more than 8.3 ft (2.5 m) high. The drink used 185 gal (700 l) of white rum, 185 gal (700 l) of soda, 500 lb (227 kg) of sugar, 150 lb (68 kg) of mint, 79 gal (300 l) of lime juice, and 4,226 lb (1,917 kg) of ice.

CALGARY SKYWALK → You can walk 11 mi (18 km) in downtown Calgary, Alberta, Canada, without having to step outside. The Plus 15 is an enclosed pedestrian walkway that connects 100 buildings by means of 60 bridges suspended 15 ft (4.6 m) above the ground.

CARROT MUSEUM → A small museum in Berlotte, Belgium, focuses solely on the humble carrot. It was founded by the local Carrot Fan Club, whose members can be identified by the prominent carrot statues in their front gardens.

The Jarramplas costume is armored to help soften the blows of thousands of tossed turnips.

TURNIP FOR WHAT

→ At the annual Jarramplas festival in Piornal, Spain, hundreds of people gather to chase a costumed man out of town—by hitting him with turnips!

Some say the Jarramplas figure, who beats a drum and wears a devil's mask and horns, represents the expulsion of a centuries-old cattle thief, but others claim it is a religious ritual that symbolizes driving out evil. As many as 15,000 rock-hard turnips are hurled toward the Jarramplas throughout the festival!

MIRROR
MOSQUE

➔ **Hundreds of thousands of pieces of colored and mirrored glass cover the interior of the Shāh-é-Chérāgh mosque in Shiraz, Iran.**

The mesmerizing mosaics reflect the name of the building, which means "King of the Light" in Persian. Shāh-é-Chérāgh started out in the 12th century as a modest mausoleum built for two brothers, but over time it has turned into an ornate place of worship and wonder for Iranians and tourists alike.

Fourteenth-century Queen Tash Khātūn commanded the glass decorations be installed because she wanted light within the mosque to be intensified a thousand times over.

IT'S LIT!

⊙ **Ubon Ratchathani, Thailand, prepares for the Buddhist Vassa with a breathtaking Candle Festival.**

This colorful celebration marks the beginning of a three-month monastic retreat and involves the carving of incredibly elaborate candles, which are then paraded as floats throughout the town. Local artisans and Buddhist devotees spend hours cutting up and melting beeswax to mold and carve by hand. Some floats weigh over 10 tons!

These huge candles are offered to the local temples to provide the monks with sufficient light during Vassa, as they must remain in their temples during this time.

HAIRDRESSER WANTED → The 800 residents of Norman Wells, an isolated settlement in Canada's Northwest Territories, had to cut their own hair for years after the last hairdresser left town. With the nearest hairdresser a 17-hour drive away in Yellowknife, some chose to let their hair grow for months at a time while others trimmed their locks with sheep shears.

HANGMAN'S BEACH → Maugher Beach on McNabs Island, Nova Scotia, Canada, used to be called Hangman's Beach because during the Napoleonic Wars of the early 19th century, the British Royal Navy used to hang the bodies of executed mutineers there—often four at a time. The bodies served as a warning to ships entering Halifax Harbor that crew members needed to behave themselves while in port.

GINGERBREAD HOUSE → Daniel Mangione and his team of pastry chefs at the Ritz-Carlton, Dove Mountain resort in Marana, Arizona, built a 19-ft-tall (5.8-m) gingerbread house inside the hotel and opened it as a restaurant. The edible house was made up of 4,000 ginger bricks, which took more than two months to bake. The house was constructed from 200 lb (91 kg) of ginger powder, 400 lb (181 kg) of honey, 350 lb (159 kg) of flour, 50 lb (23 kg) of cinnamon, 10 lb (4.5 kg) of nutmeg, and 250 eggs.

HORSE DIAPERS → Horses in Selma, Alabama, must wear diapers when on the city's streets. The law was passed by the city council in a bid to tackle sanitary problems created by the animals.

SHEEP DUNG → The meat in hangikjöt, an Icelandic lamb dish, is often smoked using burning dried sheep dung.

BOTTLE BUILDING → Engineering graduate Li Rongjun constructed a two-story office building in Chongqing, China, made partly from 8,500 empty beer bottles, held together with sand and cement. He spent four months and $11,000 on the building, the top floor of which consists of 40 layers of bottles while the lower floor is made of conventional brick.

HELL'S BELLS

➔ Hidden deep in the depths of a limestone sinkhole in Mexico's Yucatan peninsula, mysterious bell-shaped stalactites have been found. The stalactites (often called hell's bells, elephant feet, or trumpets) range in size— some are as large as an adult! They can take 100 years to grow just 1 in (2.5 cm), so these bells likely formed over thousands of years!

CHURCH RISES ➔ In 2015, the ruins of a 16th-century church, which had been hidden under nearly 100 ft (30 m) of water since a dam was completed in 1966, re-emerged from beneath a Mexican reservoir for only the second time in nearly 50 years. A prolonged drought dropped the water level in the Nezahualcoyotl reservoir by 75 ft (23 m), allowing the church's 48-ft-high (15-m) bell tower to protrude above the surface.

AIRPLANE RESTAURANT ➔ In 2016, a decommissioned Indonesian Boeing 737 jet airplane opened as a restaurant in the city center of Wuhan, China. It cost a total of $5.4 million to buy the aircraft, transport it from Indonesia, and renovate it, including building a flight simulation system to make customers think that they are airborne.

CUPCAKE TOWER ➔ A team of volunteers in Escondido, California, built a cupcake tower that was 31.5 ft (9.6 m) tall and was made up of 25,103 cupcakes.

PURPLE BREAD ➔ Zhou Weibiao, a professor at the National University of Singapore, has created purple bread, which he says is healthier and easier to digest than traditional bread. He made it by extracting anthocyanin—the natural blue pigment found in foods like grapes and blueberries—from black rice and then infusing it into bread dough.

SEASHELL STATUE ➔ Artist Radha Mallappa, of Mysuru, India, made a sculpture of the Hindu god Ganesha from hundreds of different-sized seashells. It took her four years, working 12 hours a day, to build the 12-ft-high (3.7-m), 8.5-ft-wide (2.6-m) statue.

FLYING CARS ➔ At Colin's Crest—a landmark on the Vargåsen stage of the Rally Sweden course, an intense winter car race—drivers fly 148 ft (45 m) through the air at speeds of over 100 mph (161 kmph).

CEMETERY PICNIC ➔ Every year on the Sunday after Easter, the Pontic ethnic community in the Greek village of Rizana makes their way to the local cemetery to enjoy a "Picnic with the Dead." They bring folding tables, chairs, and tablecloths and sit down to a meal amid the marble gravestones in a tradition that dates back over 2,000 years.

BALLOON DESSERT ➔ Customers at Alinea, a restaurant in Chicago, Illinois, can order an edible, transparent, helium-filled balloon for dessert. Created by head chef and co-owner Grant Achatz, the dish begins with a green apple taffy base, which is then blown up using a tube connected to a helium tank. Some diners like to pop the balloon with a pin, while others prefer to suck out a little of the helium first so that they can speak in a squeaky voice.

SLOW JOURNEY → It takes 90 days for a drop of water to travel the entire length of the Mississippi River from northern Minnesota to the Gulf of Mexico.

NOISE ANNOYS → Of the 8,670 noise complaints that Washington's Reagan National Airport received in 2015, 6,500 of them were made by the same person. That unnamed individual made an average of 18 calls every day of the year.

LEPRECHAUN MUSEUM → In Dublin, Ireland, there is a museum dedicated to leprechauns. Conceived by local architect Tom O'Rahilly, the National Leprechaun Museum offers a complete guide to the mythical little people, including a room where all of the furniture is three times smaller than normal size so that visitors can feel what it would be like to be a leprechaun.

SCORPION SMOKING → In parts of Afghanistan and Pakistan, people smoke scorpion venom as an alternative to tobacco. Some choose to burn the dried scorpion corpse on a fire and inhale the smoke, while others prefer to crush the dried tail, which contains the venom, mix it with tobacco, and smoke it like a cigarette.

STRANGE SPF

⊙ Thousands of beachgoers in China are covering up with face-kinis.

Inventor Zhang Shifan first created the masks as a way to protect her sensitive skin from the harmful rays of the sun and jelly stings. The idea caught on, and in 2014, she sold 30,000 face-kinis! The cover-ups are now available in many different colors and patterns, including designs that resemble the Peking opera's famous theatre masks. Despite their funny appearance, the masks provide better protection from the sun's harmful rays than sunscreen or hats can offer.

PARKING FINES → Under the city's Food for Fines program, drivers in Lexington, Kentucky, can pay parking fines with canned food instead of cash. A donation of 10 canned food items earns a $15 credit on citations. The scheme is designed to help stock local food banks through winter.

SMARTPHONE HAZARD → The town of Augsburg, Germany, has installed special traffic lights at ground level to make them visible to people who are constantly looking down at their smartphones. After two pedestrians were injured by quiet trams as they crossed the street without looking up from their phones, the authorities decided to fit traffic lights into the sidewalk at two busy tram stops.

PRISON PAGEANT → The Talavera Bruce women's prison in Rio de Janeiro, Brazil, holds an annual Miss Criminal beauty pageant. The 2015 winner was 27-year-old Michelle Neri Rangel who has been behind bars since 2010, when she was sentenced to 39 years for robbery.

AXE LOUNGE → The Timber Lounge, a bar in Halifax, Nova Scotia, Canada, gives customers the chance to hurl axes. There is a special area where they can throw hatchets and double-edged axes at painted wooden bullseyes—but only if they are not too intoxicated.

TWIN VILLAGE →

The Ukrainian village of Velikaya Kopanya has 122 twins among a population of less than 4,000. Villagers believe the high rate is due to health-giving properties in the local water, and its supposed effects even extend to cattle, with above-average births of twin calves, too.

SHOE CUSTOM →

On Christmas Day in the Czech Republic, unmarried women stand by a door and throw a shoe over their shoulder. If the shoe lands with the toe pointing toward the door, it is believed that they will marry within the next 12 months.

BLUE WINE →

Winemakers in Spain's Basque country have created the world's first natural blue wine. Start-up company Gik give their wine a bright blue color by mixing in anthocyanin, a natural pigment found in the skin of grapes, and indigo, a dye extracted from the *Isatis tinctoria* plant.

FUNNY FINS ⊙

Led by their lobster conductor named "The Lobster Formerly Known as Larry," over 250 rubber fish and lobsters sing and dance in synchrony on this art car created by Richard Carter and John Schroeter of Houston, Texas. The car is known as "The Sashimi Tabernacle Choir," and 5 mi (8 km) of wires are needed to make the gag gifts perform songs ranging from pop music to opera.

NATURAL MIRROR →

Measuring over 4,500 sq mi (11,655 sq km), the Salar De Uyuni salt pan in Bolivia is so flat that rain is unable to drain, creating the world's largest natural mirror.

SELLERS' NIGHTMARE →

As a result of the 1984 Freddy Krueger horror movie *A Nightmare on Elm Street*, U.K. houses on roads called Elm Street are often valued as low as half of those in surrounding streets.

DENSE FOG →

During the Great Smog of London in 1952, visibility in the streets was so bad in the dense fog that blind people led sighted people home from train stations.

CANOE MARATHON →

Competitors in the Yukon 1000 Canoe and Kayak Race, which is held every two years from Whitehorse down the Yukon River to the Alaska Pipeline Bridge on the Dalton Highway, cover 1,000 mi (1,609 km) and paddle up to 18 hours a day for 12 days.

BANKERS BANNED →

After being refused a loan, Alexandre Callet banned all bankers from his Michelin-listed restaurant, Les Écuries de Richelieu, in Paris, France. He placed a blackboard outside that read, "Dogs welcome, bankers banned (unless they pay an entry fee of 70,000 euros ($79,590)." He wanted the loan to open a second restaurant.

SEASTAR SKEWERS

⊙ Sampling street food in Beijing, China, might require a bit of an acquired taste—especially when that includes seastars! In comparison to the giant grasshoppers, dried seahorses, and baby scorpions, seastar skewers could be considered a safe bet, except for the unappetizing hard outer shell and off-putting brown color of the flesh inside. It's certainly edible, although not particularly palatable to most.

Best CRYPT Secret

⊙ **Sealed away and forgotton in a small crypt beneath a monastery in 1861, these mummies have been adopted as citizens of San Angel, Mexico.**

After San Angel's 12 most mysterious residents were rediscovered in 1917, word spread, and when the suggestion was made by a local friar to bury them, residents of the small town refused, claiming they were adopted citizens.

Recently, the mummies have been laid to rest in glass coffins, and the crypt has been fully restored and opened to the public.

Despite being 155 years old, these mummies are incredibly well preserved thanks to the volcanic environment, which allowed for them to dehydrate quickly rather than truly decomposing.

A closer look at their jewelry and wardrobe shows that these were well-to-do parishioners.

ROBOT RECEPTIONIST → Pepper, a $34,000 robot that can speak 19 different languages, is the receptionist at the AZ Damiaan Hospital in Ostend, Belgium. Pepper is able to introduce visitors to the hospital, provide information, and guide them to their correct floor and room. Fully charged, it can work for 20 hours unsupervised.

LONG STRUDEL → A strudel prepared in Jaškovo, Croatia, measured 4,851 ft (1,479 m) long—almost a mile. It used 1,815 lb (825 kg) of flour, 1,436 lb (653 kg) of apples, 110 lb (50 kg) of sugar, and 22 lb (10 kg) of cinnamon.

ILLEGAL PANTS → Under a new town ordinance, anyone in Timmonsville, South Carolina, who is caught wearing saggy pants that intentionally expose underwear faces a fine of up to $600.

RARE MEATS → Chinju-ya Restaurant in Yokohama, Japan, specializes in serving dishes made with rare meats. Its exotic menu has featured cooked crocodile feet, grilled piranha, badger curry, and battered, deep-fried whole salamander.

CORNER CITY → If you travel directly north, south, east, or west from Stamford, Connecticut, you will enter the state of New York.

ICE BREAKER → The Russian ship *Arktika*, a nuclear-powered icebreaker, is 567 ft (173 m) long—the length of 1½ football fields—more than 100 ft (30 m) wide, and can break through ice 10 ft (3 m) thick.

PIZZA ROBOT → Domino's in Queensland, Australia, has been testing pizza delivery by robot. DRU (Domino's Robotic Unit) is a 3-ft-tall (0.9-m) robot that can drive itself on roads or sidewalks at 12.4 mph (20 kmph) to any location within a range of 12-mi (20-km). The unit consists of a chiller for cold drinks and a battery-powered heated compartment that can keep up to 10 pizzas warm. It is programmed to return to the store for recharging as soon as it has finished its deliveries.

BALANCING ROCK → A huge rock measuring 20 ft (6 m) high, 16.4 ft (5 m) in diameter, and weighing an estimated 250 tons is balanced precariously at a 45-degree angle on the slope of a small hill at Mahabalipuram, India—but has remained firmly in place for over 1,300 years. Terrified that the gravity-defying rock—known as "Krishna's Butter Ball"—might slip and go crashing down the hill, locals have even brought in elephants to try to move it to a safer spot, but all attempts to dislodge the rock have failed.

WATERFALL REVIVED → After being dry for at least 200 years, the 260-ft-high (80-m) waterfall at Malham Cove in the Yorkshire Dales National Park in England began flowing again in December 2015 following prolonged heavy rain.

LAST RESIDENTS → For more than 45 years, Juan Martin and Sinforosa Colomer have been the only human residents of the abandoned Spanish village of La Estrella. It was once a busy place, with hundreds of inhabitants, a church, two schoolhouses, and several bars, but a ferocious storm in 1883 killed nearly half of the population, and over the ensuing decades the surviving families gradually drifted away. Now only the (two) Colomers are left. They have no TV, phone, electricity, or running water, and the closest inhabited town is over 15 mi (25 km) away.

SNOW ROLLERS → A windstorm in January 2016 caused the formation of thousands of snow rollers in fields near Picabo, Idaho. The rare weather phenomenon led to the creation of snowballs as big as 18 in (45 cm) that were blown across the ground, picking up more snow as they moved.

POETIC COFFEE → To mark World Poetry Day on March 21, 2016, 1,280 stores worldwide owned by the Austrian coffee retailer Julius Meinl allowed customers to pay for their coffee by writing a poem.

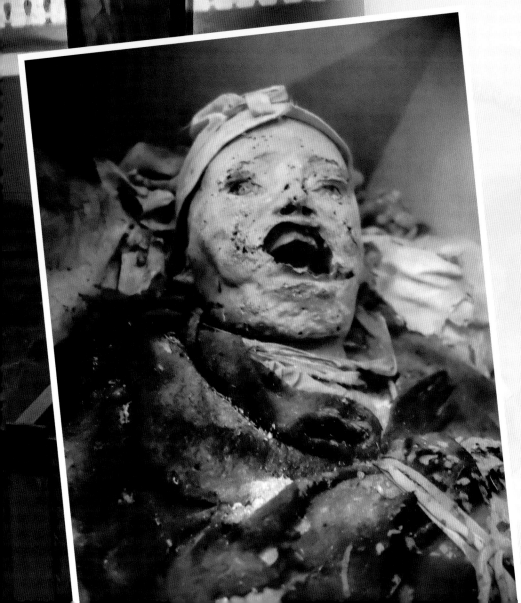

Witchetty Grub

⊙ **The witchetty grub, the larvae of moths found in Australia, is a nutritious and well-known native food source of the Australian aborigines.**

The fat, white larvae feed and live in the woody roots of the witchetty bush. Said to have an almond-like flavor, the grubs, which grow to about 2.75 in (7 cm), can be eaten cooked or raw. High in protein, just 10 grubs a day are sufficient for survival.

Aboriginal women and children dig around the roots of the plant, catching the grubs by pushing a long piece of wire or hook down the hole and pulling them out.

POTTER CAFÉ → There is a *Harry Potter*–themed coffee shop in Henderson, Nevada. The walls and tables at "Bad Owl Coffee" are decorated with Potter references, the Wi-Fi is named Hedwig for the young wizard's snowy white owl, and the menu offers such treats as butterbeer lattes.

NOISE LAW → Until 2016, it was illegal to hoot and holler in Bracebridge, Ontario, Canada. A new bylaw allows "yelling, shouting, hooting or similar noises made by a human" between 7 a.m. and 11 p.m., whereas previously those noises were banned at all times.

WILD RITUAL → Part of the Khweta ceremony requires young men to continuously dance for hours on end until they are exhausted. The ritual is practiced by several tribes in South Africa as a way of turning boys into men.

PEACE GESTURE → In an attempt to foster peace, the Hummus Bar café, near Netanya, Israel, offers a 50 percent discount to Jews and Arabs who eat together.

INSTANT VOLCANO → The Paricutín volcano in Mexico began as a crack in a cornfield in 1943 and grew to a 1,102-ft-tall (336-m) mountain by the end of the year.

RAINBOW BAGEL → At The Bagel Store in Brooklyn, New York, owner Scott Rosillo sells beautiful rainbow-colored bagels. He creates them by adding neon food coloring to the batches of dough, but the process is so complex that it takes him and his team of bakers 50 times longer to make a rainbow bagel than an ordinary one.

Ark Nova takes only two hours to inflate and can hold about 500 people.

THE BENCHES iNSiDE WERE MADE FROM WOOD SALVAGED FROM THE 2011 TSUNAMi.

ARK NOVA

→ Ark Nova is the first of its kind— an inflatable, portable concert hall. Following the devastating earthquake and tsunami that struck Japan in 2011, Japanese architect Arata Isozaki and British sculptor Anish Kapoor wanted a way to bring art, music, and hope to areas most affected. Their collaboration resulted in the giant, purple Ark Nova and a festival tour of Japan, since the concert hall can easily be deflated, packed into trucks, and moved to new locations.

WHALE BONE ALLEY → Massive whale bones line the northern coast of Yttygran Island in Russia. Stuck into the ground and towering around 16 ft (5 m) tall, the two parallel rows of ribs and jaws stretch along for 1,800 ft (550 m), earning it the nickname "Whale Bone Alley." Researchers estimate that the white spires have been there for 600 years, remnants of a time when local tribes cooperated to hunt whales for their meat and other resources.

world

89

THE PYRES OF PINARES

Precautions, such as taping the horse's tail, are taken to help ensure the safety of the horses and the riders.

⊕ Every year on January 16, horses and their riders blaze through massive bonfires during a celebration known as "Las Luminarias" in the town of San Bartolome de Pinares, Spain.

In preparation for the fiery stunt, the townspeople gather all the firewood they can find and pile it up throughout the cobblestone streets of their village. At dusk, the fires are lit and bold horsemen and women leap through the flames, which reach around 2,012°F (1,100°C), believed to "cleanse" the horses and riders for the new year. It's all a part of a festival hundreds of years old that celebrates Saint Antony, the patron saint of animals. Despite the dangers, locals insist the animals are never hurt.

world

91

DONKEY
CHEESE

DONKEY DAIRY

→ **The world's most expensive cheese does not come from your usual suspects, like cows or goats—it comes from donkeys!**

Known as Pule cheese, this Serbian cheese is made from the milk of Balkan donkeys and costs over $1,000 a pound! The crumbly white cheese comes from a single herd of donkeys that live on a farm in the Zasavica Special Nature Preserve. Milked by hand three times a day, it takes 3.5 gal (13.2 l) of milk to produce just 1 lb (.45 kg) of Pule!

TWO FACED ➋ While hiking at Ponce de Leon Springs State Park in Florida, PhD student Danny Goodding captured a bizarre sight—a two-colored woodland jumping spider! The 1-cm-long spider actually exhibited both male and female characteristics (or gynandromorphism), with its colors being split bilaterally down the center of its body.

FROZEN FISH → In January 2014, the weather was so cold that when a trout jumped out of a hatchery in Decorah, Iowa, in temperatures of –22°F (–30°C), it immediately froze to a wall.

SEAGULL CHASE → A German shepherd dog named Storm went missing for four days after chasing seagulls in Hastings, England, and was eventually rescued after being found swimming 1 mi (1.6 km) out at sea.

LIGHTNING GULP → The striated frogfish is able to swallow prey in one lightning-fast gulp, inhaling its food in just 6 milliseconds. Its mouth expands at close to the speed of a .22 rifle bullet—and that is underwater in a medium 800 times denser than air.

PROSTHETIC LEG → Mr. Ben the cockatoo has been fitted with a prosthetic leg made on a 3-D printer by a parrot rescue center in Oxfordshire, England. He used to keep falling off his perch because he only had one foot, but that did not stop him promptly eating the prosthetic leg once fitted.

SNAKES ALIVE! →
When Jacqueline Rutland moved into a new home in Verrierdale, Queensland, Australia, she kept hearing noises in her roof. She blamed them on her dog until workmen replacing the roof found 20 snake skins, the longest more than 6.5 ft (2 m) long.

GOLFING TURTLE → A snapping turtle built its nest in a sand trap at Wildwood Golf Club in McCandless Township, Pennsylvania. Club officials roped off the bunker to avoid disturbing the buried eggs, which coincidentally, are white, round, and about the size of golf balls.

MONKEY BUSINESS → Long-tailed macaques at temples in Japan and Indonesia steal cell phones, shoes, hats, and sunglasses from tourists—and only give them back in return for food.

HUNGRY HYENA

⊙ At the Mashatu Game Reserve in Botswana, Africa, this scavenger bit off more than he could chew! Wildlife photographer Mike Dexter visited an elephant's carcass just two days after it had died naturally in the wild and was shocked to find this young hyena had carried out an amputation!

EXPERT MIMIC → A tiny Australian bird, the brown thornbill, scares off would-be predators by mimicking the calls of other, much larger birds, including the pied currawong, which is about 40 times the size of the thornbill.

CALM DEVIL → Nick the Tasmanian devil—an animal usually notorious for its aggressive behavior—was fitted with a pacemaker at California's San Diego Zoo because his heartbeat was abnormally slow.

LOBSTER RETRIEVER → Alex Schulze, of Boca Raton, Florida, has taught his black Labrador retriever, Lila, to dive to the ocean floor and catch lobsters. He began by training her to retrieve toys from the bottom of a swimming pool. When he moved their trick out into the ocean and asked her to pick up a lobster, she succeeded on the first attempt.

BLOOD-THIRSTY ANIMALS

Moths are usually harmless, except for the **VAMPIRE MOTH** (*Calyptra thalictri*), which feeds on the blood of vertebrates—including humans.

Of the roughly 1,000 known bat species, only three **DRINK BLOOD**, and of those three, only one preys on mammals and humans.

The sharp-beaked ground finch of the Galápagos sometimes feasts on **BOOBY BLOOD**, earning it the name "vampire finch."

The Brazilian candirú—a tiny, **PARASITIC CATFISH**—attacks other fish by swimming into their gills.

The large, blood-sucking **TSETSE FLY** is the primary carrier of deadly **SLEEPING SICKNESS** in Africa.

Despite its charming name, the kissing bug is so named because it feeds on blood in the night, preferring to **BITE HUMANS IN THE FACE.**

Believe it or not, **VAMPIRE BATS** have more blood-sucking **PARASITES** than the average bat, meaning vampires feed on vampires.

CANNIBAL DINOSAURS → As well as eating other dinosaurs, *Tyrannosaurus rex* were cannibalistic and sometimes ate each other. They were such fearsome and compulsive meat eaters that after a battle the winner would often devour the loser.

NEW SPECIES → The dead body of a 24-ft-long (7.3-m) beaked whale that washed ashore on St. George's Island, Alaska, in 2014 belongs to a new species—and one of the few other known specimens is a skeleton hanging in a high school gym in Dutch Harbor on the Aleutian Islands.

FAITHFUL FRIEND → When a dog named Athena became trapped in a chain-link fence in Fulton County, Georgia, her canine companion Zeus stayed by her side for two days, barking constantly until help arrived.

FIRE STARTER → Brookfield, a hungry black Labrador owned by Gary and Katie LeClerc of Waterbury, Connecticut, started a house fire by turning on the stove while he was sniffing around two pizza boxes. The boxes had been placed on the cold stove but caught fire when Brookfield nudged one of the burner knobs while trying to steal a slice of pizza. Fortunately, the fire was extinguished 30 seconds later and nobody was hurt.

NEW TARANTULA → Mark Pennell, of Bristol, England, spent 10 years searching the jungles of the world for a new species of tree-dwelling tarantula—and finally found it in the Sarawak region of Borneo when one landed on his foot! The spider was subsequently named *Phormingochilus pennellhewletti* in honor of Pennell and fellow explorer Dean Hewlett.

SMOKING SNAKE → A family in Maroochy River, Queensland, Australia, noticed smoke coming from a wall socket—and when they investigated, they found a huge carpet python badly burned and trapped there. They called a snake handler, who took an hour to extricate the injured reptile.

STRONG SWIMMER → A racehorse named Rebel Rover swam 1.2 mi (2 km) out to sea after being spooked during a training session on a beach in Brisbane, Australia. Marine rescuers found the horse swimming in 13 ft (4 m) of water and, in a 90-minute operation, eventually managed to maneuver their boat close enough to the animal to lasso him.

SAILOR HEN → Explorer Guirec Soudée, from Brittany, France, spent more than two years sailing around the world with a chicken named Monique. The hen adapted so well to life at sea that in the 28 days it took Soudée's boat, *Yvinec*, to cross the Atlantic Ocean to the Caribbean island of St. Bart's, she laid 25 eggs.

BEAR ATTACK → Tosya, a little dachshund, saved two boys from being badly mauled by a huge black bear in Amgu, Russia. Stas Nagoronov, 8, and Nikita Nikonov, 12, were attacked as they left a village shop, but Tosya arrived on the scene and barked furiously at the bear. It then left the boys to chase Tosya into the forest, but she escaped. Thanks to her timely intervention, the boys suffered only minor injuries.

SPEEDY TORTOISE → A star tortoise at the Arignar Anna Zoological Park in Chennai, India, lost one of its front legs in a mongoose attack—but is now able to move around again after keepers fitted it with a set of wheels. The two small wheels, which are normally used on a sliding window, are fixed with a special resin to either side of the bottom of the tortoise's shell and are connected by a lightweight metal rod.

GLOBETROTTING TERRIER → Skipper, a Jack Russell terrier owned by Jon Taylor of Shropshire, England, has clocked up 20,000 mi (32,180 km) traveling around the world. He has sailed across the Atlantic Ocean in a 54-ft (16-m) yacht, and while in the Caribbean, he caught lobster with his bare teeth and rode on a paddleboard. The globetrotting dog has also journeyed with his owner around Europe and flown with him to the Canary Islands.

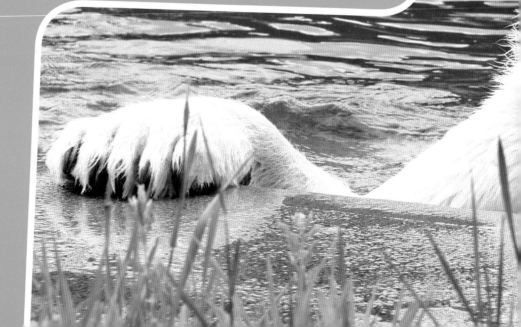

POLAR PLAYMATE

⊙ In *Dare To Look!* we revealed how animal trainer Mark Dumas took an 18-month-old grizzly bear named Billy to the pub to shoot pool. Well now Dumas shares a swimming pool and bed with Agee, a 7-ft-tall (2.1-m), 840-lb (381-kg) polar bear.

Dumas, from Abbotsford, British Columbia, Canada, has trained bears for more than 40 years and claims to be the only person in the world who can touch a polar bear, generally considered one of the most dangerous predators. By learning to read 21-year-old Agee's body language, Dumas is even able to put his head in her mouth, despite knowing that one wrong move would probably be fatal.

PUPPY LOVE → Alma Padillia, of Manchester, England, spent $3,000 on a wedding for her two Shih Tzu dogs Elvis and Bella. The canine guests enjoyed a banquet of bone-shaped biscuits and a three-tiered wedding cake made of dog food.

QUAKE SURVIVOR → Romeo, a golden retriever, was pulled alive from a mountain of rubble in Amatrice, Italy, 10 days after buildings in the region were devastated by a powerful earthquake.

ELEPHANT FIREFIGHTERS → When Riau Province in East Sumatra, Indonesia, was plagued by forest fires for nearly three months in the fall of 2015, officials brought in 23 trained elephants to serve as emergency fire trucks. The elephants were outfitted with water pumps and hoses in an attempt to control the fire and prevent it from spreading to neighboring regions.

PLAYING DEAD → Sleeper cichlid fish of East Africa fake death by lying on their sides at the bottom of lakes. When a scavenging fish approaches, the "corpse" suddenly jumps to life, snatches the investigating fish, and eats it.

CAT LADY → Lynea Lattanzio moved out of her five-bedroom house in Parlier, California, to make way for her hundreds of cats. She lives in a trailer on the grounds of her 12-acre (5-hectare) property while her cats have the run of the house. She started her sanctuary for feral and abandoned cats in 1992 and estimates that she has since lived with a total of 24,000 cats.

CROC GUARDS → A gang of suspected drug dealers in the Netherlands used crocodiles to guard their loot. When police officers in Amsterdam arrested the gang, they also seized $450,000 in cash—most of it locked in a cage with a pair of full-grown crocodiles.

Living Pesticide

⊕ **There are 800 Indian Runner ducks living at the Vergenoegd Wine Estate in South Africa!**

Twice a day they waddle quickly through the vineyard, plucking up tasty snails that would otherwise destroy the grapevines, while also fertilizing the land at the same time. The wine company is proud of their living pesticides, even naming a line of wines after them!

PET "PANDAS" → Meng Jiang of Singapore has dyed the fur of her three Chow Chow dogs black and white so that they look exactly like giant pandas. Instead of their natural white fur, the dogs—Yumi, TouDou, and DouDou—now have dyed black patches around their eyes, on their ears, and on other parts of their bodies.

ENGINE DRAMA → Paws, a six-month-old tabby cat from Rhyl, North Wales, used up one of his nine lives when he was driven for 20 mi (32 km) while trapped in a car engine. The kitten had climbed into the car of a neighbor, Andrew Higgins, who, when the car began to lose power on its journey, looked under the hood and found Paws. Luckily, the kitten survived with just a few minor burns.

SWIVEL HEAD → The three-toed sloth is able to rotate its head 270 degrees (three-quarters of the way around) because it has three extra vertebrae in its neck.

UNLUCKY MOUSE → A Victorian mousetrap exhibit at the University of Reading's Museum of English Rural Life in Berkshire, England, unexpectedly claimed the life of a mouse 155 years after being built. The wood and metal trap, which was not baited, was patented in 1861 and was used for display purposes only until an unfortunate rodent decided to make its home there in 2016.

TALENTED POODLE → Sailor, a black poodle owned and trained by Alex Rothacker, of Grayslake, Illinois, can walk a distance of 33 ft (10 m) on a globe in just over 33 seconds. He can also jump rope, clear multiple bars in one leap, and climb stairs on two legs. Rothacker rescued Sailor when the dog was six months old and was about to be put down because of his aggressive behavior.

ANIMAL FARMERS

KOPI LUWAK coffee is brewed from beans **EATEN, DIGESTED,** and **PASSED** by civets!

PIGS can sniff truffles out from as deep as **3 FEET (1 M)** underground!

DAMSELFISH grow and protect their very own algae gardens!

LEAF CUTTER ANTS have been growing their own food for over **50 MILLION YEARS,** collecting leaves to use as **FERTILIZER** for their underground fungi farms!

CASTOREUM, an ingredient commonly found in vanilla ice cream, comes from the **SECRETIONS AND URINE** of beavers!

YETI CRABS farm their food on their own arms, swaying their appendages in order to fertilize the **BACTERIA** growing on them.

SPIDER NEST → When Victoria Price, of Porthcawl, South Wales, went to the hospital complaining of a pain in her head, doctors removed a live, furry spider, which had crawled into her ear and made a nest inside.

FEATHERED FRIEND → A Magellanic penguin named Dindim swims to the coast of Brazil every year just to visit the man who rescued him. Retired bricklayer Joao Pereira de Souza spotted the penguin—starving and covered in oil—on the beach near his house in Provetá, Brazil, in 2011. He fed the bird every day until it was strong enough to leave, but Dindim refused to go. So the man rowed out to sea and dropped the penguin off, but when he returned to shore, he found Dindim waiting for him at his shanty. Dindim stayed for 11 months before finally leaving, but he now spends four months of the year breeding off the coast of Argentina and Chile and then swims all the way back to Brazil to enjoy the rest of the year with his human rescuer.

FELINE FELON → Over a period of six months, Brigit, a six-year-old Tonkinese cat owned by Sarah Nathan of Hamilton, New Zealand, stole dozens of men's underwear and socks from neighboring clothes lines.

MONSTER PYTHON → A reticulated python measuring 26 ft (8 m) in length—nearly the width of a singles tennis court—was found on Penang Island, Malaysia, in 2016. It weighed over 550 lb (250 kg) and was so heavy it needed five people to lift it.

POWER PERCH → A cat was eventually rescued in March 2016 after being stuck for three days at the top of a 30-ft-tall (9-m) telephone pole near Stranraer, Saskatchewan, Canada.

PAMPERED POOCH → Josephine Carter, from Surrey, England, has spent $45,000 in two years on clothes, pampering, and wigs for her pet Chihuahua, Queenie. The little dog has a huge selection of dresses, coats, hats, wigs, and accessories, as well as her own personalized buggy, special doggy nail varnish, and matching luxury waste bags.

MEAN MIMIC → The sabre-toothed blenny (or false cleanerfish) mimics the behavior of cleaner wrasses, which remove parasites and dead skin from larger fish. The blenny copies the wrasse's shape, markings, and movement to enable it to get close to large fish, but then instead of performing the expected cleaning duties, it bites off a chunk of flesh and flees.

WEASEL HAVOC → The $4.4 billion Large Hadron Collider—the world's largest atom smasher—was temporarily immobilized in April 2016 after a weasel broke into a high-voltage transformer near Geneva, Switzerland, and caused a power outage.

CLIFF PLUNGE → Toby, a one-year-old English sheepdog/poodle mix, somehow survived a 300-ft (90-m) fall at Gooseberry Mesa, Utah. The McInnes family of Eagle Mountain was hiking with their pet when the dog leapt off a cliff and tumbled down the steep slope.

SURROGATE MOM → Amanda Dukart, a keeper at Chahinkapa Zoo in Wahpeton, North Dakota, saved the life of Barkly the baby kangaroo by carrying her around in a special pouch all day for six months. The orphaned joey only had a 25 percent chance of survival when her mother died suddenly, but thanks to her human surrogate mom, she was soon strong enough to hop.

BALANCING ACT ⊙
Rani the goat amazes onlookers in Pakistan as she balances on all four hooves atop a platform just a few inches in diameter. She remains sure-footed and steadily climbs higher and higher as her handler, Osman Ali, gradually adds height to the small pole. Rani learned the trick in just three days and is able to hold the precarious position for up to two minutes!

FIRE RESCUE → Rex, an Alaskan malamute/German shepherd cross, saved a sleeping woman from a house fire in Vonda, Saskatchewan, Canada, by barking loudly, waking her, and even pulling her off the couch and toward the door. Feeling unwell, Noreen Lucas, whose son is Rex's owner, had taken a sleeping pill and was in a deep sleep on the couch when the fire broke out. She awoke to see flames in the hallway. The house burned down, but thanks to Rex, nobody was hurt.

PEDALING MANTIS
⊙ This unassuming praying mantis jumped onto a curled plant and looked just like he was riding a bicycle! Student Eco Suparman from Borneo captured the stunning sight in a cemetery in the Ambawang River Village.

No longer featured in the circus, an illustrated poster for the Barnum & Bailey Circus shows Mooney's all-elephant baseball team in a stadium in 1913. Harry Mooney was Barnum & Bailey's elephant trainer from 1907 to 1918.

THE BARNUM & BAILEY GREATEST SHOW ON EARTH

MOONEY'S GIANTS THE BIG LEAGUE LEADERS
THE FAMOUS ELEPHANT BASE-BALL TEAM

An elephant learning to play ball in Sarasota, Florida, around 1910.

ELEPHANT BASEBALL

For more than 200 years, elephants have been a show-business attraction, performing tricks such as riding bicycles, playing musical instruments, and even playing baseball!

In the early 1900s, Barnum & Bailey's "Greatest Show on Earth" started their own baseball league made up of nine of their circus elephants. Chief elephant trainer Harry Mooney taught his pachyderms how to swing a bat, use a mitt, and pitch, and in 1912, they played their first game. The attraction was so popular that other circuses later followed suit, creating their own tusker teams.

EQUINE ELEGANCE ❯ Morestead the horse looks dapper as he models the world's first Harris tweed suit designed for racehorses. Commissioned by William Hill, designer Emma Sandham-King used over 59 ft (18 m) of tweed to create the three-piece fashion statement. The dashing suit uses 10 times more fabric than a usual suit and was made to celebrate the Cheltenham Festival, where over 200 mi (321.8 km) of tweed are worn by attendees every year!

ANCIENT BONES ❯ In January 2016, construction workers digging in the north end zone at Reser Stadium—home of the Oregon State University football team—unearthed the 10,000-year-old bones of a mammoth, a bison, and a camel.

HALF GOAT ❯ A goat was born on a farm in China's Yunnan Province with no hind legs—but within a week, it was able to walk around happily on just its forelegs.

animals

101

METAL HIVE → Wolfgang Buttress, an artist from Nottingham, England, created a 55-ft-high (17-m) replica of a beehive made from 170,000 pieces of aluminum. *The Hive*, which weighs 40 tons, was installed at London's Kew Gardens and connected to a real beehive. The activity of the bees set off sound and light displays on the sculpture, so that anyone standing inside it could experience life in a real hive.

COW SPECIALIST → Artist John Marshall, from East Sussex, England, has painted only one subject for more than 10 years—cows. Each year, he sells around 40 cow paintings—some on canvases up to 6 ft (1.8 m) in size that can fetch over $8,000.

RAPID RACK → At the height of summer, a moose's antlers can grow an inch every day. A big bull moose can grow an 80-lb (36-kg) rack, adding close to 1 lb (0.45 kg) of bone a day.

COW PRIZE → The prize for achieving the top score in the Tunisian cell phone game Bagra is a real live cow. Players earn points in the game, which is named after the Arabic word for "cow," by abducting their opponents' cows with a UFO while protecting their own.

HAPPY ENDING → William Lindler of the Hanahan Fire Department, South Carolina, saved three-week-old pit bull puppy Jake from a raging fire by giving him mouth-to-snout resuscitation. Although the dog suffered serious burns, Lindler adopted him, and Jake has now become an honorary firefighter and the department's official mascot, visiting schools to help educate children about fire safety.

SNAKE SHOCK → When angler Andy Warton, from Darwin, Australia, caught an estuary cod near Melville Island, he was shocked to discover that the fish had a live, venomous spotted black snake inside its mouth.

DESIGNER SKULLS → Artist Jason Borders, originally from Lexington, Kentucky, uses a rotary grinding tool to turn animal skulls and bones into intricately patterned works of art that sell for thousands of dollars. He obtains many of his dead animal parts from farmers and uses the tool to engrave a series of dots and lines into the bone until they form beautiful patterns.

NIGHT FRIGHT → Jitendra Mishra, of Lakhimpur Kheri, Uttar Pradesh, India, woke up one morning to find 184 snakes slithering across his room. The snakes had made their way into the house through a wall after gaining access to the basement.

STAR WEEVIL → Scientists have named a new species of beetle after *Star Wars* character Chewbacca. The flightless weevil *Trigonopterus chewbacca* was discovered in Papua New Guinea and was named for Han Solo's first mate because the dense scales on its head and legs reminded the scientists of Chewbacca's thick fur.

RESOURCEFUL PUP → When Nick Haworth's 18-month-old German shepherd/husky mix pup Luna fell overboard into the Pacific Ocean during a 2016 fishing trip off San Diego, California, he feared that she had drowned—but five weeks later, she miraculously turned up safe and sound 2 mi (3.2 km) away on San Clemente Island. After swimming to dry land, she had likely survived by eating rodents and dead fish that had washed ashore.

LUCKY ESCAPE → Li Shou, a nine-month-old pure Birman kitten owned by Sandie Meadows, of West Sussex, England, had a lucky escape after swallowing a 16-in (40-cm) car antenna that was as long as her body. The antenna narrowly missed the cat's vital organs before becoming stuck, and it was only able to be removed by surgery.

> On the same weekend in May 2016, two different fishermen caught rare blue lobsters off the coast of Nova Scotia, Canada— beating odds of around four million to one.

TECHNO MONKEY → Izumi, an 11-year-old snow monkey at Lincoln Park Zoo, Chicago, Illinois, chose Iwaki as the name for her newborn baby by using touch-screen computer technology.

WAITING GAME → A loyal cat sat in the exact same spot in a street in Belgorod, Russia, every day for over a year, waiting hopefully for his owners to return. The cat's owners sold their nearby apartment and moved away from the area, but chose to leave their pet behind. The animal survived on the street by living off food given to him by neighbors.

SCHOOL HOME → A mother duck named Vanessa returned to the Village Elementary School in Hartland, Michigan, for the 13th straight year in 2016 to lay her eggs in the school courtyard. Once they have hatched, she leads the ducklings through the school corridors to a nearby pond.

SAFETY FIRST → The male nursery web spider ties up its mate to avoid getting eaten during sex. The female spider is larger and more aggressive, so the male produces silk to wrap around some of her front legs before mating takes place.

FISH BRACE → After Mr. Hot Wing the goldfish was born without a lower jawbone—a condition that made it difficult for him to eat and breathe because his mouth could not stay open—Lehigh Valley, Pennsylvania, veterinarian Brian Palmeiro performed surgery to open the fish's mouth and then helped it remain open by creating and fitting a special fish mouth brace made from a plastic credit card.

AIRPORT PATROL → Border collie K-9 Piper helps ensure airline passenger safety by clearing unwanted wildlife from Cherry Capital Airport in Traverse City, Michigan, even while airplanes are landing nearby. He works four 10-hour shifts per week, removing foxes, ducks, and geese from the runways and detecting rodents that would otherwise encourage birds of prey to hunt in aircraft flight paths. He always wears reflective spectacles to keep out the dirt and debris that fly up off the runways and ear muffs to protect his hearing.

A baby northern fur seal was found in March 2016 in the front yard of a home in Fremont, California, having wandered at least 4 mi (6.4 km) from the nearest stretch of ocean.

GREAT ESCAPE → In 2016, Inky the octopus made a daring nighttime escape from his tank at New Zealand's National Aquarium in Napier and fled to the ocean. He slipped through a gap left by maintenance workers at the top of his tank and, judging by the telltale suction cup prints, made his way across the floor to a 6-in-wide (15-cm) drain. He then squeezed his body—about the size of a soccer ball—into the drain and slid down a 164-ft-long (50-m) drainpipe that dropped him into the Pacific.

LONG FLIGHT → Although only 0.08 in (2 mm) long, the corn leaf aphid often travels around 620 mi (1,000 km) from Texas to Illinois in search of food.

PUFFER PATTERNS

→ When these intricate patterns were first discovered on the ocean floor in 1995, they were a mystery to divers—remaining so until 2013 when the culprits were caught.

Male pufferfish create these circles, laboriously flapping their fins for up to nine days, in order to attract mates. When the circle is completed, it is inspected by the female, who then lays her eggs in the center. Even though these fish are only about 5 in (12.7 cm) long, their formations can reach 7 ft (2.1 m) in diameter!

LONG WALK → A stray dog that was badly injured in a road accident in Russia walked 185 mi (296 km) to find the woman who had nursed her back to health. Suffering from two broken legs, Shavi was picked up from the side of the road in Rostov-on-Don by Nina Baranovskaya, who then took care of her at her apartment. However, Nina was unable to look after the dog in the long term, so she found Shavi a home with friends in Voronezh Oblast, nearly 200 mi (322 km) away. A few days later, Shavi went missing and turned up back in Rostov near Nina's home—a journey that would have taken her about a week.

BROKEN HEARTED → A dog named Pirata—meaning "pirate" in Spanish, on account of the black patches around its eyes—refused to leave the San Antonio de Padua Hospital in Rio Cuarto, Argentina, after its owner died there. The dog had accompanied its owner to the hospital for an operation, but after the man's death, despite the best efforts of hospital staff to persuade the dog to leave, it kept wandering the corridors and returning to the room where it had last seen him.

IGUANA ALERT → A man was turned away from the Boulder County Justice Center in Colorado for trying to sneak his pet iguana into the courthouse. Security staff detected the reptile hidden in a bag as it passed through an X-ray machine.

Zaman Iqbal, of Aberdeen, Scotland, is plagued by seagulls who brazenly walk into his shop and steal packets of food from the shelves.

PROFANE PARROT → U.S. President Andrew Jackson's pet parrot, Poll, had to be removed from his funeral service in 1845 for squawking foul language.

HAMSTER CONCERN → A man called a police hotline in England to complain that his ex-girlfriend was overfeeding their hamster.

BAD MOVE → A suspected burglar jumped into a lake in Barefoot Bay, Florida, to escape a police search team—only to be killed and eaten by an 11-ft-long (3.4-m) alligator. The man's remains were later discovered in the reptile's stomach.

INDIAN BIRDMAN → Every day, an Indian man named Sekar gets up at 4:30 a.m. and prepares to feed 4,000 parakeets that flock to his home in Chennai, India. His interaction with the birds started in 2004, following the Indian Ocean tsunami, when he fed a pair of parakeets some rice. Soon he was attracting thousands of feathered visitors as other pairs began nesting nearby. A camera repairman by profession, he spends about 40 percent of his income feeding the birds.

MONKEY VANDALS → A gang of 100 monkeys raided a polling station in northern Thailand and tore up voter lists ahead of a 2016 referendum on a proposed constitution. It is thought the macaques were attracted by the lists' pink color.

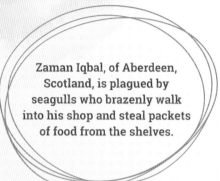

ANIMAL ORCHIDS

→ The *Dracula simia* species of orchid looks just like the grinning face of a little monkey! The scientific name of these rare orchids has some relevant meaning as well—"Dracula" referring to the long spurs that hang down and look like vampire fangs, and "simia" meaning "monkey" in Latin. The *Caleana major* of Australia is also called the flying duck orchid (for obvious reasons) and can only be seen in the wild.

Ironically, when fully blossomed, the monkey orchid smells just like a ripe orange, not a banana.

SPIDER PHOBIA → Gemma Wright, of Chelmsford, England, has conquered her phobia of spiders by living with more than 50 tarantulas. She used to be so afraid of spiders that she could not even look at one.

CAT FIGHT

→ **With prey hanging limp from her mouth, this frightening photo shows the aftermath of a rare fight between a tigress and a leopard in Sariska Tiger Reserve in India.**

The clash was witnessed by a group of tourists on an early morning safari, who saw the tiger climb a tree, push the leopard out, and then pounce on it from a 10-ft (3-m) distance. Within just five minutes, the tigress emerged victorious—after shaking the young leopard like a rag doll. The fatal encounter is quite unusual to see, as tigers rarely eat other carnivores, let alone a feline cousin.

SWEPT AWAY → In December 2015, a pregnant cow feared dead after being swept away by floods in Cumbria, England, was found alive and well two days later, quietly munching grass on a golf course 18 mi (29 km) away.

CLEAN LIVING → Some wild boars mimic humans by washing any food that is dirty before eating it. At an experiment at Basel Zoo in Switzerland, several European wild boars took dirty apples to a stream and carefully washed them with their snouts before devouring them. When presented with clean apples, however, they did not go to the stream and ate the fruit right away.

CANINE COMPANION → After getting lost on an expedition in Mexico's Sierra Madre Oriental mountain range, 14-year-old Juan Heriberto Trevino survived for 44 hours in the wilderness—thanks to a Labrador retriever named Max, whom he had only met a few hours earlier. When Juan slipped down a ravine, Max followed him and stayed by his side for the next two days, lying on the boy's legs at night to keep him warm. The next day, Max found a puddle for both of them to drink from, staving off thirst. The pair were eventually rescued by a search party.

PAINTED PONIES → Wild ponies in Dartmoor, Devon, England, have been painted with reflective blue stripes so that car drivers can see them at night. More than 60 ponies were killed in collisions with vehicles in 2015.

MERCY MISSION → After Min Tims, from Mount Isa, Queensland, Australia, accidentally ran over a little green tree frog with her lawnmower, she felt so guilty that she patched up its head wounds and flew the injured amphibian 625 mi (1,000 km) to a frog hospital in Cairns.

THIRSTY LEOPARD → A leopard in northern India got its head stuck in a metal pot for six hours after it went looking for a drink. Eventually forest officials tranquilized the animal, freed it, and released it back into the wild.

NIGHT MILK → Milk collected from cows at night can help a person sleep better. A South Korean study found that night milk is exceptionally rich in tryptophan and melatonin—two natural sleeping aids—compared to milk taken from cows during the day.

WHITE WILD

Albinism is caused by genetic mutations that result in the absence of melanin, a pigment found in the skin, hair, and feathers of humans and animals. Leucism, on the other hand, is a partial loss of pigmentation and often mistaken for albinism. A good way to tell the difference is by the eyes: albino eyes tend to appear pink or red in color, while leucistic eyes are generally dark and unaffected. The two vastly different conditions appear in nature, creating a stunning and rare sight in some species.

SPIRIT BEAR

One of the rarest (and most revered) bears on Earth, the Kermode bear, is actually a white black bear! The white fur trait is recessive, meaning both parents must pass on a copy of the mutated gene. The spirit bear, as they are also called, is found almost exclusively in the Great Bear Rainforest of Canada.

CRYSTAL LOBSTER

Most lobsters are a dark, greenish-brown color, but several naturally occurring genetic mutations can transform them into a variety of colors. Albino lobsters, lacking in colored pigments, are the rarest variety—one in 100 million. Amazingly, a person is more likely to get attacked by a shark than see an albino, or "crystal," lobster.

WHITE LIONS

This stunning white lion is not albino, but a genetic rarity found only in the Greater Timbavati region of South Africa. The recessive gene carrying the leucistic pigment also gives the lions blue or green-gray eyes instead of the usual brown. There are many more white lions in captivity than there are in the wild—where only 13, including cubs born in 2014, remain.

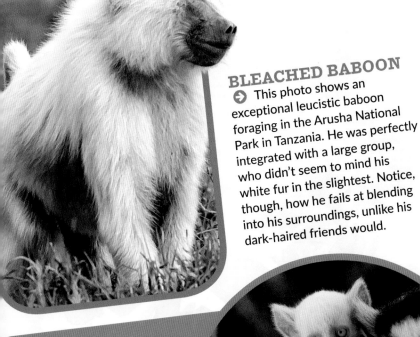

BLEACHED BABOON

➔ This photo shows an exceptional leucistic baboon foraging in the Arusha National Park in Tanzania. He was perfectly integrated with a large group, who didn't seem to mind his white fur in the slightest. Notice, though, how he fails at blending into his surroundings, unlike his dark-haired friends would.

WAXEN WALLABIES

➔ Believe it or not, albino wallabies thrive on Bruny Island in Tasmania, their numbers swelling up to 200, due to the lack of predators. With their pink eyes, claws, and nose, these wallabies are true albinos—and therefore also have vision problems, are prone to cancer, and are sensitive to sunlight.

LIGHT LEMUR

➔ This rare all-white ring-tailed lemur baby, named Sapphire, stands out against a dark-colored adult lemur. Not all albino or leucistic animals thrive. According to a PBS documentary that features Sapphire and her family, she was later abandoned and probably perished.

SILVER SKUNK ➔ Skyla the albino skunk looks striking without the usual distinct black-and-white skunk coloring. Skyla's owner Emily Campbell even entered her into a beauty pageant for skunks held in the United Kingdom!

Albino Humpback Whale

➔ First spotted in 1991 off Queensland, Australia, Migaloo is the only documented albino humpback whale in the world.

Scientists were originally skeptical about Migaloo's albinism because his eyes are brown instead of red or pink, but after researchers analyzed his DNA in 2011, they confirmed that he is indeed albino. Elders of the local aboriginal collective in Hervey Bay, Queensland, gave this special whale his name, which means "white fella."

STINGRAY C-SECTION

➔ In 2016, the Ripley's Aquarium of the Smokies in Gatlinburg, Tennessee, to our knowledge, was the first to successfully deliver a cownose ray pup via C-section!

After a pregnant cownose ray retained her baby for an extra six to eight weeks, the aquarium team decided to perform the cesarian section, and now both pup and mother are alive and healthy.

BABY STINGRAY

MONKEY PIG ➔ A piglet born in Ciego de Ávila, Cuba, in 2016 had the head and face of a monkey, with a simian jaw, short snout, and protruding forehead. The strange mutatation may have been caused by environmental pollution or by a rare brain development disorder called holoprosencephaly.

STRAWBERRY CRABS FOREVER

➔ Thanks to this tiny crab's size, color, and little hairs, it bears a striking resemblance to a strawberry! Discovered in Taiwan's Kenting National Park by a team of marine biologists lead by Professor Ho Ping-ho of National Taiwan Ocean University, the cute crustacean is only about 1 in (2.5 cm) long.

ACTUAL SIZE!

LUCKY FISH ➔ A single Asian arowana—or dragon fish—can sell for as much as $300,000. The Chinese believe that the tropical freshwater fish is a symbol of good fortune due to its red color and coin-like scales.

DOG EXORCIST ➔ A pet spa in Japan's Kagoshima Prefecture offers to exorcise any possessed dogs. The 30-minute exorcism costs almost $300 and is performed by a Shinto priest, who drives away the animal's evil spirits.

ITSY-BITSY SPIDER

➔ Photographer Duncan McMorrin was taking macro photos in his home garden when he noticed a tiny money spider trapped inside a single raindrop! The Surrey, England, native said it was an "incredibly lucky find" and managed to snap fantastic photos despite the wind swaying the clothes line. Unfortunately, the itsy-bitsy spider did not escape the raindrop alive.

HERMAPHRODITIC FISH ➔ The chalk bass (*Serranus tortugarum*)—a fish native to the Caribbean—changes its sex up to 20 times a day. The fish repeatedly vary their gender roles during reproduction.

LOBSTERS FREED ➔ A group of Buddhist monks on Prince Edward Island, Canada, bought 600 lb (272 kg) of live lobsters from restaurants and released them back into the ocean.

ADOPTED CROW ➔ Vikkie Kenward, of West Sussex, England, adopted an orphaned baby crow that she had found abandoned by the side of a road, and three months later, the pair were inseparable. The bird, named Fagin, follows her everywhere. He sits on her head, watches TV with her, and even jumps in her truck when she goes for a drive.

SWAN TERROR ➔ An aggressive male swan smashed up eight model boats—each worth thousands of dollars—at a lake in Suffolk, England. The bird's reign of terror stopped model boaters from using the lake, prompting one boat owner to write to Queen Elizabeth II, who owns all of the swans on the River Thames, asking for help.

WHALE DRIP ➔ The blue whale skeleton suspended from the ceiling of the New Bedford Whaling Museum in Massachusetts slowly oozes oil, almost 20 years after the whale had been struck by a tanker in 1998 off the coast of Nova Scotia.

CAT WASH ➔ A Bengal crossbreed cat called Bobby, living in Nottingham, England, survived a spin in a washing machine. The nine-month-old cat had climbed into the machine for a nap under a duvet but was quickly awakened when the wash cycle began. Hearing a thudding sound, owner Lisa Keefe stopped the machine and found Bobby soaked and in a state of near collapse. Happily, after receiving urgent veterinary treatment, Bobby made a full recovery.

TARANTULA EATS SNAKE ➔ In October 2015, a graduate student in Brazil stumbled upon a scene never before witnessed in the wild—a tarantula eating a snake. The large tarantula (*Grammostola quirogai*) ripped the front and middle of the 1-ft-long (0.3-m) snake to shreds. Researchers speculate the unfortunate snake accidentally surprised the spider in its rocky hiding place.

↑ YOUR UPLOADS

ROLES REVERSED → One-year-old Lorenzo Ferreira Figueira killed a grass snake by biting it on the head while playing in the garden of his home in Mostardas, Brazil. His mother Jaine found the boy with the snake in his mouth and blood on his clothes and, fearing that he had been bitten, rushed him to hospital for medical attention that turned out to be unnecessary. The doctor confirmed that baby Lorenzo had bitten the snake close to the head, immobilizing and preventing it from attacking.

> The heart of a pygmy shrew beats 1,200 times per minute—more than 12 times faster than the human heart.

THAWED OUT → Scientists in Japan successfully brought back to life tiny water-dwelling creatures that had been kept frozen for over three decades. The eight-legged water bears, or moss piglets, were retrieved from frozen moss samples collected in Antarctica in 1983 and stored at –4°F (–20°C). Once revived in 2015, they reproduced and laid 19 eggs, 14 of which hatched.

TEDDY SNACK → A carpet python in Queensland, Australia, underwent an emergency C-section operation to remove a purple teddy bear from its stomach. The snake had eaten the toy thinking it was a tasty meal.

FROZEN SOLID → A New Zealand cricket-like insect called the mountain stone weta survives harsh winters by temporarily freezing 80 percent of its body solid. It has developed special proteins that prevent ice crystals from forming inside its cells in sub-zero conditions. However, when temperatures rise, the weta thaws out and resumes activity, effectively coming back from the dead. It can do this repeatedly, even freezing, thawing, and re-freezing its body daily when temperatures fluctuate.

SINGER'S SPIDER → A 6-in (15-cm) tarantula discovered in California has been named after Johnny Cash. *Aphonopelma johnnycashi* lives near Folsom Prison, which the country singer made famous with his 1955 song "Folsom Prison Blues." Its black body is also reminiscent of Cash, who always wore dark clothing.

Five-Legged Frog

Janice Savage, from Fort Valley, Virginia, contacted Ripley's with this photo she took of a frog with five legs! She found the funky amphibian while cleaning the fish pond in front of her house—originally thinking the extra appendage was in fact a twig stuck to the frog.

LOYAL COMPANION → When Phoebe the basset hound fell into an old cistern in a ravine on Vashon Island, Washington, and was unable to climb out, her Irish setter/spaniel mix companion Tillie stood guard over her for a whole week. Tillie did occasionally try to summon help by running out and running back to the cistern, and finally she managed to attract the attention of a passerby. Tillie's devotion was recognized when she was subsequently presented with a Washingtonian of the Day award by the state governor.

AMAZING MEMORIES → Gray squirrels remember the exact location, with 62.5 percent accuracy, of the 3,000 nuts they bury each winter.

ATHLETIC DOG → Ludivine the bloodhound ran the entire 13.1 mi (21 km) of the 2016 Elkmont Half-Marathon in Alabama. Her owner, April Hamlin, who lives on a nearby farm, had let the dog out to relieve herself, but instead she went to the start line and took off with all the runners, eventually finishing 7th out of 165 competitors in just under an hour and a half. She was the highest placed female. Although Ludivine had not signed up as an official participant, she was awarded a medal by the race organizers.

ROCKING ROOSTER

⊙ Wendy Jarvis's musical cockerel, Cooper, entertains customers at her thrift store in Southampton, England, by playing the guitar with his beak! Named for rock legend Alice Cooper, the bird is so popular that people come into the store just to see him perform.

BIRD-CEPTION

→ Thousands of tiny birds flew together and formed the shape of a giant bird!

This beaky scene in Staffordshire, England, was a flock of starlings and lasted around 45 minutes. Scientists think starlings group together intricately like this, known as a murmuration, to stay safe from predators like falcons and hawks who find it hard to target a single bird in the middle of a moving mass.

CANINE BODYGUARDS → A colony of little penguins—the world's smallest penguins—on Middle Island off the coast of Victoria, Australia, is guarded round the clock from predatory foxes by a team of dogs. The penguin population dwindled alarmingly around the year 2000 when a buildup of sand in the 100-ft (30-m) stretch of water separating the uninhabited island from the mainland allowed foxes to make the crossing at low tide. A local chicken farmer then suggested using large Maremma sheepdogs as bodyguards for the penguins, and now the foxes keep away. At one point, the penguin population on the island was down to just four, but now there are over 100.

HUMAN WALKER → Arsenal, a gray poodle owned by Xu Ligang from Shanghai, China, is able to climb stairs using just his hind legs. Using just two legs, he can climb 20 stairs in under eight seconds.

SKIN ALLERGY →
Mitzi the Jack Russell terrier has to wear a Onesie because she is allergic to her owner, Erin Arnold, of Penyffordd, North Wales. The dog has an allergy to dander—the tiny particles that are constantly shed from human skin.

SALAD LIZARD → When a 3-in-long (7.5-cm) green anole lizard was found in the organic tatsoi leaves of kindergarten student Faye Steingart's homemade salad, it was cold and lifeless, having spent several days in a refrigerator—but once it was warmed up, it came back to life and was adopted by Riverside Elementary School in Princeton, New Jersey, as a classroom pet.

OH DEER! → A wild deer was rescued by a police officer after getting its head stuck in a plastic light fixture in the woods in Centereach, New York. Officer Jeff Hull tossed his coat over the globe, and as the deer pulled back, the light fixture came free.

BEAR DIP → A black bear took a dip in the swimming pool at the home of Denise and Tony Diering in Vancouver, British Columbia, Canada. It then climbed into the adjoining hot tub, relaxing there for 15 minutes, before calmly wandering off back through the hole it had made in the Diering's fence.

Stallions kick, bite, and do whatever it takes to win the affections of a female at a festival in China!

In a tradition that goes back at least 500 years, over 50 horses are paired up to battle at the Xinhe Festival in South China. When a mare (female horse) is brought into the company of the stallions (males), it causes them to go into a frenzy—ready to passionately fight to get her attention and establish dominance. Curious spectators watch and bet on the stallion they believe will be the ultimate champion! While it may seem inhumane, it is actually a natural breeding behavior in wild horses, and event organizers insist the horses are treated well.

LOVE BITES

SHEEP HALO → A blind sheep at Edgar's Mission Farm Sanctuary in Lancefield, Victoria, Australia, wears a specially designed wide plastic halo around his head to prevent him from walking into objects. The halo was originally created for blind puppies, but a new model was built to fit a sheep. To help the sheep find his way around, he was also trained to listen for and follow another member of the flock who was fitted with a bell.

TORTOISE WALKER → New Yorker Amanda Green placed an ad on Craigslist In March 2016 for someone to take her 16-year-old African tortoise, Henry, for walks in Central Park. Animal-lover Amalia McCallister beat almost 400 applicants—some from as far away as Australia—to land the $10-an-hour job.

EXTRA CLAWS → A lobster caught in Canadian waters in 2016 had four fully formed claws instead of the usual two. Given the name Clawdette, it had three claws on one arm and one on the other, the result of a genetic mutation. It was bought by a seafood wholesaler in Portland, Maine, who vowed to spare the meaty crustacean from the dinner table and instead give it to the state's Department of Marine Resources for research purposes.

COURTSIDE CONDO

→ After flooding and habitat damage left harvest mice without homes, a conservation program in England helped set up cozy tennis balls as artificial nests. Wimbledon and other tennis clubs donated hundreds of their discarded tennis balls, which are similar to the round nests the tiny rodents build on long stalks of grass.

PET CROC → Albert, a fearsome saltwater crocodile, has been kept as a pet in the garden of a house in Darwin, Australia, since 1958. Now 13 ft (4 m) long and over 70 years old, Albert was inherited by Helen Haritos when her father George, who had caught the croc in the wild, died in 1992.

SQUEAKY TOYS → Jasper, a six-month-old Cane Corso puppy owned by Michael Ehrlich, underwent surgery in Levittown, Pennsylvania, to remove two plastic squeaky toys from his stomach. The two balls were so big they filled most of his stomach. The previous year, Dr. Scott Joudrey, who carried out the operation, treated a bulldog that ate three pacifiers and helped a mixed-breed dog that wolfed down a pair of calf-high boots.

TRIGGER HAPPY → In a freak accident, a dog named Trigger shot its owner, Allie Carter, of Avilla, Indiana, in the foot during a waterfowl hunt. When Carter laid her 12-gauge shotgun on the ground, her 11-year-old chocolate Labrador stepped on the gun, depressing the trigger and causing it to fire.

POWER WALK → Chacha, a 24-year-old chimpanzee, escaped from Yagiyama Zoological Park in Japan and made his way through a nearby residential area by scaling poles and walking along overhead power lines. He was on the loose for over an hour before being recaptured.

BUZZING BLOCK → Residents in an apartment block in Madrid, Spain, lived for two years unaware that 25,000 bees were hidden behind their walls. The bees had settled into a cavity between the bricks and plaster and had even started to build a honeycomb.

GIRAFFE POWER → Dung from giraffes at Doué-la-Fontaine Zoo in western France is being used to help power 1,700 homes in the nearby city of Angers. The giraffe poop is mixed with dung from local cattle to produce methane gas.

FLYING RABBIT → Bumper the pet rabbit was blown onto the roof of a house in Omagh, Northern Ireland, by a storm in January 2016. The strong winds caught the rabbit's hutch and hurled him up onto the roof, but he was rescued unharmed.

SCARY STUDENT → A male leopard entered a school in Bangalore, India, in February 2016 and injured six people before it was tranquilized and released back into the wild.

animals

Ripley's Exhibit
Cat. No. 172088
Metal Orangutan
Made of recycled kitchen
utensils and copper scouring
pads by Justin La Doux
c. 2016

DOGGY PADDLE → Wispa, a seven-year-old chocolate Labrador, saved the life of her drowning owner by jumping into a swollen river and giving him a piggyback ride to safety. Seventy-three-year-old Pete Alderson had fallen into the River Wye near his home in Hereford, England, and, unable to swim, had disappeared beneath the surface. He was just about to lose consciousness when Wispa carried him from the water.

BEST BUDDIES → Sequoia, a huge 550-lb (250-kg) black bear, has an unusual best friend at Folsom City Zoo, California—a small stray cat. The feral cat first wandered into the bear enclosure a few years ago in search of food and soon became a frequent visitor, regularly hanging out with Sequoia.

RUFF SERVICE → French brewery Kronenbourg 1664 opened a pop-up bar in London, England, where all the bartenders were dogs. Customers were served by a team of German Shepherds wearing small beer barrels around their necks.

CLEVER DOG → Cooper, a two-year-old Shih Tzu dog owned by Kirsty Forrester, of Lancashire, England, can solve mathematical problems faster than an 18-month-old human toddler. The clever dog can count, solve shape-sorting puzzles, and knows 60 different commands.

HUNGRY CHICK → In the first two weeks of its life, a baby great tit—a small bird native to Europe and Asia—will eat 1,000 caterpillars.

ALLIGATOR BLOCKAGE → After people in Fort Myers, Florida, complained about blocked drains, engineers discovered the cause was a dead, 11-ft-long (3.4-m) alligator. The reptile measured 3 ft (0.9 m) wide and was found in a 4-ft-wide (1.2-m) space in a storm drain catch basin.

TORTOISE HUNT → When Zuma, a 90-year-old pet tortoise, snuck into a trash bag, council workers saved him from being burned alive by scanning 1,000 garbage bags to find him with a thermal imaging camera. His owner, Sarah Joiner, had reported him missing, and after searching through 10 tons of waste for two and a half hours, workers from Westminster City Council in London, England, finally located him just before the bags were incinerated.

OH MY!

→ A lion, a tiger, and a bear lived harmoniously together in the same enclosure at the Noah's Ark Animal Shelter in Locust Grove, Georgia, since 2001. The affectionate trio—Leo the African lion, Shere Khan the Bengal tiger, and Baloo the American black bear—were all rescued as cubs from the basement of an Atlanta home and had not been separated until Leo died in 2016.

BAT CUDDLES

⊙ **Baby bats in Texas huddle so closely together that there can be as many as 500 of them within 1 sq ft (0.1 sq m)!**

Caves, tunnels, and bridges are overrun with millions of Mexican free-tailed bats, aka Brazilian free-tailed bats, each spring in central Texas. Many of them are pregnant females, who usually give birth to just one pup each. Despite the overwhelming number of babies, the mothers are almost always able to find their own young within the writhing mass dangling from the ceiling by recognizing their unique voice and scent.

⬆ The 20 million-strong bat population of Bracken Cave in Texas nearly doubles once the pups are born!

ARNIE'S BACK → Arnold Schwarzenegger, a cat owned by Leah and Allen Elphick of East Sussex, England, has survived being shot twice in two years.

BAD DRIVERS → Two dogs drove a car into the wall of a Walmart store in Wayne County, West Virginia, after their owner had left them inside the vehicle. The owner had left the car engine running so that the dogs could stay cool while she shopped, but one of the pets then managed to put the car into forward gear.

TINY HOME
⊙ This hummingbird nest and eggs were found in Monte Verde, Costa Rica. These miniscule birds build nests that are about the same circumference as a U.S. quarter. Hummingbird mothers build these petite dwellings with plant fibers and lichens to provide camouflage, and use spider silk to help hold it all together.

Hummingbird nests are elastic, stretching as the young birds grow!

animals

119

FLYING PIG → A 250-lb (113-kg) pig escaped with nothing worse than minor road rash after flying out of a trailer that was being pulled at 65 mph (105 kmph) on Interstate 25 near Windsor, Colorado.

HIGH JUMP → Bailey, a three-year-old kelpie dog owned by Tegan Eagle, of Melbourne, Australia, can jump a height of 9.5 ft (2.9 m)—1.5 ft (0.45 m) higher than the world high-jump record for humans.

BEAR DETERRENT → Chase Dellwo, of Belgrade, Montana, fought off an attack from a 375-lb (170 kg) male grizzly bear by shoving his arm down the bear's throat. When the bear began to maul him, Dellwo remembered his grandmother's advice given to him years ago that said large animals have bad gag reflexes. It worked, and the bear backed off.

MONKEY VILLAGE

The village of Xianfeng in Sichuan, China, was overrun with 600 angry monkeys after its once-successful tourism ploy backfired. In an effort to boost its economy, the villagers lured more than 70 wild monkeys from the nearby mountains, giving them a new home in town. After an initial wave of tourists, commercial support for the attraction fell through—leaving all the monkeys to run rampant and terrorize the locals by destroying crops, breaking into homes, and starting fights among themselves. The government removed 300 monkeys from the village, but the other half still remain.

DISTRACTION ROBBERY → A monkey threw a piece of fruit into a jewelry store in Piduguralla, Andhra Pradesh, India, and then, while workers were distracted, opened a drawer and snatched 10,000 rupees (around $150) in cash.

BURST BELLY → A red-bellied black snake, which had apparently been swallowed by a brown snake, managed to slither its way out of its captor's body. It seems that the brown snake was enjoying its lunch in Griffith, New South Wales, Australia, when it was hit by a car, causing its stomach to burst and allowing the black snake to escape through the hole in its side.

SURPRISE GUEST → When Natalie Biggins married Jamie Richardson in Newcastle upon Tyne, England, the wedding rings were handed to the best man by a Rhesus macaque monkey named Rosie. It was the groom's idea to surprise his bride by hiring Rosie who, after doing her duties, posed for pictures with the couple and their guests.

EXTRA TOES → Originally bred for hunting puffins that nest in narrow caves on steep cliffs, the Norwegian Lundehund dog has six toes on each foot for extra grip. Unlike most other dogs, it can also close its ears by bending them either forward or backward, so that the ear canal is protected against dirt and water. At one point, the breed was so rare there were only five in existence.

TWO NOSES

Toby, a two-year-old Australian Shepherd dog, has two noses. He was born with the defect and, abandoned by his previous owner, was about to be put down when he was rescued from the streets of Fresno, California, and adopted by Todd Ray, the founder of the Venice Beach Freakshow.

TRASHY HOMES

HIDING IN A SODA CAN!

⊙ There are 5.25 trillion pieces of plastic debris in the ocean, causing great harm to the ocean's many inhabitants—but some creatures seem to make the best of a bad situation.

In Shizuoka, Japan, a yellow pygmy-goby (*Lubricogobius exiguus*) pair find refuge in a can. This tiny species of fish usually thrives in mucky sand, living in holes, under pieces of plastic, and even in toothpaste tubes. In the Maldives, this hermit crab was caught scurrying along with his plastic cup home. Crabs are opportunistic, so if they can't find a suitable shell, they'll use bottle caps and other debris that offer protection.

CAT'S VIEW → Japanese tourism chiefs have created a Google Maps-style street view of the city of Onomichi from a cat's perspective. The map lets users explore the streets from 8 in (20 cm) above the ground—a cat's height—in an attempt to encourage people to visit Onomichi, which is home to about 150,000 cats.

EYES UP → When born, a flounder has an eye on each side of its head, but after a few days, the eyes move to the same side of the head. As an adult, the flatfish lives at the bottom of the ocean with its eyed side facing up so that it can spot predators.

DIGGING TEETH → The naked mole rat of East Africa has huge teeth that are located outside its mouth, so that it can use them to shovel earth to build its burrow home without actually eating dirt.

BEAR MYSTERY → An inquisitive bear somehow managed to end up inside a locked Subaru station wagon in Jefferson County, Colorado, without breaking any windows. The trapped bear was released from the vehicle after a deputy carefully opened the trunk. The animal then ran off, leaving behind a shredded interior.

BIG PATIENT → Dentist Dr. Alex Smithson had to treat Alyona, a rare 252-lb (114-kg) Amur tiger at Blackpool Zoo, England, for toothaches. The eight-year-old big cat needed root canal surgery on all four of her razor-sharp, 5-in-long (12.7-cm) canine teeth that are more than five times the size of their human counterparts.

SURFING DUO → Brazilian surfer Ivan Moreira and his five-year-old Labrador dog Bono rode a stand-up paddleboard on the treacherous Mearim River tidal bore for a distance of 1.06 mi (1.7 km) in March 2016. The pair have been practicing their hobby together since 2012, when Bono was just six months old.

SIX TAILS → After suffering a severe injury to its tail, a young tegu lizard in Argentina regenerated six new tails at the same time.

DEAD OTTER → When U.S. National Park Service paleontologist and Grateful Dead fan Kari Prassack identified an extinct species of otter in Idaho, she named it *Lontra weiri* for the band's guitarist Bob Weir.

DOG CONCERT → American experimental musician Laurie Anderson staged a concert for 50 dogs in New York's Times Square, producing electronic violin and keyboard sounds at a frequency that only dogs could hear. Their human owners were able to listen in on headphones.

FIGHTING HEADS → A two-headed baby cobra at Nanning Zoo, China, repeatedly tried to eat itself. Since each head had its own brain, the two halves moved independently, and one head would attempt to swallow the other.

TINY SNAIL → *Angustopila dominikae*, a newly discovered species of land snail from Guangxi Province, China, is so tiny that almost 10 of them would fit into the eye of a needle. Its shell measures just 0.86 mm in height.

MANED LIONESSES → A pride of lionesses in Botswana's Moremi Game Reserve boast bushy manes and produce deep roars, fooling other lions into thinking that they are males. Wildlife experts believe that the phenomenon is caused by a genetic condition, which affects only the lionesses in that area.

BAT EMERGENCY → The emergency room of a hospital in Kilgore, Texas, was forced to close temporarily in February 2016 after a number of bats began to appear. The bats had moved into the walls and ceilings of the building and had spread into the area that receives ambulances.

Monkey LOVE

→ A pet monkey and a chicken fell in love after meeting at a market in the Banyuwangi district of Java, Indonesia.

The two are regularly seen at the market, with the monkey cuddling up to his feathered friend and the chicken content to rest in his arms.

63 CATS → A real estate agent visited a vacant house in Washington, D.C., and found two women squatting there with 63 cats.

PET SOUNDS → Professional cellist David Teie, from Washington, D.C., has created a music album that appeals solely to cats. The music is matched to the frequency range that cats use to communicate and is designed to relax them by mimicking purring and mewing sounds.

POLITE OCTOPUS → Instead of grabbing its prey like other cephalopods, the Pacific striped octopus gently taps its prospective meal on the shoulder and startles it into its tentacles. It is also the only octopus that kisses and cuddles while mating and even feeds its partner.

BEAR RIDE → A black bear hitched a ride for 65 mi (104 km) in the back of a California garbage truck. The bear climbed into a trash compactor that was picked up by a disposal truck in the Hume Lake area and, unbeknownst to the driver, rode with him all the way to a dump near Fresno.

An amazing 60 million to one billion monarch butterflies hibernate in massive clusters in the Monarch Butterfly Biosphere Reserve in Mexico, migrating every winter in a journey spanning more than 2,500 mi (4,023.4 km). Blanketing the forest in stunning orange and black, the sheer weight of them sometimes causes tree branches to bend or snap.

ANCIENT SPONGE ➔ A deep-sea sponge from the species *Monorhaphis chuni* lived to be 11,000 years old.

PUPPY CLONES ➔ Phillip Dupont, a veterinarian from Lafayette, Louisiana, loved his favorite dog Melvin so much that he has spent $100,000 on creating two clones of the Catahoula/Doberman mix. The puppies, Ken and Henry, were created by a South Korean company using DNA taken from one of Melvin's skin cells.

NEW SPECIES ➔ A new species of snake, the Alai pit viper (*Gloydius rickmersi*), was discovered after a specimen was found squashed on a road in Kyrgyzstan in 2013.

HALF-MILE WEB ➔ In a scene reminiscent of a horror movie, a northern suburb of Memphis, Tennessee, was overrun by millions of tiny spiders, which joined forces to spin a huge web measuring 0.5 mi (0.8 km) long across a field.

GIANT SLUG

⊙ Coyote Peterson, host of exploration show *Brave Wilderness*, found and held a 2-ft-long (0.6-m) sea slug on the California coast! Commonly found in tidal pools, California black sea hares, virtually harmless to humans, are the largest species of sea slug and feed mostly on algae and kelp. They get their name from the small tentacles on their heads that look like rabbit ears. Holding the massive slug, Coyote said it was "so unbelievably slippery!"

animals

123

PINK HIPPO

➔ This hippo is pretty in pink! French photography couple Laurent and Dominique Renaud snapped this hippo at Kenya's Masai Mara National Reserve. Experts speculate about the cause of this discoloration, as the animal's normal eye color rules out albinism.

BEE DANCE
➔ Sara Mapelli, of Portland, Oregon, dances with up to 15,000 bees blanketing her body in a layer 8-in (20-cm) thick. Although she has frequently been stung, the Bee Queen, as she is known, performs her routine to help cure people of their fear of the insects.

WORLD TOUR
➔ A migrating Arctic tern flew all the way from Britain to Antarctica and back—a roundtrip journey of 59,650 mi (96,000 km)—in under a year. The small sea bird, which weighs less than an iPhone, left its breeding grounds on the Farne Islands off the coast of Northumberland, England, in July 2015 and reached Antarctica via the west coast of Africa four months later. It then returned to the United Kingdom in 2016, arriving in May to complete a total journey that was more than twice the Earth's circumference.

PEST CONTROLLER
➔ In 2011, Felix, a nine-month-old kitten, was appointed to keep Huddersfield train station in West Yorkshire, England, free of mice—and she proved so successful and so popular that in 2016 she was promoted to senior pest controller, a position that came with a safety vest uniform and a name badge. Following her promotion, the number of her Facebook page fans rocketed from 3,000 to over 90,000.

HUNCHBACK DOG
➔ Cuda the pitbull is one of 17 dogs in the world known to have short spine syndrome. The six-year-old canine has just as many vertebrae as a typical dog, but rather than being evenly spread out, hers are concentrated near her neck and tail. Cuda is capable of doing just about everything other dogs can do and is even a certified therapy dog!

BARNACLE BEAST

GIANT PENGUIN → The extinct "colossus" penguin, which lived around 40 million years ago, stood 6.7 ft (2 m) including its beak—as tall as NBA star LeBron James.

⊙ **This alien-like barnacle stumped crab fisherman Mathew Wallace with its rainbow-colored accents and eerie appendages—but it's no mystery!**

Caught at Port Hueneme Pier, in Oxnard, California, this creepy crustacean is actually a cluster of six California barnacles scientifically known as *Megabalanus californicus*. Slippery and spiky on the outside, each individual barnacle has an opening out of which extends hairy feelers that may look extraterrestrial but are actually the animal's legs!

ALBINO TURTLE → A rare albino turtle with pink flippers and red eyes—a 1-in-100,000 occurrence—emerged from a green turtle nest on Australia's Sunshine Coast in 2016.

FLIGHT DIVERTED → A 2015 Air Canada flight from Tel Aviv, Israel, to Toronto was diverted to Frankfurt, Germany, to save the life of a dog passenger. Simba, a seven-year-old French bulldog, was being transported in a crate in the cargo hold while his owner traveled in the cabin above, but when the heating system in the hold broke down, the temperature there dropped to below freezing, putting the animal's life in danger—so the pilot made a $10,000 unscheduled landing, after which Simba was transferred to another airplane to complete his journey.

TOP CAT → Bossy, a Scottish fold cat, earns a salary equivalent to $216 a month as the communications manager of Romanian retailer Catbox. He was chosen over 700 humans to land the job.

EXPERT HUNTERS → The dogs that battled freezing temperatures to rid Macquarie Island of introduced pests were honored on a set of Australian postage stamps in 2015. The dogs, mostly Springer spaniels and Labrador retrievers, spent up to three years hunting and eradicating rabbits and rodents from the island, which lies partway between New Zealand and Antarctica.

SCARY JOURNEY → Tigger the kitten traveled up to 300 mi (480 km) by hunkering down inside a car bumper for hours. The tiny cat was eventually discovered by Lt. Nick Grimmer when he arrived in Cornwall, England, after driving his BMW all the way from Birmingham.

TOILET ATTACK → While using the toilet in his home in Chachoengsao, Thailand, 38-year-old Atthaporn Boonmakchuay was bitten on the groin by an 11-ft-long (3.4-m) python that had slithered up sewer pipes. As the snake ferociously clamped its jaws on his flesh refusing to let go, Boonmakchuay grabbed its head and tied it to the bathroom door with a rope seconds before passing out due to loss of blood. He was rushed to a hospital for treatment while fire crews used hammers to smash the toilet and drag the snake from the pipe.

BIRD FEEDER → Cary Campbell, an artist from Whistler, British Columbia, Canada, wears a dress that she designed herself solely for feeding hummingbirds. The voluminous red gown is adorned with flowers and cups filled with sugary water to entice hummingbirds.

125

CRAZY CATERPILLAR

➜ This bizarre, bushy-haired bug was discovered in the Peruvian Amazon by wildlife photographer Jeff Cremer. It is known as the flannel moth caterpillar, but locals call it "ovejillo," which means "little sheep" in Spanish. However, despite its adorable appearance, close contact with this critter can be painful! It is covered in urticating hairs, which have tiny, spiny hooks on them that can inject venom.

Sporting a golden tuft, some scientists have noted the caterpillar's resemblance to a certain U.S. president's famous hairdo.

TINY VENOMOUS BARBS!

WINNING TICKET ➜ Ruby the Labrador retriever found a $225,000 winning lottery ticket that her owners had forgotten about. Jane and Alan Slater, from the Isle of Wight, England, had already won $225,000 on the EuroMillions lottery when Ruby uncovered a second lucky ticket for the same draw—hidden away inside a catalog.

FALLING COW ➜ A cow was rescued by fire crews in West Yorkshire, England, after it had plunged 20 ft (6 m) from a field down onto the rooftop sun terrace of a house.

THREE EARS ➜ A three-eared cat found abandoned in Norfolk, England, was taken to an animal rescue center where he was dubbed Captain Kirk due to his "final front-ear."

DOG SONGS ➜ The Laurel Canyon Animal Company from Los Angeles produces music CDs for dogs. The company works with animal communication experts and even psychics to translate a dog's sounds into a song. The final version of each tune is chosen from the dog's response to the song when it is played back.

BABY JUMP ➜ To avoid predators, barnacle geese build their nests on mountain cliffs—but at just three days old, the tiny goslings must jump as far as 400 ft (122 m) to reach food on the ground.

WARTHOG GROOMING ➜ In an act of grooming, South African helmeted turtles pluck parasites and other insects from warthogs when they come to drink at muddy water holes.

GIANT OYSTER ➜ On a beach at Knokke, Belgium, the Lechat family from Luxembourg discovered an oyster that measured a staggering 15.2 in (38 cm)— equivalent to a U.S. size 20.5 men's shoe and three times bigger than the average oyster.

MY LAKE! ➜ In Asheville, North Carolina, 67-year-old Betsy Bent was attacked by a beaver while she was paddleboarding . . . on Beaver Lake.

SHARP VISION ➜ The eyesight of Europe's griffon vulture is so good it can see a dead rabbit on the ground nearly 2 mi (3.2 km) away.

NOISY GIBBON ➜ A species of southeast Asian gibbon called the siamang has a throat sac that can expand to the size of its head. It uses the enlarged sac to make loud territorial calls.

AGILE BEAR ➜ A hungry black bear risked electrocution by climbing to the very top of an electric tower in Wood Buffalo National Park, Alberta, Canada, to eat the eggs from a raven's nest. Despite being attacked by the birds, the bear nimbly scaled the metal footings to reach the nest some 50 ft (15 m) above ground.

FLIP-FLOP BIRD ➜ This mockingbird's shoes serve both fashion and function! Suffering from "knuckling," a condition which makes it hard for birds to uncurl their toes and hinders their ability to walk or perch, this lucky bird's life was saved by a pair of makeshift flip-flops! California Wildlife Center vet Lorraine Barbosa created the shoes in order to reset the bird's alignment.

EAGLE SNATCH → Dutch police have been training white-tailed eagles to snatch illegal or enemy drones from the sky. The birds' scaly feet and talons are so tough that they are able to grab drones without suffering injury from the blades.

ANGRY BIRDS → In the summer of 2016, mail workers in Maryport, Cumbria, refused to deliver letters to addresses in the town because they came under attack from seagulls.

TWISTED BEAKS → For more than 20 years, a mystery virus has caused thousands of Alaska's wild birds— including crows and black-capped chickadees— to have deformed, twisted beaks. The condition, known as avian keratin disorder, can be fatal because the birds have difficulty feeding and can freeze to death because they cannot groom their feathers.

THREE HORNS → A three-horned cow was born on a farm in Uzbekistan, its third horn growing from the middle of its head like a unicorn.

SHARP RIBS → Found in Morocco, Portugal, and Spain, the Iberian ribbed newt has sharply pointed ribs that it can stick through its sides to protect itself against predators.

SKIN TRAP → A python at Alice Springs Reptile Center, Australia, became trapped in his own skin for more than three hours after shedding it in a perfect circle. With his tail in his mouth, Tim the Stimson's python did lap after lap inside his old skin before finally breaking free.

REINDEER GAMES

⊙ **Reindeer give it their all as they drag their herders across the ice and snow in frigid Nadym, Russia!**

Once a year, indigenous nomads from across Russia meet in the arctic to celebrate their lifestyle on Reindeer Herders' Day. Competitions include wrestling, high jumps, and of course, reindeer racing! One of the top prizes is a snowmobile, for which both the herder and reindeer are thankful.

animals

127

LOVE RAGE → On Valentine's Day 2016, a lovesick elephant, who had lost his mate to a rival male, went on a rampage and smashed up more than a dozen cars in Xishuangbanna, southern China.

BAT INVASION → More than 100,000 fruit bats descended on the town of Batemans Bay, New South Wales, Australia, in May 2016. They covered almost every surface and every tree and forced many residents to stay inside their homes, afraid to open their windows.

SURPRISE PACKAGE → A Siamese cat named Cupcake survived an eight-day, 260-mi (418-km) journey by mail in a sealed cardboard box. Her owners, from Cornwall, England, sent a package of DVDs to East Sussex unaware that Cupcake had climbed into the box. It was more than a week later when the recipients opened the package that they found the scared cat tucked up inside.

WHALE DIALECT → Sperm whales "speak" in their own local dialect, enabling them to identify other social groups in their area. They communicate via a series of spaced clicks called codas, and a six-year study found that sperm whales in the Caribbean used codas that were unique to their regional groups.

FIRST BATH → In 2016, the world's oldest land animal, a 184-year-old giant tortoise named Jonathan, was given his first-ever bath. Using a loofah, a soft brush, and surgical soap, almost two centuries' worth of dirt was scrubbed off his shell by Dr. Joe Hollins, the veterinarian on the British island of St. Helena in the South Atlantic Ocean.

TIGHT SQUEEZE → A baby elephant was rescued by a group of men after falling down a narrow drain near a main road in Hambantota, Sri Lanka. The unlucky baby had somehow slipped down the uncovered drain and was unable to climb back out.

Family is important to elephants, thus the team kept families like this one together so they'd wake up next to each other after sedation wore off.

MILITARY HERO → Lucca, a German shepherd dog, sniffed out thousands of explosive devices while working with the U.S. Marines, saving countless lives. She completed over 400 missions in six years, during which not one member of the military was killed. Lucca herself lost her front left leg after stepping on an explosive in Afghanistan, for which she was awarded the Dickin Medal, the highest honor for service animals.

PRINTED FEET → After losing his feet to frostbite, Phillip the duck was able to waddle again with the help of a pair of new prosthetic feet made on a 3-D printer. The feet were built over a period of six weeks by teacher Jason Jischke and his class at South Park Middle School in Oshkosh, Wisconsin.

REFUGEE CAT → A refugee cat that traveled on a crowded rubber boat with his family fleeing war-torn Iraq, but ran off on the Greek island of Lesbos, was eventually reunited with them four months later in Norway at the end of a 2,500-mi (4,000-km) adventure. Kunkush jumped out of his basket on reaching Lesbos but was later found by volunteers and flown to Berlin, Germany, where he was fostered until his family made contact through a Facebook page that had been set up in the cat's name.

Ripley's Exhibit Cat. No. 18144
Wasp Nest Deer
Deer with a wasp nest caught in its antlers

MAMMOTH MANEUVERS

→ Using helicopters, cranes, and a ton of determination, a team in Zimbabwe safely relocated nearly 80 elephants!

The elephants had escaped from a wildlife sanctuary, which helps keep them safe from poachers. A team initially used a helicopter to herd the hefty creatures into small groups, and then veterinarians tranquilized the animals. In a race against the clock, cranes were used to gently pick the pachyderms up and place them onto trucks that returned them to the safety of their home.

BEETLE FAN → The harmless bushveld lizard of southern Africa perfectly mimics the markings of the oogpister beetle, a fearsome insect that sprays formic acid at predators, sometimes causing blindness. The little black-and-white lizard has even learned to walk the same way as the beetle.

WRONG PRIORITIES → A team of sniffer dogs employed at England's Manchester Airport at a cost of $1.7 million failed to detect any illegal class A drugs during their first seven months of operation, but they did prove adept at discovering sausages and cheese.

BEE CHASE
→ After a queen bee became trapped in the trunk of her car, Carol Howarth, of Pembrokeshire, Wales, was followed by a swarm of 20,000 bees for two days!

BALD HEDGEHOG

➔ Meet Nelson, the completely bald hedgehog. It's hard to say what made his spikes all fall out, but animal rescue volunteers guess that it might be stress-related alopecia caused by some trauma out in the wild. Nelson now lives at Foxy Lodge Wildlife Rescue in Norfolk, England, where he receives 30-minute massages every day to try to get his spikes to grow. Unfortunately, his pleasant massage therapy has yet to produce results.

GOAT ATTACK ➔ A rescue helicopter that landed in a paddock near Adelaide, Australia, to take a road accident victim to a hospital was grounded after a territorial goat rammed the chopper and damaged a window.

TURTLE SMUGGLER ➔ Dong Yan, of Windsor, Ontario, Canada, was banned from owning turtles for 10 years after trying to smuggle 38 reptiles into the country from the United States by hiding them in his pants.

ADOPTED MONKEY ➔ Tatyana Antropova's 16-year-old pet cat Rosinka adopted a baby squirrel monkey that had been abandoned by its mother at a zoo in Tyumen, Russia.

FAST POPPER ➔ Twinkie, a Jack Russell terrier owned by Doree Sitterly, of Westlake Village, California, can pop 100 balloons in 39 seconds.

LUCKY PEARL ➔ A Filipino fisherman found a huge 75-lb (34-kg) pearl with a speculated value of $100 million—but, having no idea of its worth, he kept it under his bed for 10 years as a good luck charm. He discovered the 2-ft-long (0.6-m), 1-ft-wide (0.3-m) pearl—thought to be by far the biggest ever found in the world—a decade ago inside a massive clam in the sea off Palawan Island. It wasn't until he showed the pearl to a local tourism officer that he learned how valuable it was.

FOUR-LEGGED FANS ➔ Sitting in outfield seats, 1,122 dogs attended a Chicago White Sox baseball game against the Cleveland Indians on September 13, 2016.

REALISTIC COLLAR ➔ Police officers in Newport, England, responding to reports of an injured otter lying by the side of a road, instead found a faux fur collar from a coat.

ESCAPED SHEEP ➔ After escaping from their shepherd who had fallen asleep, 1,300 sheep ran through the streets of Huesca, Spain, on the night of June 7, 2016.

TITANIUM BEAK ➔ Gigi the macaw was fitted with a new 3-D printed titanium beak by veterinarians in São Paulo, Brazil, when her own beak became too damaged to eat solid food.

MISMATCHED PAIR

➔ David Bowie's dog has eyes very similar to his late owner's. While Max the dog actually has two differently colored eyes, a condition known as heterochromia, Bowie's mismatched eyes were the result of a childhood fight with a friend who accidentally sliced the late artist's eye with his fingernail, leaving Bowie's right pupil permanently dilated.

CHERISHED CHOMPER

animals

➔ **Nobumitsu Murabayashi's beloved pet may not be as soft as your cuddly animal companion, but he loves it just the same. It's a caiman, affectionately named Caiman!**

Living inside his Hiroshima, Japan, home, Murabayashi caters to Caiman, petting him, brushing his teeth, and even walking him on a leash! At home, Caiman roams freely, spending most of his time in the tatami room—a traditional Japanese room floored with rice straw, which Murabayashi has to replace yearly thanks to his heavyweight housemate. Inseparable for 35 years, the two are expected to share at least 20 more years together!

Full grown, Caiman tips the scales at 101 lb (46 kg) and measures a whopping 6 ft 10 in (2.1 m)!

131

TREE LION → Deng Dingrui and a team of artists from Myanmar spent three years carving a 47.5-ft-long (14.5-m), 14.3-ft-high (4.3-m), 13-ft-wide (4-m) lion sculpture out of a single redwood tree trunk. Once completed, the huge "Oriental Lion" was transported 3,125 mi (5,030 km) for display in a square in Wuhan, China.

MARZIPAN MICHAEL → The Szabo Marzipan Museum in Szentendre, Hungary, is home to a life-size sculpture of Michael Jackson made from marzipan and white chocolate.

KETCHUP FAN → English singer-songwriter Ed Sheeran has images of a ketchup bottle and a cup of tea tattooed on his left arm to remind him of home. He also has a teddy bear tattoo on his right arm because his childhood name was Teddy.

FAST WORK → The Beatles earned $90,000 in 35 minutes for their show in Minneapolis, Minnesota, in August 1965—which is almost $700,000 today when adjusted for inflation.

DISNEY TREE → For Christmas 2015, workers built a 46-ft-high (14-m) tree made up of 2,000 soft toys at St. Pancras International Station in London, England. All of the toys were Disney characters, with a giant Mickey Mouse at the very top.

Eternal
CAGE

Laveau's visitors often scribble Xs on her mausoleum for good luck!

⊕ In 2010, actor Nicolas Cage purchased a plot in New Orleans, Louisiana's oldest cemetery—the heavily populated St. Louis Cemetery No. 1—constructing a monstrous cement pyramid for his future dead self.

Alive and well, Nicolas Cage is known for his eccentricities, and at 9-ft-tall (2.7-m) and peculiarly modern amidst crumbling crypts, the pyramid will carry on his loopy legacy after death. There is no name on the grave yet, but it is adorned with "Omni Ab Uno," Latin for "Everything from One."

Cage will be kept in good company, sharing St. Louis No. 1 with the likes of the city's first mayor, Etienne de Boré, and even Voodoo Queen Marie Laveau. Renowned in life and revered after her 1881 death, some say Laveau continues to work her magic from beyond the grave.

OMNIA AB UNO

PRINCESS AND THE FROG

⊙ One frog plus two snails equals . . . Princess Leia? Photographer Tanto Yensen of Indonesia was taking pictures of his dumpy tree frog outdoors when a couple of snails showed up and wanted to play. The frog sat patiently as its two new friends slimed all over its head and body while Yensen snapped away behind the camera, capturing this iconic *Star Wars* hairdo.

MONEY SAVER → The famous scenes in the 1975 movie *Monty Python and the Holy Grail* where the knights bang coconuts together to represent the sounds of horses' hooves were done out of necessity because the production team could not afford real horses.

SECRET STORYLINE → English actor Kit Harington, who plays Jon Snow in *Game of Thrones*, used the TV show to get out of paying a speeding ticket. A patrol officer pulled him over and threatened to arrest him unless he told him whether or not Snow lived in the next season. Harington had promised not to tell anyone his character's fate but was allowed on his way without punishment after revealing that Snow lived.

POKÉMON HUNTER → Tom Currie, from Auckland, New Zealand, quit his job so that he could spend two months traveling the country to hunt for all the Pokémon characters in the cell phone game *Pokémon Go*.

MULTITALENTED → Iceland's goalkeeper at the Euro 2016 soccer tournament, Hannes Þór Halldórsson, directed the video for the country's 2012 Eurovision Song Contest entry.

CONNECTING DOTS → For the 2016 Niagara County Fair in Lockport, New York, local artist Michael Weber created a giant 2 ft × 3 ft (0.6 m × 0.9 m) connect the dots puzzle made up of 10,389 dots, which took more than nine hours to complete.

DONALD BANNED → A 1943 Donald Duck cartoon was banned in Russia until 2016 because its content was thought to be too extremist.

WASTE APP → A smartphone app allows users to order leftover food that restaurants would otherwise throw away. Chris Wilson and Jamie Crummie launched the Too Good to Go app in the United Kingdom as a way of cutting down the amount of food waste.

REAL SMART → The average smartphone has more processing power than the computers that took *Apollo 11* to the Moon.

It also includes hidden word searches with phrases like, "LIVE LONG AND PROSPER," "SPOCK," and "STAR TREK."

Ripley's Exhibit
Cat. No. 172060
Spock Keyboard Art
Computer keyboard portrait
by Doug Powell
3,830 keys! Origin: Oviedo, FL

135

URBAN MEOWkover

CATS

DIAMOND SNEAKERS → In 2016, New York luxury brand Bicion and designer Dan Gamache created a pair of diamond-encrusted sneakers costing $4 million. The sports shoes are adorned with hundreds of diamonds and blue sapphires set in 18-karat gold.

RELEASE DAY → French custom stipulates that all new movies in that country must be released on a Wednesday.

PARALLEL LIVES → Although Danbi Shin lives in New York City and Seok Li lives in Seoul, South Korea—14 hours and over 6,800 mi (10,880 km) away—the artistic couple maintain a sense of unity by photographing themselves doing the same things simultaneously. They find similar backgrounds in the two cities, align the two photos to make a single image, and then post the collages on Instagram.

TWO DOCTORS → British actress Georgia Moffett has a former Doctor Who for a father (Peter Davison) and another former Doctor Who for a husband (David Tennant).

UPSIDE DOWN → In honor of Philippine Independence Day, on June 12, 2016, Facebook posted a banner image of the country's flag—but accidentally posted it upside down, with the red half and not the blue half at the top, a gesture that signified that the Philippines had gone to war!

NEW AUDIENCE → In December 2015, in the first 48 hours after their music became available to stream online, Beatles songs were played 50 million times.

DANCING FEET → Irish *Riverdance* star Michael Flatley had an artwork accepted by the National Collection of Art in Ireland—that he painted with his famous feet. Flatley created the abstract piece, titled *The Walking Dead*, by dipping his shoes in paint and dancing on a large canvas.

GRANNY BAND

⊙ Japanese band KBG84 consists of 33 singing and dancing grandmothers with an average age of 84. When their first single, "Come On and Dance, Kohama Island," topped Japan's music charts in 2015, their oldest member, Haru Yamashiro, was 97.

→ In a cute crowdfunded campaign, all 68 ads at Clapham Common Underground station in London, England, were replaced with cat posters.

Every giant poster, billboard, and stick-on turnstile was given a feline photo, with every furry friend being a stray cat from two rescue groups. The project, dubbed Citizens Advertising Takeover Service (CATS), was executed by Glimpse—a collective that aims to "use creativity for good."

BABY BAND → New York writer/director Jake Fertig launched a new parody boy band in 2016 called Baby Boiz, whose youngest member was only 4. At the time of the release of the band's first single, Ravi was 4, Caleb 6, Julian 9, Gavin 11, and Jake himself—twice the height of the rest of the band—was 23.

ROADSIDE CONCERT → Drivers stuck in a long traffic jam on the M5 motorway in Somerset, England, were entertained by an impromptu roadside concert staged by a string quartet. The musicians were traveling home from a concert in Devon and decided to relieve the boredom for other drivers by setting up their instruments and performing Johann Pachelbel's "Canon."

FIELD PAINTING → Renowned landscape artist Stan Herd, of Lawrence, Kansas, used plants to create a larger-than-life replica of Vincent Van Gogh's painting *Olive Trees* in a field near Minneapolis, Minnesota. It took Herd six months of digging, planting, and mowing to form the 1.2-acre (0.5-hectare) artwork, which could only be viewed properly from the air. He achieved the different colors of green, yellow, orange, and gold by planting kale, squash, cucumbers, oats, and wheat, and as the crops grew, he cut the meadow into the required shapes for the image and dug furrows to add a 3-D effect.

STONE FACES → Since 1976, Joe Resendes, of Taunton, Rhode Island, has used a sharp box cutter to carve more than 3,000 peach pits into whimsical face sculptures. He has enjoyed a long association with peaches, as he was born in the Azores, where children learn to carve peach pits into miniature baskets.

HAND STAMPING → Russell Powell, an artist and elementary school teacher from San Jose, California, paints detailed portraits of famous people such as Bob Marley and John Lennon on the palm of his left hand before stamping them on a paper canvas to create permanent imprints. He calls the process "hand stamping" and has to work fast to keep the paint on his hand from drying before he can make the imprint.

FUTURE BIRTHPLACE ⊙
In 1985, the city of Riverside, Iowa, was looking for a theme to center their annual town festival around when city council member Steve Miller proposed they celebrate their location as the future birthplace of *Star Trek*'s James Tiberius Kirk. Miller had read a book written by the show's creator that stated Kirk's origin was a small town in Iowa and thought, why couldn't it be Riverside? The city loved the idea and embraced its new identity, eventually erecting this memorial stone in the bold captain's honor and holding a *Star Trek* festival every year.

RIVERSIDE IOWA

FUTURE BIRTHPLACE OF CAPTAIN JAMES T. KIRK

MARCH 22, 2228

SALT ART

➡ **Croatian artist Dino Tomic creates detailed pictures by spreading kitchen salt onto a black background.**

He carefully sprinkles the salt onto a giant canvas from a plastic bottle or a paper cone and uses his fingers to add any finishing touches. He decided to use salt as a medium because his wrist had started to hurt from too much conventional drawing.

When the colors of Dino's artwork are inverted, they have a totally different appearance! ➡

POOP MUSEUM →
A traveling art exhibition that opened at Sandown Zoo on the Isle of Wight, England, in 2016 lifts the lid on poop, featuring real-life examples from the animal and human world. The National Poo Museum was created by members of the art collective Eccleston George and features moose and lion excrement, tawny owl feces containing bones and teeth, as well as poop from a human baby. There are also samples of fossilized poop—or coprolites—dating back 140 million years.

REPORT INTERRUPTED →
A TV station was doing a live update about a bank robbery that had taken place the previous day, when the suspect returned to rob the same bank for a second time. Iowa station KIMT-TV was filming outside Sterling State Bank in Rochester, Minnesota, in December 2015 when a bank employee suddenly ran out and pointed out the robbery suspect, prompting reporter Adam Sallet to break off his story and call 911. A man was arrested nearby and later charged with two counts of robbery.

DARK DESTROYER → Drew Wissler, of Pittsburgh, Pennsylvania, completed an entire video game—with all its levels and challenges—while blindfolded. It took him 103 hours of sightless play to finish *The Legend of Zelda: Ocarina of Time*, relying solely on his memory.

RESOURCEFUL FAN →
David Spargo managed to meet his favorite band, Australian electronic dance duo Peking Duk, by editing their Wikipedia page with a fake entry claiming that he was related to one of them. He then showed his ID and the Wikipedia page on his cell phone to a security guard at a Peking Duk concert in Melbourne and was allowed backstage. The band was so impressed by the lengths to which Spargo had gone that they shared a few beers with him.

⊙ These stunning patterns are made up of dead bugs! Wisconsin artist Jennifer Angus used about 5,000 insects to create this creepy-crawly exhibit for the Smithsonian American Art Museum in Washington, D.C. All the bugs are real and have not been painted or altered in any way, except for positioning. Even the paint is made up of bugs! Crushed up cochineal insects were used to create the shocking pink hue.

BYTE-SIZED BUDDHIST → A Buddhist temple in China developed a robot monk that can roll around, answer questions, and recite mantras! The wise android, Xian'er, was originally a cartoon character created by Master Xianfan of the Longquan temple near Beijing. In order to reach people who were more familiar with their cell phones than their inner selves, the character of Xian'er was lifted off the page and turned into something people could interact with.

pop culture

139

TWITTER FRENZY →
Around 500 million tweets are sent each day—enough to fill a book containing 25 million pages.

DISCARDED GUM →
Dutch photographer Sanne Couprie displays more than 1,400 pictures of discarded chewing gum on his Instagram account—and they have won him more than 10,000 followers. He started the social media project after discovering three pieces of neatly arranged gum on the steps to a museum in Milan, Italy, and now takes pictures of any interestingly shaped gum that he finds on footpaths, cracks, and sidewalks. Some lumps are freshly chewed, while other older pieces bear the telltale marks of a person's footprint.

BAND NAME → Canadian band Nickelback took their name from band member Mike Kroeger saying "Here's your nickel back" when he worked at Starbucks and gave customers their change at the register.

50 SONGS → To prepare for his role as the late Jim Morrison in the 1991 movie *The Doors*, Val Kilmer learned 50 of the band's songs. He sang them so well that the remaining members of the band could not tell Kilmer and Morrison's voices apart.

SPLINTER SUIT
→ A novelty for bathing beauties, yet sufficiently buoyant, these 1920s swimsuits are fashioned from spruce wood veneer! Modeled by the "Spruce Girls" these suits also helped promote Washington State's booming lumber industry.

BIG FEET → A Cambridge University, England, study found that Spider-Man would need sticky 43-in-long (109-cm) hands and U.S. size 114 feet to stick to a wall without falling off.

SECRET PHOBIAS → In real life, American tough-guy actor and pro wrestler Dwayne "The Rock" Johnson is afraid of spiders, roller coasters, and miniature horses.

LONG NAME → Pablo Picasso's full name has 23 words. Named after various saints and relatives, he was baptized Pablo Diego José Francisco de Paula Juan Nepomuceno María de los Remedios Cipriano de la Santísima Trinidad Martyr Patricio Clito Ruíz y Picasso.

HARBOR HOAX

→ The Staten Island Ferry Disaster is the greatest tragedy you've never heard of. That's not due to it being buried in the news the day of the Kennedy assassination, as literature on the disaster suggests, but because it never actually occurred! To perpetuate this hoax, Joe Reginella of Staten Island erected a 5-ft-tall (1.5-m) bronze memorial, created a website, produced a short "documentary" about the tragedy, handed out pamphlets, and even directed concerned tourists to the Staten Island Ferry Disaster Memorial Museum—which was as imaginary as the event itself. The nonexistent museum even promised an octopus petting zoo!

DEDICATED IN LOVING MEMORY TO THE PASSENGERS AND CREW OF THE CORNELIUS G KLOFF WHO LOST THEIR LIVES ON NOVEMBER 22, 1963 IN ONE OF THE MOST MYSTERIOUS AND TRAGIC MARITIME DISASTERS IN AMERICAN HISTORY ERECTED BY THE STATEN ISLAND FERRY MEMORIAL FOUNDATION AND CHEMICAL BANK

A giant octopus *never* dragged the ferry and its passengers to the depths of New York Harbor!

Thrift Clothing

VIEW FROM ANOTHER ANGLE!

➔ At the Museum of Fine Arts in Richmond, Virginia, artist Noah Scalin used thrift store clothing to recreate a portrait originally taken by 19th-century photographer James Conway Farley, the first prominent African-American photographer in the United States.

Scalin picked up a couple bags of clothing from a local thrift store, threw the contents on the floor, and then arranged the pile of shirts, socks, and pants into a remarkably accurate anamorphic image. To see the image arrangement, the viewer had to stand in a certain spot; otherwise the image appeared distorted.

pop culture

141

Valeriano created an amazing watermelon carving of Game of Thrones's Night King!

IncrEDIBLE CARVINGS

➔ **Italian artist Valeriano Fatica carves detailed animals and pop culture characters out of fruits and vegetables.**

The 28 year old originally wanted to become a Japanese manga artist, but he soon realized his true passion for sculptures, creating intricate watermelon carvings for his family's restaurant La Roccia. Valeriano posts the fruits of his labor on YouTube, where his time-lapse videos of his masterful carvings fascinate fans from start to finish.

Q Which carving is your favorite?

A I can't really tell, because any time I make a new one I think it is the best one. If I had to choose, maybe I'd choose the Night King.

PUMPKIN CARVED INTO A LIFELIKE WHITE WALKER FROM GAME OF THRONES!

Horror fiction author H. P. Lovecraft's Cthulhu character carved from a watermelon.

Q How did you get into carving fruit?

A Ever since I was I child, I loved art. I went to the art high school in Campobasso, and afterward, I left the art academy of Rome to return to my hometown, because I thought art school was a waste of time. I then started working in my family's restaurant, La Roccia. In 2011, I started to carve fruit for buffets and ceremonies. After a year, I decided that I wanted this to become my job.

Where do you draw your inspiration from?

I try to get my inspiration from the characters that made my childhood so beautiful.

How many carvings have you completed so far?

At the beginning, I did a lot more sculptures—I did almost a hundred. Now I prefer to do less of them.

Do you eat any of your carvings after they are complete?

A lot of them! I ate the turtle, for example. I'm actually trying to find a way to make them last a long time, but I'm unable to do it at the moment.

Is there a carving you are most proud of?

Besides the Night King, I'm also very proud of the open-mouthed dragon.

How long does it take you to complete a piece?

It usually takes me about 20 hours, about two days. It depends on the difficulty of the project.

Have you carved on any other medium besides fruit?

Of course! When I was younger, I started making sculptures with clay, and I did several plaster casts. Lately I've also started to carve stone.

If you could carve anything into any medium, no matter the size, what would it be?

I would like to carve a giant watermelon dragon with open wings.

What is the most difficult part about what you do?

The most difficult part is to fulfill the very strange requests of my clients, and most of all, it's hard to negotiate the price for my unique work.

Batman's Joker carved out of a pumpkin!

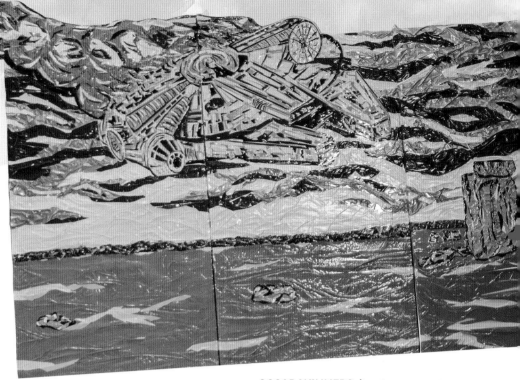

EMOJI TUNES → For Valentine's Day 2016, former Beatle Paul McCartney wrote a series of tunes to accompany emojis on the video chat service Skype. He created short sounds, ranging from hard electric guitar hooks to gentle progressions on the harpsichord and xylophone, for 20 different emotions, including blushing, flirting, and love.

CHAMELEON SNEAKERS → New York designer David Coelho has created a range of sneakers that change color at the touch of a button. His ShiftWear shoes feature e-ink display screens, allowing the wearer to decide what goes on the screens in terms of color and design by using a smartphone app.

BURGER GIRLS → Japan's Hamburgirl Z is the world's only hamburger-themed girl band—and most of their songs are about burgers. Each of the 15 members dresses as a different burger ingredient, including beef, lettuce, bacon, pickle, chicken, green pepper, and pineapple. There are also two onions, played by twins.

SELFIE DEFENSE → Martial arts classes in Moscow, Russia, teach people how to use selfie sticks as weapons to fight off muggers.

DISTANT COUSIN → Tom Hanks is a third cousin, four generations removed, of Abraham Lincoln through the former president's mother, Nancy Hanks.

FAMOUS EAR → When Vincent Van Gogh chopped off his ear in Arles, France, in 1888, he gave the severed body part to a local cleaner named Gabrielle.

OSCAR WINNERS → When Ben Affleck starred in *Batman v Superman: Dawn of Justice*, he was the third Academy Award winner to play Batman, following after Christian Bale and George Clooney.

PORCELAIN PAGODA → The centerpiece of the 2015 Festival of Light display in Wiltshire, England, was a 66-ft-tall (20-m) porcelain pagoda created by Chinese workers from 80,000 cups, bowls, and plates.

YOUNG CRITIC → Seven-year-old Iain Armitage, of Arlington, Virginia, watches as many as 50 stage plays a year and reviews them online. He saw his first play at age three and regularly travels with his parents to New York City to catch Broadway productions.

TONE DEAF → Nadine Cooper, of Nottingham, England, established the Tuneless Choir for 60 people who can't sing. As a child, she was told to stop singing by her school music teacher because she was so bad she was spoiling it for everyone else.

SKY BALLET → Members of the U.S. dance troupe Bandaloop performed ballet routines around the windows of a skyscraper in Shanghai, China, swinging from wires more than 100 ft (30 m) above the ground.

SNAP, CRACKLE, POP!

⊙ New York City food artist Jessica Siskin makes sculptures from Rice Krispies. She spends up to two hours on each artwork, ranging from an edible Chanel handbag, cute dogs, and emojis, to portraits of pop culture icons such as David Bowie, Kim Kardashian, and Homer Simpson.

BODY RIPPING → By painting directly onto a model's skin, Chilean artist Jeampiere Dinamarca Poque creates grotesquely realistic body art illusions that appear to show a woman tearing her body in half.

BLUE PERIOD → In a 2016 art installation staged by New York artist Spencer Tunick, 3,200 people in Hull, England, stripped naked and painted themselves in four shades of blue to celebrate the city's relationship with the sea.

That's no moon—it's a pancake! The planet it orbits is a flapjack as well, and both are floating in a sea of olive oil, flour, cinnamon, cumin, and seasoned salt.

SPACED-OUT SCANS

⊕ Believe it or not, these spacey scenes were made by mixing things you could find in your own kitchen cabinets!

Using ingredients like cinnamon, salt, pancakes, soy sauce, and cat fur, Seattle-based photographer Navid Baraty creates images that look like something taken by the Hubble Space Telescope. He arranges the elements onto a sheet of glass on top of a flatbed scanner and then scans it with the lid open to achieve a black background. The result is a fictional space scene good enough to eat (except for the cat fur)!

pop culture

145

July 6, 2016
Only 13 hours after its release, Pokémon Go became the number one highest-grossing mobile app.

July 7, 2016
Thanks to the game's augmented reality (AR) feature, John Coniglio was able to catch this screenshot of a giant Lickitung seemingly joining a New York Mets baseball game.

July 8, 2016
Shayla Wiggins of Wyoming stumbled upon a dead body while playing the game!

July 10, 2016
Plays of the Pokémon theme song more than tripled on the music streaming service Spotify on the weekend Pokémon Go was released.

POKÉDOG COSPLAY
→ Georgia cosplayer Carissa Grall created this incredible costume for her dog, Jaguar, that makes her look just like the Pokémon character Umbreon! Carissa cleverly used chopsticks to hold the tall ears up and mesh for the eyes so Jaguar could see.

ILLUSTRATOR
ポケモンイラストレーター

ポケモンカードゲームイラストコンテストにおいて、あなたのイラストは、優秀であることが認められました。そこで、あなたをポケモンカード公式認定イラストレーターと認め、その栄誉をたたえます。

PRICEY PIKACHU → One of the rarest Pokémon cards in the world is the Pikachu Illustrator card—only six are known to exist. They were prizes for the winners of the Japanese Pokémon Card Game Illustration Contest held in 1997. One once sold for $20,000 (£15,224), and in 2013, Scott Prate of Illinois attempted to sell one on eBay for $100,000 (£76,123). These cards have no English counterpart and are the only Pokémon cards that say "Illustrator" rather than "Trainer."

GOTTA SPEND'EM ALL → Every year, the small island country of Niue releases new coins featuring pop culture characters—2001 was the year of Pokémon!

July 11, 2016

Less than a week after the release of Pokémon Go, the market value of the gaming company Nintendo went up by $7.5 billion.

July 13, 2016

The hashtag #PokémonGo made nearly 6 BILLION impressions within the first week the game was released.

July 22, 2016

Nintendo shares dropped 18 percent after the company announced that Pokémon Go would have a "limited" financial effect for shareholders.

HE EVEN TRAVELED TO EUROPE, ASIA, AND AUSTRALIA!

August 4, 2016

Nick Johnson of Brooklyn, New York, became the first person to catch all the original 145 Pokémon first released with the game, including region-specific species!

PIKACHU OUTBREAK!

⊕ Every year, dozens of giant Pikachu flood the streets of Yokohama, Japan, during the Pikachu Outbreak festival!

Pokémon is one of the most well-known franchises in the world, and even people who don't watch the show or play the games recognize the adorable yellow character, Pikachu!

During the week-long Pikachu Outbreak, Yokohama is covered in images of the cuddly creature—taking over restaurants, train stations, and malls. Hundreds gather from all over the world to celebrate their love of Pokémon and watch oversized versions of their favorite pocket monster dance, sing, and play.

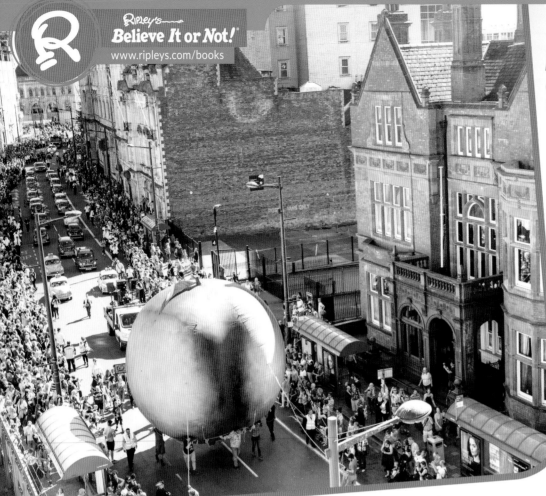

PEACHY PROCESSION

➲ In September 2016, a giant inflatable peach was paraded through the streets of Cardiff, Wales, during a giant celebration to commemorate children's author Roald Dahl, who was born in the city 100 years ago. The 30-ft-tall (9-m) peach, from Dahl's beloved book *James and the Giant Peach*, rode along atop a car as thousands of fans cheered and held signs that read, "Don't Slice the Peach" and "Power to the Peach." When the fruit model reached Cardiff Castle, it was sliced open to reveal James. Beloved characters from Dahl's other works were represented as well.

HIDDEN PAINTING → Sixteen years after buying Pablo Picasso's masterpiece *La Gommeuse* (*The Nightclub Singer*) for $3 million, U.S. billionaire Bill Koch learned that there was another portrait—also by Picasso—hidden under the lining on the back of the canvas. It turned out that the then penniless Picasso had painted his art dealer and friend, Pere Mañach, in the style of a Hindu god and had presented it to him as a gift before asking for it back so that he could reuse the canvas. When Koch discovered the secret, he displayed the two paintings at his mansion in Palm Beach, Florida, by cutting a hole in the wall so that the two artworks could be viewed from separate rooms. In 2015, he sold the pair for a combined $67 million.

LONG SHOWS → British comedian Ken Dodd still performs five-hour-long evening stand-up shows at age 88. Audience members are warned in advance that they have little chance of catching the last bus or train home.

DISTRACTED GAMER → Frenchman Romain Pierre was detained for straying onto an Indonesian military base while playing Pokémon Go on his smartphone. He had accidentally entered the complex in Cirebon as he hunted Pokémon while jogging.

NOVEL APPROACH → Russian-American author Vladimir Nabokov (1899–1977) wrote some of his novels on index cards while he was working as a curator of butterflies at Harvard University. When he had finished, his wife Vera would type up his handwritten cards. When he died, he left instructions for his heirs to burn the 138 handwritten cards that made up the rough draft of his final and unfinished novel, *The Original of Laura*, but Vera refused, and the book was published posthumously.

LUNAR PUMPKIN → For the 2015 Louisville Jack-O-Lantern Spectacular, Chicago-based sculptor Edward Cabral carved a Halloween pumpkin, recreating the iconic image of Buzz Aldrin's 1969 moon walk on the *Apollo 11* mission. The carving copied the picture down to the smallest detail, showing Aldrin in his spacesuit, with fellow crew members reflected in the visor of his helmet.

ROYAL FLUSH → Artist Mateo Blanco, of Orlando, Florida, created a life-size Queen Elizabeth II out of 4,000 playing cards and hundreds of dice. It took him more than five months to complete the 5.3-ft (1.6-m) sculpture.

THREE GENERATIONS → Like his father and grandfather before him, rapper Sean Paul is a former member of the Jamaican national water polo team. He played with them from age 13 to 21 but then gave up the sport to launch his music career.

PENCIL HEARTS → Working under a magnifying glass, Russian micro artist Salavat Fidai used a craft knife to carve the tip of an ordinary pencil into two tiny interlinking hearts. He has also replicated works by Vincent Van Gogh onto little pumpkin seeds and has painted pictures of characters from the TV series *Breaking Bad* and from the *Star Wars* movies onto pumpkin seeds. Fidai only took up miniature art after losing his office job in 2013.

SPOCK ROCK → An asteroid discovered in 1988 was renamed in 2015 for the late *Star Trek* actor Leonard Nimoy. The asteroid, 4864 Nimoy, is about 6 mi (9.6 km) across and orbits the sun once every 3.9 years. There is also an asteroid called 2309 Mr. Spock, which was discovered by American astronomer James Gibson and was named in honor of his cat. Gibson had named his pet after the *Star Trek* character because he said it was intelligent, logical, and had pointed ears.

Over a period of 11 hours, keen video gamer Ryan Hart, from London, England, beat 260 consecutive opponents on *Street Fighter V*.

SAND SCULPTURES → Scottish artist Paul Blane builds incredibly detailed sand sculptures that recreate such diverse subjects as *The Simpsons* and Leonardo da Vinci's painting *The Last Supper*. He can earn up to $1,000 a day from his artworks, which take around a week to build but can last for weeks if nobody destroys them. They are so valuable that he hires security guards to protect them at night.

MERMAID PARADE

➲ **Every year since 1983, a few hundred thousand locals and tourists soak up the sun in the sparkly Coney Island Mermaid Parade!**

Marching bands and sea creatures dance their way down the street, celebrating the start of summer. Elaborate costumes and homemade floats delight the half a million spectators that turn out for the aquatic-themed spectacle. According to the Coney Island website, the parade is the largest art parade in the United States, "a celebration of ancient mythology and honky-tonk rituals of the seaside."

BUFFETT LUNCH → A lunch with American business magnate Warren Buffett sold for $3.5 million on eBay in 2016. The winning bid was placed anonymously, and the proceeds went to charity.

24-HOUR PICTURE → Artist Quentin Devine, from Surrey, England, created a portrait of actor Kiefer Sutherland as Jack Bauer in the TV series 24 from 1,485 London postcards. He created the mosaic by gluing the cards onto a 24-sq-m (258-sq-ft) canvas in 24 hours, laying an average of one postcard every minute.

RICE TURTLE → Sculptors in Xiamen, China, made a giant model of a turtle from almost 1,000 bags of rice. The turtle measured 38 ft (11.6 m) long, 25 ft (7.6 m) wide, and 5.2 ft (1.6 m) tall, and was created from precisely 66,000 grams of rice because the number 6 is considered lucky in Chinese culture.

NAME CHANGE → The Hanna-Barbera cartoon *Top Cat* was retitled *Boss Cat* when it was shown in the United Kingdom to avoid a name clash with a popular brand of canned cat food.

CREATIVE DESK → Sting wrote the song "Every Breath You Take" at the same wooden desk where Ian Fleming used to write his James Bond novels—located at Fleming's old villa, called GoldenEye, in Jamaica.

ROYAL COLLECTION → Margaret of London, England, has collected mo than 10,000 items of memorabilia re to the British royal family, including li mannequins of the Duke and Duches of Cambridge. She began collecting seriously during Queen Elizabeth II's Jubilee in 1977.

STADIUM CONCERT → An orchest 7,548 musicians performed a 45-minu concert in a soccer stadium in Frankfu Germany, on July 9, 2016. To ensure th of the musicians were able to play on c a 5,920-sq ft (550-sq m) video screen v erected so that director Wolf Kerschek be seen 52 ft (16 m) tall from every cor of the stadium.

EVERYDAY DESIGNS → Armenian fa illustrator Edgar Artis takes stylized pap cutouts and turns them into imaginative dress design drawings using everyday ite such as leaves, seashells, soap shavings, matchsticks, cheese, slices of beetroot, a salt. One pale blue evening gown illustra is formed entirely of squeezed toothpast while another design depicts a short fring skirt made of French fries, complementec by a bright red top made from blobs of tomato ketchup.

CELEBRITY HYBRIDS → As a hobby, Norwegian Pedro Berg Johnsen likes to combine portraits of celebrities to create hybrid photos of people who do not actua exist. Using Photoshop and a computer program called Sqirlz Morph, he has create dozens of new people by blending the hea and faces of celebrities such as Taylor Swif and Emma Watson, Arnold Schwarzenegge and Colin Farrell, Ethan Hawke and Brad Pitt, and Megan Fo and Angelina Jolie.

DIP DYE

⊙ In 2016, flower crowns, floppy hats, and other festival fashions got some competition! Created by Brad Lawrence of Detroit, Michigan, Black Light Visuals introduced body marbling to the festival scene—transforming concertgoers into glowing works of art! A swirling kaleidoscope of colors is transferred onto the skin by dipping body parts into a tub full of skin-safe acrylic paint and water. With motion, the mixture creates a beautiful marbled effect that glows in the dark!

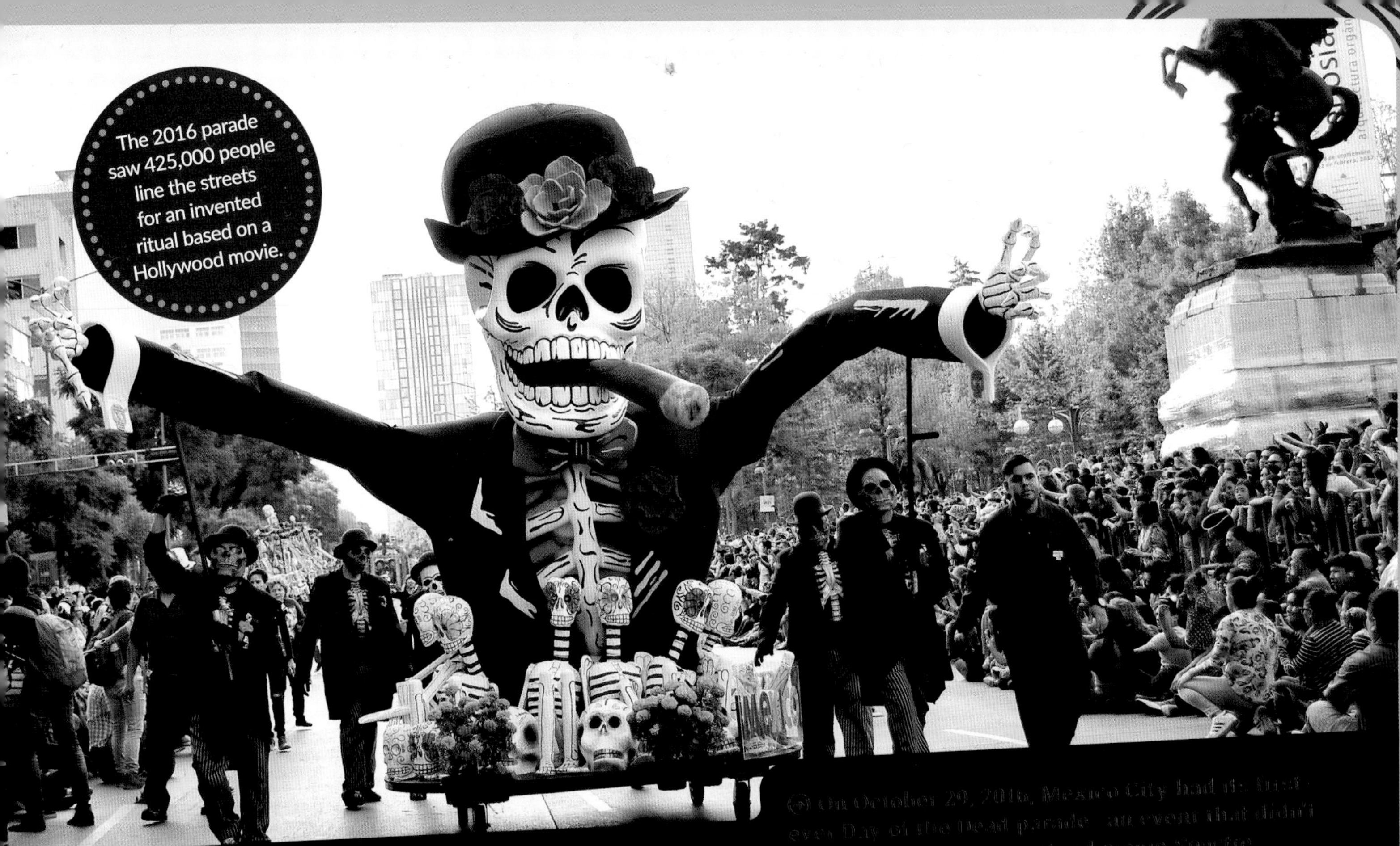

The 2016 parade saw 425,000 people line the streets for an invented ritual based on a Hollywood movie.

SPECTRE-LIKE PARADE

On October 29, 2016, Mexico City had its first-ever Day of the Dead parade—an event that didn't exist before the James Bond movie *Spectre*.

After Mexico City officials vied for the movie's production to film in their city, the movie featured a huge chase scene in the middle of a made-up Day of the Dead parade. Once the film was released and city officials expected an influx of tourists, they didn't want to disappoint 007 fans that came to experience a (nonexistent) Day of the Dead parade like in the movie—so they created one.

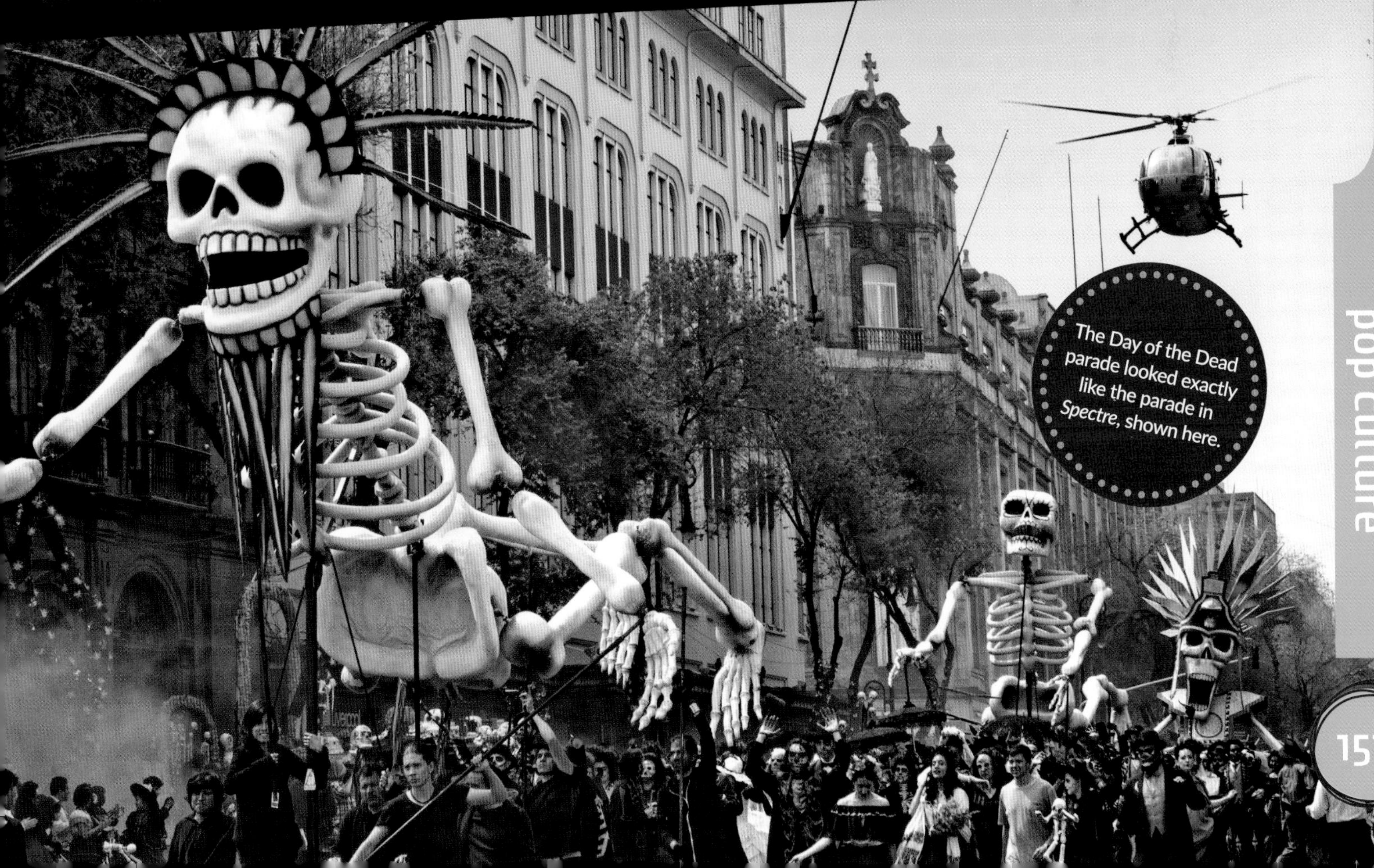

The Day of the Dead parade looked exactly like the parade in *Spectre*, shown here.

➡ In May 2016, a giant pedal-powered hamster slowly made its way around the streets of London, surprising locals and tourists.

The 12-ft-long (3.7-m) hamstermobile was created by U.K. car repair company Kwik Fit to celebrate the story of Jaffa—the hamster who was rescued from his owner's car after he got stuck. The Kwik Fit team took three months to create the mechanical Jaffa, which is made from more than 98 ft (30 m) of fake fur.

HAMSTERMOBILE

DOUBLE DEATH ➡ Two members of Jefferson Airplane—guitarist Paul Kantner and the band's original singer, Signe Toly Anderson—both died separately on January 28, 2016.

COMEBACK PLEA ➡ The day after the announcement of David Bowie's death in January 2016, more than 1,500 fans signed a petition—started by Italian Bowie fan Andrea Natella—for the musician to be brought back from the dead.

SLEEPYHEAD FASHION ➡ In 2016, Jurys Inn Hotel Group along with celebrity costume designer Wendy Benstead created an outfit of superior comfort—a suit and duvet combo called The Suvet! The two-piece ensemble combines comfort with functionality, letting the wearer take the coziness of bed with them while they're on the go. Perpetual snoozers take note: enough interest in this plushy prototype could prompt a limited edition run of this delightful bedroom couture.

SLEEP PROBLEM ➡ Washington Irving (1783–1859)—the author of *Rip Van Winkle*, the story of a man who fell asleep for 20 years—suffered from insomnia.

WATER PAINTING ➡ Turkish artist Garip Ay recreates Vincent Van Gogh masterpieces on the surface of water. He mixes black dye and carrageenan, a thickening agent, into a bowl of water before dropping in various oil colors. He then uses a metal rod to maneuver the paint into images such as "Starry Night" or the Dutch artist's famous self-portrait. To keep a permanent copy of the artwork, he carefully places a piece of paper on the water, and the painting magically transfers to it.

EXTREME SELFIE ➡ On the red carpet of the U.K. premiere of the 2016 movie *Zoolander 2* in London, actor Ben Stiller posed for a picture with his co-stars using a selfie stick that measured 28.1 ft (8.6 m) long.

GHOST ENCOUNTERS ➡ The grandfather of *Ghostbusters* star Dan Aykroyd once attempted to build a radio that was designed to reach the spirit world and enable him to speak to the dead.

BLESSED PHONES → Georgiy Machavariani, the manager of a cell phone store in Tbilisi, Georgia, called in a priest to bless all his store's Apple products because some people thought the iPhone was the "device of the devil." They had refused to buy iPhones because they associated the Apple logo with the forbidden fruit eaten by Adam and Eve, but after the priest sprinkled holy water around the store and blessed the entire stock of iPhones, sales improved greatly.

UNLUCKY NUMBER → In the 61 years the annual Eurovision Song Contest has taken place, no song has ever won from the number two position in the order of performance.

FOAM MAN → James Muldoon, from Aughnacloy, Northern Ireland, spent 11 months building an Iron Man suit out of foam yoga mats. He cut out the shapes from the 3-mm-thick foam, glued them together to make the suit, and then spray-painted the design. Finally, he added LED lights to the eyes and touch lights on the chest.

WAX JESUS → Artist John Eagan, of Freehold Township, New Jersey, made a 16-in-high (40-cm) bust of Jesus from the wax of more than 40 lb (18 kg) of partially melted white church candles.

SOCK MONKEY → Jody Lewis, of Somerset, England, cut up 66 pairs of calf-length socks and stitched them back together to create a giant 10.5-ft-tall (3.2-m) sock monkey. She then stuffed it with 33 lb (15 kg) of polyfiber.

SAME BIRTHDAY → Canadian musician Bryan Adams and U.S. singer/songwriter Ryan Adams share the same birthday, November 5.

ROLLERCOASTER RESTAURANT

⊙ Alton Towers, a theme park in Staffordshire, England, has opened Rollercoaster Restaurant, where dishes are served to customers via a tiny rollercoaster car. The food travels around two gravity-defying loop the loops before dropping 26 ft (8 m)—the equivalent of two double-decker buses—down a spiral to the tables.

153

ABITA MYSTERY HOUSE

From voodoo and vampires to swamps and Spears (Britney, that is), Louisiana has its fair share of oddities. Tucked away in Abita Springs, this folk art Mystery House takes the king cake!

The Abita Mystery House is a rambling labyrinth of buildings, where each house is a different collection. Entering through a vintage gas station and into an old Creole cottage, curious visitors are overwhelmed with the odd. Artist and Mystery House curator, John Preble, has spent years collecting found objects and creating unusual inventions for this roadside attraction!

THIS MUSEUM HAS NO LIVE SNAKES ON DISPLAY!

the AMAZING BASSIGATOR

22 FOOT EXHIBIT

SEE IT LIVE AT THE UCM MUSEUM IN ABITA SPRINGS, LOUISIANA

IN HER

BAG

Preble's collection includes interactive dioramas of Southern life. He used a variety of recyclable materials, lights, and motors to make this Mardi Gras scene move! The French Quarter balcony rocks and the float riders dance!

Preble used his taxidermy skills to create Darrel the "Dogigator." Half alligator, half dog, Darrel guards a collection of antique barbed wire!

See DARREL the DOGIGATOR

MARVEL of SCIENCE

DARREL

SEE IT LIVE AT THE UCM MUSEUM IN ABITA SPRINGS, LOUISIANA

DARREL

BOOKINGS BOOM → Dozens of Japanese fans have flocked to the Russell Hotel in Sydney, Australia, after it was featured in an episode of the anime series *Free! Eternal Summer*. Many arrive dressed as characters from the show and specifically request room 25 (the one featured in the episode), booking up to a year in advance. The small hotel has also sold more than 500 of the Australian flora and fauna–themed key rings used by the characters online to customers in countries including Mexico, China, and Canada.

RICE GRAIN → Taiwanese artist Chen Forng-Shean painstakingly created a portrait of Taiwan's new president, Tsai Ing-wen, on a single grain of rice. He used the point of a needle to outline Tsai's face and then filled in the grooves with black paint. It took him three months and 10 attempts to get it right.

KIDNEY STONE → *Star Trek* actor William Shatner once sold a kidney stone he had passed for $25,000. The stone was so big he said, "You'd want to wear it on your finger." The money went toward building a Habitat for Humanity home in Louisiana.

NEW MAC CANDLE ➡ As a joke, Apple accessory firm Twelve South created 100 candles that smell just like a new Mac—which promptly sold out. The hand-poured candles, each $24, carry hints of mint, peach, basil, lavender, mandarin, and sage. For those who love the smell of tech, all is not lost! Twelve South ramped up production of the "New Mac Candle" and is currently still selling the hot ticket item.

New Mac
HAND POURED SOY CANDLE

FAMOUS NAME → American author Nathanael West's 1939 novel *The Day of the Locust* features a character called Homer Simpson.

MICROSCOPIC BIBLE → Researchers at the Russell Berrie Nanotechnology Institute in Israel have engraved the entire Hebrew Bible on a chip the size of a grain of sugar.

UFO QUEST → Tom DeLonge left American rock band Blink-182 in 2015 so that he could devote more time to researching UFOs and aliens.

HUMBLE BEGINNINGS → J. K. Rowling is worth an estimated $1 billion, but her first book advance for *Harry Potter* was just $2,250.

BUZZ LIGHTYEAR → In honor of his favorite movie hero, Sam Stephens, from Devon, England, has legally changed his name to Buzz Lightyear, and, following a year-long battle, he finally won the right to be issued a driver's license with his new name. He also has a large collection of *Toy Story* memorabilia and a tattoo of Buzz on his leg.

HUMAN ORCHESTRA → American beatboxer Kenny Muhammad, aka "The Human Orchestra," can simultaneously generate an entire orchestra of sounds from his mouth.

COMIC COVER → A comic book cover that hung on a bedroom wall for 30 years was bought at an auction in 2016 by a collector from Ohio for $50,000. The original artwork for Marvel Comics' superhero Thor from December 1968 was designed by Jack Kirby, who created many of Marvel's major characters, including the Fantastic Four, the X-Men, and the Hulk. The issue is considered significant, as it was when Thor first realized he was a superhero.

STRAWZILLA

⊙ Run! It's Godzilla! In celebration of the recent success of the latest Godzilla movie released in Japan, *Shin Godzilla*, more than 100 people gathered to help create this 23-ft-tall (7-m) and 33-ft-long (10-m) straw recreation of the famous *kaiju*, or "strange beast." The grassy Godzilla is lit up with LEDs in its eyes, chest, and tail, and was one of the main highlights of the 2016 Kagashi Matsuri scarecrow festival held yearly in Chikuzen, Japan.

STAR MAKEOVER

→ Someone, somehow, reached the top of this Russian building's spire and turned its Soviet symbol into Spongebob Squarepants's best friend, Patrick Star!

In the dead of night, a determined individual or group of people managed to give the star atop of building 48 in Voronezh, Russia, a silly makeover. While many onlookers found the prank funny and suggested the building should be painted to resemble Spongebob, others, including the police, deemed it vandalism of an important piece of Russian history.

CENTENARIAN MODEL → To mark the British edition of *Vogue*'s centenary issue, Bo Gilbert, from Warwickshire, England, modeled for the fashion magazine in 2016 at age 100.

TIMELORD SUPERFAN →
Fourteen-year-old Ianto Williams of Carmarthenshire, Wales, has collected more than 2,100 items of *Doctor Who* memorabilia, including books, autographs, letters, DVDs, and toys.

DISAPPEARING ACT → French artist JR made the 68-ft-tall (21-m) iconic metal and glass pyramid that stands at the front of the Louvre museum in Paris disappear for a month in the summer of 2016 by covering it with a giant paper photograph of the museum itself.

BALLET STRENGTH → During a single performance, a male ballet dancer lifts as much as 1.5 tons worth of ballerinas—the same as picking up an adult hippopotamus. A three-hour ballet performance uses up energy equivalent to running 18 mi (29 km) or playing two full games of soccer back-to-back.

MUTANT BURGER
→ Australian restaurant Ribs & Burgers introduced a blue-bunned burger to celebrate the release of X-Men: Apocalypse on Blu-ray. Dubbed the Mutant Burger, its bright bun protects a slab of fried chicken, chili, and blue cheese!

ALIEN

BAR

⊙ Sci-fi fans and art aficionados alike will find the *Alien*-themed HR Giger Bar in Château St. Germain, Gruyères, Switzerland, a masterpiece worthy of breaking quarantine for.

With a surreal skeletal structure winding its way throughout, it's no surprise the otherworldly architecture was designed by legendary artist H. R. Giger himself, based on his Academy Award-winning concepts and special effects for the film *Alien*. Everything—the ceiling, walls, floors, tables, and chairs—is modeled after the biomechanical environment in the film.

FLAME-GRILLED FRAGRANCE
→ On April Fool's Day 2015, Burger King Japan sold a limited-edition Whopper-scented perfume! Available for just one day, Flame-Grilled (the name of the fragrance) came with a Whopper and cost roughly $41 (5,000 yen).

CHEESE SCULPTURE →
In celebration of National Cheeseburger Day, sculptor Troy Landwehr created a 1,524-lb (682-kg) sculpture of a cheeseburger, complete with a pickle on top—entirely out of cheese. The sculpture, which was carved in 30 hours from a 1-ton block of Wisconsin cheddar, stood 45 in (1.1 m) tall and 38 in (0.9 m) wide.

LOST DISNEY → *Sleigh Bells*, a long-lost 1928 animation featuring Oswald the Lucky Rabbit, the first-ever Disney character, was rediscovered almost 90 years later in the archive of the British Film Institute. Unseen since its original release, the print was restored by Walt Disney Animation Studios and screened as a world premiere on December 12, 2015. Although a rabbit, the star of the six-minute movie has big, black floppy ears and is the precursor to Mickey Mouse.

MINIATURE LANDSCAPES →
Photographer and macro artist David Gilliver, from Glasgow, Scotland, creates a miniature world where tiny, 2-cm-tall figures interact with everyday food items. His dioramas include a little rock climber scaling a slice of kiwi fruit, a group of hikers walking across a head of broccoli, and a waterskier crossing a bowl of shark-infested breakfast cereal.

LIFELIKE DOLLS → Using polymer clay, Michael Zajkov, an artist from Moscow, Russia, patiently hand-sculpts dolls that are so realistic they look human. Each doll has 13 joints and is fitted with eyes made from German glass and a wig from French mohair.

NO COLOR → More than 9,000 homes in the United Kingdom still have black-and-white television sets.

Ripley's Exhibit
Cat. No. 171332

Paper Art Beyoncé

Origin: Daegu, South Korea

ELVIS HAIRCUT → The Chaffee Barbershop Museum in Fort Smith, Arkansas, is dedicated to a single haircut—the G. I. buzz cut received by Elvis Presley when he was called up to join the U.S. Army in 1958. Exhibits include an emotional letter sent by three teenage girls to President Dwight D. Eisenhower, vowing that they could not cope if the army cut off Elvis's sideburns.

SPOON SCULPTURES → Artist James Rice, from Tacoma, Washington, creates amazing sculptures of motorcycles using nothing but shiny bent spoons. He had the idea when his wife Jeny realized she had a whole box of metal spoons she could not use and asked him to make something cool—and now his sculptures sell for up to $4,000 each.

GEORGE'S BAR → "George's Bar," a bar in Melbourne, Australia, is dedicated solely to neurotic *Seinfeld* character George Costanza. The walls are decorated with posters of him and quotes by him, and a sign outside encourages customers to "Be more like George."

COIN MOSAIC → At Heathrow Airport, London, England, a team of seven artists took six hours to build a 33 ft x 26 ft (10 m x 8 m) mosaic of an image of the Statue of Liberty from 600,000 coins.

COMIC FACES → Lianne Moseley, a makeup artist from Calgary, Alberta, Canada, transforms people into living comic book characters. Over a period of two hours, she paints their faces so that they look like 3-D cartoon characters—including Captain Planet, Archer, and Superman.

BORN PERFORMER → In elementary school, Jim Carrey's teacher struck a deal with him to control his misbehavior. She said that if he would sit quietly during class, he could have a few minutes at the end of each lesson to perform his routines for his classmates.

HE'S EVEN HOLDING A MONKEY!

MONKEY KING

A 36-ft-high (11-m) Transformer stands tall in Qingdao, China. Made from discarded car parts, the statue resembles the Monkey King, or Sun Wukong—a mythological character from the 16th-century Chinese classical novel *Journey to the West*. Those familiar with the legends will recognize his gold-banded iron rod, the Monkey King's favorite weapon.

AUCTION BOOM → Since 2007, eBay has sold more than 240 million pairs of shoes worldwide and enough wristwatches, laid end to end, to stretch for more than 1,300 mi (2,080 km)—all the way from New York City to Havana, Cuba.

ROYAL ARTIST → Watercolor paintings by His Royal Highness Prince Charles have sold for more than $9 million in combined sales since 1997, making him one of the United Kingdom's most successful living artists.

BANANA FACES → Davonte Wilson, of Plano, Texas, earns $100,000 a year by giving bananas faces and individual personalities. For his business, Bananas Gone Wild, he creates customized bananas for $10 each, decorating the fruit with marker pens, glitter, fake beards, mustache stickers, and miniature eyeglasses.

BLANK STARES → When Leonardo da Vinci's *Mona Lisa* was stolen from the Louvre art gallery in Paris, France, in 1911, the empty space left on the wall attracted more visitors than the painting had.

COMING AND GOING ● Fashion label Hood by Air revealed these dual-sided cowboy boots at the spring 2017 New York Fashion Week. The unusual footwear certainly turns heads, causing anyone who sees them to do a double-take!

BEFORE

AFTER

LAST LETTER → Canadian actor/director Mike Myers owns the last letter ever written by former Beatle George Harrison. The letter praised Myers for the *Austin Powers* movies and asked him for a "Mini Me" doll. Myers received the letter on the day of Harrison's death—November 29, 2001.

FEEDBACK ALBUM → The compilation album *Arc* by Canadian singer/songwriter Neil Young consists almost entirely of guitar feedback. It is 35 minutes of loud white noise, song endings, and vocal asides from various Neil Young and Crazy Horse gigs on their 1991 U.S. tour.

BINGE VIEWER → Alejandro "AJ" Fragoso, from Brooklyn, New York, watched television for 94 hours straight in April 2016. Sitting in a Manhattan apartment, over the course of five days, he watched back-to-back episodes of shows including *Battlestar Galactica*, *Curb Your Enthusiasm*, *Game of Thrones*, and *The Twilight Zone*. He started with two companions, but Louise Matsakis dropped out after 10 hours, and Molly Ennis broke eye contact with the screen at the 59-hour mark and was disqualified.

FORCE FAÇADE

● A statue of Vladimir Lenin scheduled for "decommunization," or demolition, in Odessa, Ukraine, received a Sith-tastic makeover courtesy of local artist Alexander Milov. He encased the existing Lenin statue with a titanium façade, transforming it into the world's first monument to Darth Vader. Vader's helmet even provides Wi-Fi for those who feel the pull to the dark side.

CA$H MONEY

⊕ **Artist Evan Wondolowski, of Boston, Massachusetts, creates portraits of celebrities from real money!**

He uses thousands of paper strips from shredded, discontinued bills and then glues the pieces into position to form amazingly accurate images of the likes of rapper Biggie Smalls (aka the Notorious B.I.G.), comedian Stephen Colbert, rapper 50 Cent, and even Dennis Rodman (in Won, the official currency of North Korea). He buys the shredded notes on eBay, and each portrait takes him approximately a month to complete. Besides bills, he also made an image of Barack Obama out of old U.S. pennies.

GREEN LANTERN FUNERAL →
In February 2015, the embalmed body of 50-year-old Renato Garcia, of San Juan, Puerto Rico, stood propped up against a wall in his sister's apartment during his wake—dressed as the Green Lantern. Although the family had never discussed his funeral wishes, his neighbors and friends suggested dressing him as the comic book superhero after Garcia started wearing the costume daily in the weeks leading up to his death.

CORNFLAKE GIRL → Anne Griffiths, an artist from Oxfordshire, England, categorizes and classifies cornflakes in the same way that 19th-century naturalists did with butterflies. She has created a display of more than 30 distinct cornflakes, each slightly different in size, shape, and color.

BOND BREAKTHROUGH → The 2006 James Bond movie *Casino Royale*, starring Daniel Craig, was the first Bond movie shown in China. The previous 20 had all been banned by Chinese government censors.

POTTER SPIES → The contents of J. K. Rowling's *Harry Potter* books were guarded with such secrecy in the days leading up to publication that Britain's spy agency, GCHQ, scoured the Internet for possible plotline leaks.

WEIRD TREND → After U.K. band Radiohead announced the release of their new album—*A Moon Shaped Pool*—on May 6, 2016, fans celebrated by eating pictures of singer Thom Yorke. The strange trend began when a disbelieving fan posted on the online community Reddit, saying, "If [the new album] is announced or released tomorrow, May 6, I will eat a photo of Thom Yorke."

EXPENSIVE POTATO → A photograph of a potato on a black background that was taken in 2010 by celebrated Irish visual artist Kevin Abosch sold for over $1 million in 2016 to an unnamed businessman.

CREW MEMBER → In 1996, Canadian singer Michael Bublé appeared in two episodes of *The X-Files* as an uncredited member of a submarine crew.

GAMING MARATHON → Chris Cook, from Birmingham, England, played the soccer video game *FIFA 15* nonstop for 48 hours 49 minutes—the equivalent of playing 32 actual matches or almost an entire season.

EXPERIENCED TRIO → The Golden Senior Trio, a three-man jazz band based in Kansai, Japan, have a combined average age of 83. Its members are vibraphonist Naoteru Nabeshima, aged 89, pianist Zensho Otsuka, 81, and bassist Naosuke Miyamoto, 79.

TALENT SHOW → A four-hour-long Chinese TV talent show, *Chunwan Gala*, attracts an audience of up to 800 million people each year. Screened to welcome the Chinese New Year, the entertainment extravaganza takes 12 months to prepare.

FIRST BOOK → The first book published by L. Frank Baum, author of *The Wonderful Wizard of Oz*, was a guide to rearing, mating, and managing chickens.

COSTLY TRIP → A 12-year-old boy tripped in an art gallery in Taipei, Taiwan, and in trying to regain his balance, accidentally put his fist through *Flowers*, a 17th-century painting by Italian Paolo Porpora, valued at $1.5 million.

LOVE TOKEN → Tong Aonan, a 27-year-old mechanic from Shenyang, China, built a huge 8.5 ft x 4.3 ft (2.6 m x 1.3 m) pixelated portrait of the girl he loved from 840 Rubik's cubes. He spent two months mapping out a design and $460 on the cubes, which he then had to solve so that they fit the pattern. Finally, he spent three nights stacking them individually in a large wooden frame to create the impressive likeness of her face. Alas, when he presented it to her, she rejected it.

Pencil SCULPTURES

→ Taiwanese artist Chien-Chu Lee carves tiny, detailed sculptures into the lead of pencils.

He has carved the entire alphabet into a 0.9-mm-thick pencil, as well as pop culture characters such as Buzz Lightyear, Batman, E.T., and even an intricate model of the Great Wall of China.

THAI DYE BUFFALO

➡ Thai artist Maitree Siriboon, of the Isaan region, uses live water buffalos as his canvas! Painting pop art on these beautiful beasts, he hopes to break the Thai stereotype of buffalo being a symbol of the country's labor class, elevating the creatures and respecting them.

SURROUND SOUND ➡ *Zaireeka*, a 1997 album by U.S. experimental rock band The Flaming Lips, consisted of four CDs, which were all meant to be played simultaneously on four separate audio systems to produce a harmonic sound.

FAKE EXHIBIT ➡ Disappointed by some of the items on display at the San Francisco Museum of Modern Art, 17-year-old TJ Khayatan decided to put a pair of eyeglasses on the floor as a fake exhibit to see how other visitors to the gallery would react. To his delight, most people thought it was a genuine piece of artwork and soon gathered around it to take photos.

PRINCE TRIBUTE ➡ Following the death of musician Prince in April 2016, retired farmer Gene Hanson paid tribute by climbing on his tractor and plowing a giant version of Prince's famous love symbol into his cornfield in Edgeley, North Dakota.

PERSONAL COLOR ➡ Rapper Jay Z has his own color: Jay Z blue. He asked designers to create an entirely new color for him—pearly blue with tiny flecks of platinum—with the intention of releasing Jay Z brand editions of motorboats and jeeps.

MODEL SON ➡ Dutch designer Marieke Voorsluijs spent two months knitting a life-size model of one of her two teenage sons—complete with baseball cap and headphones—because he had reached an age when he would no longer let her cuddle him.

SMELL DATING ➡ A new dating service promised to help single people find their perfect match by sniffing each other's dirty T-shirts. Artist Tega Brain and editor Sam Lavigne created Smell Dating, a project where 100 clients were sent a T-shirt to wear for three days without bathing. The clients then mailed the T-shirts back to the "Sweat Shop" at New York University, where the garments were cut into swatches. Batches of 10 mixed swatches were then sent out for the clients to sniff, and a match was made if two people expressed a mutual liking for the other's odor.

ARTWORK DESTROYED ➡ An artwork called "Where are we going to dance this evening?" that was intended to represent the decadence of 1980s Italy was accidentally thrown out by cleaners at the Museion Bozen-Bolzano in northern Italy because they thought its arrangement of empty champagne bottles, confetti, and scraps of paper was just trash left over from a party.

SINGING GOATS ➡ In 2015, the Swedish branch of charity ActionAid released an album of Christmas songs all performed by goats. *All I Want for Christmas Is a Goat* features goats bleating and baaing to festive favorites such as "Jingle Bells," "Silent Night," and "Rudolph the Red-Nosed Reindeer."

REVERSE TATTOO ➡ Barbadian singer-songwriter Rihanna has a tattoo saying "Never a failure, always a lesson" inked across her collarbone in reverse so that she can read the inspirational motto in the mirror.

ONE BOOK ➡ A bookstore in Japan only stocks one book at a time. Instead of selling a range of titles, Yoshiyuki Morioka's tiny store in the Ginza district of Tokyo stocks multiple copies of only one title per week, partly so that the customer is not burdened with having to make a choice.

MICKEY GAS MASK

➔ **In the 1940s, Walt Disney helped create gas masks that looked like Mickey Mouse.**

The threat of chemical warfare during World War II prompted a new child-friendly design to help American children overcome the fear of wearing a gas mask. Intended to fit kids aged 18 months to 4 years old, the mask was supposed to be worn as if it was a game. Although the Sun Rubber Company produced around 1,000 Mickey Mouse gas masks, they were thankfully never used and are now stored in military museums.

JOKE GIFTS ➔ American actor Jared Leto became so immersed playing the Joker in the 2016 movie *Suicide Squad* that he would not break character on set, even when he wasn't filming. He introduced himself to the rest of the cast by sending them a dead pig and also sent "Joker-like" gifts to individual actors, including a live black rat to actress Margot Robbie.

COMPUTER EPISODES ➔ Andy Herd, of Dundee, Scotland, programmed a computer to generate new episodes of the TV show *Friends*. He put every script in the show's history into his computer, and as it learned to recognize sequences in the scripts, it began to create its own scenes.

DJ FATIGUE ➔ DJ Obi from Nigeria stayed at the decks in a Lagos café for 240 hours—10 whole days. He tried to deal with the fatigue by taking two-second naps while standing up but still began hallucinating after day four or five.

VALUABLE ARTWORK ➔ The original artwork for the last two pages of a 1939 *Adventures of Tintin* comic book sold for more than $1.1 million in 2016. The work in blue watercolor, gouache, and ink is from the eighth installment of the adventures of the boy reporter Tintin by Belgian artist Hergé (the pen name of Georges Prosper Remi).

TEA BAGS ➔ New York-based artist Ruby Silvious paints miniature works of art on used tea bags. She uses the soggy, stained tea bags as blank canvases, and during 2015, she produced a new tea bag painting, drawing, or collage on 363 days of the year.

BAD MOVE ➔ Scottish actor James McAvoy shaved his head for his role as the traditionally bald Charles Xavier in the 2011 movie *X-Men: First Class*, only to learn that in this prequel his character still had a full head of hair. So he had to wear hair extensions on-screen.

FREE SHOWS ➔ A total of 3,629 shows were staged at the 2016 Edinburgh Fringe Festival in Scotland—one of the world's biggest arts festivals. Of those shows, 643 were free, and at another 164 shows, audience members could pay what they thought the show was worth.

A monument in Sofia, Bulgaria, built to honor Soviet soldiers who died during World War II has become the site of pop culture protest and vandalism. Since being built in 1954, the statue and the surrounding park have become a popular hangout for young people. Countercultural radicals regularly redecorate the military figures into pop culture icons such as Superman, Ronald McDonald, Santa Claus, Wonder Woman, and the Joker.

TAXI SERVICE → Emilio Cacho, a cab driver in Minatitlán, Mexico, offered his services to drive people around in search of Pokémon for the smartphone game craze *Pokémon Go*. He charged $7 for the first hour of pursuit and then just over $5 for each subsequent hour, and he received more than 20 calls in just the first few days from keen Pokémon hunters—even though the game was not yet officially available in Mexico.

STRICT DIET → English actor Christian Bale lost 63 lb (28.6 kg) in less than four months to play insomniac Trevor Reznik in the 2004 movie *The Machinist*. He only ate one can of tuna and one apple a day and saw his weight drop from 173 lb (78.5 kg) to 110 lb (50 kg).

50,000 CANDLES → To celebrate its 17th birthday, U.S. beverage brand Mike's Hard Lemonade lit 50,151 candles on a giant birthday cake in Los Angeles, the number of candles matching the number of people who had "liked" their Facebook post.

The sound of the T. rex's roar in the 1992 film *Jurassic Park* was made up of tiger, alligator, and baby elephant noises.

MUD MURALS → Bernie Mitchell of Pigeon Lake, Ontario, Canada, uses drywall mud to sculpt intricate 3-D murals of birds, animals, and landscapes onto plain walls. The tools of his trade include taping knives, paint brushes, and spoons.

LEAR BAN → All productions of Shakespeare's *King Lear* were banned in Britain between 1810 and 1820 because the government deemed the play inappropriate in view of King George III's madness.

Ripley's Exhibit 27,000 seeds!
Cat. No. 172061
Seed Dinosaur
Artist Wilmer Lam took four months to create this piece

pop culture

THINK YOU CAN HANDLE THE HEAT?

The chip in this box is made with the hottest chili pepper on the planet, the 'Carolina Reaper,' created for the sheer pleasure of intense heat and pain. Subjects can expect short-term loss of speech, followed by extreme profanity, heavy breathing, enhanced sinus function, and impaired vision from heat-induced tears.

FEAR THE REAPER, and consider yourself warned.

HOW TO ENTER THE ONE CHIP CHALLENGE

TRY IT: Eat the chip. (Don't say we didn't warn you...)

PROVE IT: Take a video of your attempt or a picture of your reaction. (Make sure the chip and package are in view.)

POST IT: Tag @PaquiTortillas on social media and include #onechipchallenge and #sweeps. (Your profile must be public for us to see your post!)

Free bag of Paqui chips with participation. Every submission enters you for a chance to win the grand prize. 5 grand prize winners will win a year's supply of Paqui chips and a GoPro® HERO4 Silver. See Paqui.com/reaper for details.

FEAR THE REAPER.

THE REAPER IS WAITING. ANY LAST WORDS?

SPICY CHIP

➡ The Carolina Reaper Madness chip by Paqui Chips is so spicy that they are only sold one at a time! So deadly hot it is packed in a coffin-shaped box, the chip gets its flavor from the Carolina Reaper pepper (the hottest chili pepper on Earth), ghost peppers, and chipotle seasoning!

PIRATE MOM ➡

Mother-of-four Amanda Large, from Belfast, Northern Ireland, loves *Pirates of the Caribbean* hero Jack Sparrow so much that she has spent more than $6,000 turning herself into the character, even legally changing her surname to Sparrow. She dresses as him every day and has now become a Jack Sparrow impersonator, complete with her own replica tattoos, dreadlocks, and gold teeth.

BUTTON PORTRAITS ➡

San Francisco artist Lisa Kokin has made portraits of activists Rosa Parks and Cesar Chavez and a bust of her pet dog Chico from hundreds of buttons. She builds a chicken wire structure and covers it in old and new buttons of different shapes and sizes that are carefully stitched together.

PRIVATE VIEWING ➡

Celal Göger, a cell phone repairman from Bismil, Turkey, has invented a pair of special eyeglasses that interact with a smartphone screen so that only the wearer can see it. To everyone else, the screen appears white. He came up with the idea while traveling on public transport when he noticed fellow passengers trying to read the e-mails on his phone.

COLORFUL COAST

➡ An embankment in Qingdao, China, has been painted to resemble a rainbow! The vibrant installation is designed to prevent flooding and has become popular in the area. Many people visit the embankment to attach locks to the fence that runs parallel to it, in hopes that their wishes will be granted.

TOOTHPICK HORSE ➡

Liu Xuedong, from Changchun, China, created a 3-D artwork of a wild horse from 500,000 toothpicks. The piece measures 10 ft (3 m) long and 3.25 ft (1 m) wide, weighs 374 lb (170 kg), and took him three months to complete.

HOMEMADE BATCAVE ➡

Batman fan Darren Wilson, from Wiltshire, England, spent 18 months turning the spare room of his home into a replica Batcave to store his $22,000 collection of comic book memorabilia.

CLEAN SOUNDS ➡

Martin Schmidt and Drew Daniel, who make up experimental music duo Matmos, released a 2016 album, *Ultimate Care II*, that features only the sounds generated by a washing machine in the basement of their home in Baltimore, Maryland. They created a single, 38-minute track by drumming on, rubbing, tapping, and doing laundry in their Whirlpool Ultimate Care II washing machine.

NO HANDS ➡

Artist Mariusz Kedzierski, from Swidnica, Poland, draws incredibly realistic pictures on paper despite being born without hands. By pressing the ends of his arms against a pencil, he manages to complete around 100 drawings a year. In the past seven years, he estimates that he has put in 15,000 hours of work, and in 2013, he won second prize in the Best Global Artist competition in Vienna, Austria.

MONOPOLY MANIA

⊙ **Neil Scallan of Crawley, England, owns 2,700 sets of the popular board game Monopoly.**

His collection began 10 years ago when he started bringing sets home as souvenirs from his travels. Since then, it has turned into somewhat of an obsession, leading him to buy 104 sets during a recent trip to Los Angeles! The games have outgrown his apartment, and now many of them are stored at his parents' home.

WOODEN FISH → Japanese artist Seiji Kawasaki carves blocks of wood into lifelike replicas of food, including fish, prawns, croissants, and chili peppers. After carving the wood, he coats it in layers of acrylic paint to make the sculpture look amazingly edible.

UNIQUE GUITAR → Engineering students at the University of Queensland, Australia, built an acoustic guitar made entirely from old helicopter parts.

ROYAL ILLUSTRATOR → Margrethe II, the Queen of Denmark, illustrated the Danish edition of J. R. R. Tolkien's *The Lord of the Rings*.

SLOW SPEED → The village of Miserden in Gloucestershire, England, has such a slow broadband speed that it can take 11 hours to download a movie.

PEEKING PANDA

⊙ An actual "giant" panda casually greets visitors while scaling the top of a building in Chengdu, China. Artist Lawrence Argent created the 49.2-ft-tall (15-m) panda sculpture titled *I Am Here*. Weighing 13 tons, the massive steel panda took three weeks to build, transport, and install.

REAR VIEW!

HIS COLLECTED SWEAT

SWEATY SALTY

→ In an amusing twist, Japanese-language news blog RocketNews24 made salt from their own reporter's sweat and then tasted some human sweat-garnished rice balls!

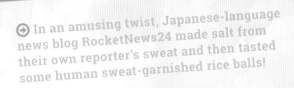

Before making the rice balls, Mr. Sato tried his own sweat salt and said it had a much stronger salty taste than he had expected. Unfortunately, it also stank like sweat!

In Japan and all across South Asia, musubi is a simple and delicious dish where triangular rice balls are filled or topped with almost anything, including salted salmon or other sour ingredients. To source the seasoning, reporter Mr. Sato brought his preserved perspiration from a sauna visit back to the office and wrung it out into a bowl. After evaporating the liquid in a frying pan, what was left was, as they called it, Sato-sourced sodium! Once the rice balls were formed, Mr. Sato sprinkled his salt on top and tasted his perspiration. Although it tasted like ordinary salt at first, the extremely salty taste and the punishing smell proved too strong.

SWEAT

Scraping the salt from the pan, they realized it was actually an icky yellow color instead of the expected white.

MAILBOX MISSION → Paul Snelling, a retired mailman from Worthing, England, has traveled the United Kingdom taking pictures of more than 4,000 red mailboxes. He hopes eventually to take pictures of all 115,000 red Royal Mail boxes in the country.

BABY SKIER → Aged just six months and 26 days, Zyla St. Onge water-skied for 686 ft (209 m) across Lake Silver in Winter Haven, Florida, in May 2016—even though she was still too young to walk.

SPONGEBOB SAVIOR → When Brandon Williams, a 13-year-old boy with autism, saw classmate Jessica Pellegrino choking on a piece of apple at Barnes Intermediate School in New York City, he saved her life by administering the Heimlich maneuver—a procedure he had learned by watching *Spongebob Squarepants*.

LANDMARK RACE → Riding the 100:1 outsider Prince of Penzance in the 2015 Melbourne Cup, Australian Michelle Payne became the first female jockey to win the prestigious horse race in its 155-year history.

PEN FRIEND → For around 40 years, V. T. Jolly, of Kochi, India, has been collecting over 6,000 varieties of writing pens from more than 30 countries, including one pen that is 80 years old and another that has a cigarette lighter on the top.

CAN FAN → Barry Steiner, a dairy farmer from Galatea, New Zealand, has a collection of more than 12,000 beer cans from 160 countries. His most prized item is the world's first beer can, made in 1935. One of a pair sold by the Gottfried Krueger Brewing Company in Richmond, Virginia, it is now worth about $3,000 to $5,000.

SCALY SKIN

⊙ A rare skin disease has left a Chinese woman with hands that appear to be covered in fish scales.

According to ImagineChina news agency, the affliction showed up when she was just three months old and caused her to go bald. Now past 20 years of age, the woman wears a wig and has become very shy due to the large amount of attention she received from curious strangers while growing up. She is one of only 20 known cases of the disorder worldwide and the first known case in China.

BLIND FAITH → As part of the Super Bowl 50 celebration in San Francisco, California, on February 5, 2016, the Indianapolis Colts's Pat McAfee kicked a 40-yard field goal while blindfolded.

WRONG RACE → Twelve-year-old LeeAdianez Rodriguez accidentally ran a half-marathon in Rochester, New York, after joining in the wrong race. She had registered for the 5k race but ended up running an extra 10 mi (16 km). She realized about halfway through that she was in the wrong race but decided to keep going to the finish.

ONE-HANDED CATCHES → On February 5, 2016, in the buildup to Super Bowl 50, Pittsburgh Steelers wide receiver Antonio Brown completed 40 one-handed catches in one minute from balls thrown to him at a distance of just over 33 ft (10 m) by Washington Redskins quarterback Kirk Cousins.

PUSH-UP KING → Jeffrey Warrick, of Buffalo, New York, can do 175 push-ups in one minute, averaging almost three push-ups per second. He has also completed a staggering 46,400 push-ups in 24 hours.

FATHER'S FOOTSTEPS → Andre Dozzell came on as a substitute for English soccer team Ipswich Town on April 16, 2016, and scored in his debut as a 16 year old—32 years after his father Jason had also scored as a substitute in his debut for Ipswich at age 16.

FINAL CUT → On December 31, 2015, 90-year-old Rhode Island barber Tony Manzi finally retired after 68 years of cutting people's hair. The man known simply as "Tony the Barber" trimmed five generations of hair at Manzi's Barber Shop in Cranston.

YOUR UPLOADS

Gum Art

Diana Lepe, of Mexico City, Mexico, sent Ripley's photos of her incredible gum art—which she made using only her mouth. Starting when she was just nine years old, she says it takes her about 10 minutes to an hour to complete a gum figure, depending on how defined the details of the subject are. Diana has now created a collection of more than 400 figurines!

HANDSKATING

Mirko Hanßen of Germany has combined rollerblading and handstands into a new sport—handskating! With incredible balance and arm strength, Hanßen is able to swerve around traffic cones, glide on one skate, and jump ramps on his handskates. Things get even crazier when he puts skates on both his hands AND feet, as he is able to switch from one to the other by doing a front- or backflip!

OLIVE Oatman

⊕ **A deadly encounter in the mid-1850s left pioneer teenager Olive Oatman with distinctive facial tattoos and a story that raises more questions than answers.**

In 1851, the Oatman family was traveling through the southwestern United States when a confrontation with Native Americans from the Yavapai tribe left six of the nine family members dead. Fifteen-year-old Lorenzo was left for dead, while his sisters Olive, 14, and Mary Ann, 7, were kept as laborers until being traded a year later to the Mohave tribe. The sisters spent years at a village, where they received blue cactus needle tattoos on their faces and arms. Sadly, due to a famine, Mary Ann died of starvation at the age of 10. Olive was finally reunited with her brother Lorenzo in 1856, after U.S. government intervention.

According to interviews given soon after her return, Olive had many opportunities to reveal herself as an abductee, as hundreds of white men traded with the Mohave tribe, but she chose not to. She often spoke with fondness of the women who took care of the two sisters and snuck her food during the famine. She suffered severe depression upon her return to Western society, and many of her friends believed her unhappiness was linked to her separation from her second family—the Mohave tribe.

She was later interviewed by author Royal Stratton for his book *Life Among the Indians*, later renamed *Captivity of the Oatman Girls*—but much of what she said contradicted her previous statements of a caring Mohave family. In her lectures to promote the book, she claimed that her blue chin tattoos were a means of identification, should she escape. Conflicting with her story, however, facial tattoos were common amongst Mohave women, to ensure recognition of fellow tribal members in the afterlife.

BURGER BOXES → Fast food fan Serge Zaka, from Lusignan, France, has traveled the world since 2011 collecting more than 300 McDonald's burger boxes from over 30 different countries—including Australia, Japan, Russia, Colombia, and the United States.

ONE FINGER → Shi Liliang, a monk from the Shaolin Temple in Eastern Quanzhou City, China, can do a handstand while balancing on only one finger. He practiced the stunt by doing regular handstands and push-ups, and as he built up his strength, he gradually reduced the number of fingers he needed to support himself.

PACIFIC CROSSING → In 2015, John Beeden, from England, became the first person to row, from mainland to mainland, solo and nonstop across the Pacific Ocean. The 53 year old rowed from San Francisco, California, to Queensland, Australia—a voyage of 8,610 mi (13,856 km). It took him almost seven months, rowing 15 hours a day in his 19.7-ft-long (6-m) boat *Socks II*.

SUN POWER → An airplane flew around the world on a 26,000-mi (41,843-km), 16-month journey without using a single drop of fuel. The sun-powered *Solar Impulse 2* completed 500 hours of flying in 17 stages, taking off from Abu Dhabi on March 9, 2015, and returning to the United Arab Emirates capital on July 26, 2016. Piloted in turn by Swiss explorers Bertrand Piccard and André Borschberg, the plane has 17,000 solar cells that store solar energy and use it to power the batteries. *Solar Impulse 2* has a longer wingspan than a Boeing 747 jumbo jet but weighs only 2.3 tons—similar to a family car—compared to a Boeing's 300 tons.

MIGHTY DREADLOCK → Sixty-year-old Savjibhai Rathwa, from Vadorara, Gujarat, India, has a thick dreadlock that is 62 ft (19 m) long. He has to walk with it coiled around his arm like a snake, but he is also able to create a turban out of it and even threads it through the roof of his house. He has been growing his hair for decades, spending three hours washing it every two days, and to keep it strong and healthy, he avoids eating spicy foods.

ANT EATER → Australian grandfather Reginald Foggerdy, 62, survived in the remote outback for six days without water by eating ants. He became lost while camel hunting in bushland 100 mi (161 km) from Laverton, an isolated town in Western Australia. He ate nothing for four days but then found a nest of black ants, and he ate 12 of them one day before eating 18 the following day. He kept out of the heat by finding shelter under a tree until he was finally rescued by search teams.

In October 2015, Gareth Sanders, of Bristol, England, ironed for 100 hours straight, during which time he pressed nearly 2,000 garments.

COAST-TO-COAST → World War II veteran Ernie Andrus completed a 3,000-mi (4,828-km) coast-to-coast run across the United States—at age 93. Running at a pace of up to a marathon per week, he set off from San Diego, California, on the Pacific coast on October 7, 2013, and reached St. Simon's Island, Georgia, on the Atlantic coast two years and 10 months later on August 20, 2016.

TATTOO PROSTHESIS → JC Sheitan Tenet, from Lyon, France, tattoos his clients using an arm prosthesis modified with a tattoo machine. He lost his right hand in 1994 but trained himself to use his left hand to do tattoos until an engineer friend, Jean Louis Gonzales, mechanized a spare prosthetic limb for JC.

EXTRA MILE → Car mechanic William Medcalf traveled 15,000 mi (24,140 km) from London to Mongolia via South Korea just to carry out a 10-minute repair and to fit a $120 spare part. The Bentley specialist took two flights and then drove through the desert for seven hours to help client Bill Cleyndert, who was taking part in the 2016 Peking (Beijing) to Paris rally when a wheel bearing failed on his 1924 Bentley Super Sports.

LUCKY BET → In 1930, hockey manager Conn Smythe was able to buy star defenseman King Clancy for the Toronto Maple Leafs from the Ottawa Senators after winning $15,000 on a horse priced at odds of 108 to 1.

SNAKE CHARMER → Iqbal Jogi can insert a 2-ft-long (0.6-m) venomous snake through his nose and then pull it out of his mouth. The 30-year-old snake charmer from a village near Karachi, Pakistan, earns a living by performing his dangerous routine at schools and weddings. He was once bitten in the mouth during his act, which left him fighting for his life for three days.

Olive stopped lecturing after marrying a rancher in 1865, and the two adopted a baby girl, settling in Sherman, Texas. Despite what may seem like a happy ending, letters found after her death reveal that she battled depression and chronic headaches throughout her life, haunted by the loss of not one, but two families. She died in 1903 at the age of 65, taking the true story of her time living with the Mohaves with her

➔ Short E. Dangerously has traveled the globe wowing audiences with acrobatic feats, fire-breathing, and glass-walking—all on his hands!

Short E. was two years old when a condition led to the amputation of both his legs. His "half-man" status has led him to be featured in TV shows, music videos, and magazines. One of his role models is Johnny Eck, an early 20th-century performer who was also billed as a "half-man." Eck was famous in his day and in 1937 even performed at the Ripley's Believe It or Not! Odditorium in Cleveland. Ripley's invited Short E. to our headquarters for an exclusive photoshoot and to find out more about his life in the sideshow business.

Johnny Eck, a 20th-century half-man and one of Short E.'s role models.

Q *Where did you grow up, and what was your life like before you joined the sideshow world?*

A I'm originally from the Midwest, Michigan and Ohio. I moved down to Florida about 12 years ago 'cause I was tired of the snow and the cold. My life was not really normal for obvious reasons. I was a nightclub DJ before I got into sideshow and was looking for something different. Sideshow came along and the rest is history.

How long have you been performing?

This will be my fifth year. I'm relatively new, but a lot has happened in that short time.

Who are you currently performing with?

I started out with World of Wonders, Ward Hall's show, and that's where I got my start and learned how to be on stage, that sort of thing. Now I travel full-time with Hellzapoppin, Bryce Graves's show, and we travel 7 to 10 months out of the year. We travel with the biggest bands in the world, the biggest rock tours, motorcycle rallies, Riot Fest. It's definitely an adventure every year.

Where is the most interesting place you've performed?

Well, it wasn't sideshow related, but I spent six weeks in Brazil with a magic show I used to work with a couple years ago. I've done a lot of international stuff—Brazil, Venezuela, Australia, New Zealand. All those places were just incredible.

What kind of stunts do you perform in your shows?

I do acrobatics. I breathe fire. I do handstands on bowling balls, and I also walk on glass on my bare hands while it's on fire. The bowling balls used to get the biggest reaction—now it's the glass. When I set the glass on fire before I jump into it, that's when people are the most shocked, the most in disbelief. I've actually seen a woman crying as I got ready to jump off the chair into the pile on fire; she was right in front of me literally crying because she was so afraid for me. She came up to me after the show and asked me if I was okay and I told her I was fine.

SHORT E. DANGEROUSLY

Q Do you find there are different types of reactions around the world?

A Absolutely! Definitely with the magic show it's more of a polite clapping because it's a theatre atmosphere—it's seated, it's two or three thousand-seat theatres. With Hellzapoppin and Riot Fest, we're in a tent—it's a thousand people and they're losing their minds! You walk out on stage and they're roaring! It's nonstop; it's energy that you feed off of. And reactions are different around the world, too, depending on the cultures and language barriers. As far as the sideshow goes, with Hellzapoppin it's always ravenous. Every other show is polite clapping, but even as you travel around the country, reactions are different.

What are some of your hobbies?

I play a lot of video games when I'm not on the road. For me it's kind of about sitting on my couch and relaxing. Sideshow is more of a lifestyle and when I'm out on tour it consumes everything I do. So when I'm out on tour and when I'm not on the road, I just like to be relaxed. I rarely leave my house. Something I've been kind of getting into a little bit lately is a small bobblehead collection that my mom left me, sports figures and things like that. But sideshow is my hobby. I guess you could say I'm married to my career.

Is there anyone you admire?

Yes. My mother, my father. Johnny Eck, for sure. Johnny is a personal hero of mine. He paved the way for guys like me. I hope to live up to his legacy and surpass it at the same time. I know that he never did fire-breathing or glass-walking or any of that stuff, but back in those days, being an oddity and a freak was enough—and now it's not enough. Like, you've got to be a performer, too. You've got to have the personality, the charisma, and the stage presence. You can't just go out there and sit on the stage. It doesn't work that way anymore.

people

181

APPALLING GALLSTONES

Minati Mondal, 51, from Kolkata, India, had an astonishing 11,950 gallstones surgically removed from her body after going to the doctor complaining of extreme stomach pain. It took 50 minutes to remove the stones, which were between 2 mm and 5 mm in size, and four hours to count them. Her surgeon said he never thought a gall bladder could contain so many stones.

HEROIC EFFORT → Despite being blind, Robin Braidwood, of Peregian Springs, Queensland, Australia, managed to conquer the infamous Tough Mudder endurance event—an 11-mi (18-km) obstacle course of high walls, mud pits, and barbed wire. He was accompanied by running coach Norbert Petras, who ran alongside Braidwood and guided him over and under each obstacle.

WATERFALL LEAP → Nick Coulter jumped 131 ft (40 m) off the top of Burney Falls, California, and performed a backflip on the way down before landing safely in the pool below.

365-DAY RIDE → Kurt Searvogel, from Sheridan, Arkansas, cycled 76,076 mi (122,432 km) in a single calendar year starting on January 10, 2015, and averaging 208 mi (335 km) a day.

HIGHLINE TRIBUTE → In 2015, as a tribute to the soldiers who died there a century earlier during World War I, 26 daredevils gathered at Monte Piana, Italy, and walked across a 685-ft-long (209-m) highline stretched above a deep ravine in the Dolomite Mountains, before sitting in a line of rainbow hammocks 160 ft (49 m) above ground.

FAVORITE HILL → From the age of 63, devoted hiker Keith Heaviside walked 1,049 ft (320 m) to the summit of Roseberry Topping, a hill in North Yorkshire, England, six days a week for 20 years—the total distance traveled being the equivalent of climbing Mount Everest 220 times. He climbed the hill 6,100 times, even when he was waist-deep in snow or on his hands and knees because the wind was so strong it was impossible for him to stand up.

HORSE POWER → Russian body builder Elbrus Nigmatullin won a tug-of-war contest against two huge horses in Chelyabinsk when he succeeded in pulling them toward him. Looping his arms through two lengths of rope, he took the strain while the horses pulled in opposite directions. The strongman has also lifted a camel, manually spun a Ferris wheel with a diameter of 105 ft (32 m), and pulled a 30-ton wooden house over a distance of 10 ft (3 m).

FIRE MASSAGE

The way to a healthier you might be in setting yourself on fire! The spa treatment huǒ liáo, otherwise known as the Chinese fire massage, is not for the faint of heart. The alarming treatment is an uncommon form of therapy, where towels soaked with alcohol and a special elixir are placed over the body and set aflame for a few seconds before being extinguished. The process is repeated a few times. The cloth can be placed over the face, back, legs, belly, or other problem area, since the massage is believed to help improve blood circulation, eliminate wrinkles, relieve joint pain, and even cure a cold, among other ailments.

FACELESS Woman

Khadija Khatoon from Kolkata, India, was born with a facial condition that has left her with no discernable eyes and small slits where her nose should be.

One neurosurgeon said 21-year-old Khadija suffers from neurofibromatosis, a genetic disorder that causes tumors to grow throughout the body. Her condition has worsened over time, and now doctors believe there's a possibility of a tumor inside her face. Despite her struggles, Khadija remains optimistic and says she is "happy in this life."

183

TRAIN TRAVELER → David Brewer, from Lancashire, England, has visited all 2,552 train stations in the United Kingdom and has taken pictures of each one.

HIGH ACHIEVER → By age 17, Moshe Kai Cavalin, of Los Angeles, California, had two college degrees, was a published author, learned how to fly, and was working for NASA helping develop surveillance technology for airplanes and drones. He enrolled at the East Los Angeles College before he was 10, becoming the youngest college student in the United States. He graduated at age 11 and wrote a bestselling autobiography that same year. At age 15, he graduated from the University of California with a bachelor's degree in mathematics. He also had a second book published—based on his experience of being bullied—and has won dozens of martial arts trophies.

TINY JEANS → Kasim Andac, a tailor from Konya, Turkey, used a sewing machine to make a pair of jeans that are just 0.9 cm long.

CHRISTMAS CRACKER → When leading Australian soccer teams Sydney FC and Central Coast Mariners met on Boxing Day 2015, instead of flipping a coin, captains Alex Brosque and Nick Montgomery stood on the field and pulled a Christmas cracker to decide which team would kick off.

SEVEN-MONTH ROUND → On October 6, 2015, golfer Kevin Reinert was standing on the 18th tee at Starmount Country Club, Greensboro, North Carolina, when he was hit by a stolen car. The 61-year-old retired U.S. Air Force colonel suffered two broken kneecaps, a broken femur, torn ligaments, and an injured shoulder. He was told it would be at least a year before he could play golf again, but just seven months later, on May 6, 2016, he returned to the 18th hole to complete his round.

BABY STROLLER → New mother Jessica Bruce ran the full 26.2-mi (42-km) 2015 Abingdon Marathon in Oxfordshire, England, in 3 hours 17 minutes 26 seconds while pushing a baby stroller containing her seven-month-old son Daniel. Her time was only 23 minutes slower than that of the fastest woman finisher, who was running unencumbered. Jessica's husband David ran alongside and even managed to feed Daniel a bottle of milk as they went.

CASKET KEEPSAKES

Humphrey **BOGART'S** cremated remains were laid to rest with a small **GOLD WHISTLE**, inscribed "If you want anything, just whistle."

Bela Lugosi, the most famous **DRACULA** on both the stage and screen, was buried in his Dracula **CAPE**.

Charlie and the Chocolate Factory author Roald **DAHL** was buried with some **CHOCOLATE**.

President John F. **KENNEDY** was laid to rest with a 9.5-in-long (24-cm) **WHALE TOOTH**.

The family of Arch West, the inventor of Doritos, **SPRINKLED NACHO CHEESE DORITOS** into his open grave.

Actor James Doohan, who played *Star Trek* engineer **SCOTTY**, had his remains fired 72 mi (116 km) **INTO SPACE.**

Pop artist Andy **WARHOL** loved wearing **PERFUME** so much he was buried with a bottle of Estée Lauder.

STANDING STILL → To raise money for charity, Garrett Lam, a neurobiology and philosophy double-major at Harvard University, stood balanced on a plastic workout ball for 5 hours 25 minutes 36.9 seconds in Boston, Massachusetts, on September 18, 2015.

HUMAN ARROW → On May 29, 2016, wingsuit flyer Jeb Corliss, from Venice, California, successfully performed the "Human Arrow" stunt by plummeting 6,000 ft (1,829 m) from an airborne helicopter at a speed of 120 mph (193 kmph) and hitting an apple-sized target that was suspended above the Great Wall of China.

FAST WORKER → Software engineers Jay Flatland and Paul Rose, from Kansas City, Missouri, built a robot that can solve a Rubik's cube in 0.9 seconds.

Ripley's Exhibit
Cat. No. 17883

Bela Lugosi
Life Mask

Made from molds taken from the film star while he was living.

OTA BENGA

➲ **A shocking and sad tale, Ota Benga, a pygmy from the Congo, was ripped from his home in 1904 and brought to the U.S. to be displayed as a human zoo exhibit.**

Standing only 4 ft 1 in (1.25 m) and weighing 103 lb (47 kg), Benga was the biggest draw of the century. Initially on display at the St. Louis World's Fair with a completely different tribe, the Ainu people of Japan, he attracted gawkers from around the world. Two years later, Benga was forced to call a new place home—the New York Zoological Gardens, now known as the Bronx Zoo.

Kept in the primate house, Benga entertained visitors—500 people at a time—by shooting a bow and arrow, weaving, and interacting with the other animals in his enclosure. In 1906, as many as 40,000 people flocked to Benga each day!

Benga shared his space with an orangutan whom he became quite attached to.

Following a custom of his tribe, Benga's teeth were filed into sharp points.

Ota Benga stands second from the left at the 1904 World's Fair, also known as the Louisiana Purchase Exposition.

people

185

YOUR UPLOADS

Nail Saver

Nahuel Cheruse of Argentina sent Ripley's photos of his fingernail and toenail collection—he kept his nail clippings for more than 15 years! He says he got started after he saw characters from the Nickelodeon show *Aaahh!!! Real Monsters* doing the same thing. Wanting to keep a home sample of his DNA, he kept the collection in a bottle in a nightstand drawer.

TANK PULL → Using a special metal ladder fixed to the ground so that his feet could obtain traction, Russian powerlifting champion Ivan Savkin managed to pull an enormous 37-ton, Soviet-era tank for a distance of almost 6.5 ft (2 m) in Vladivostok. He says that of all the things he has moved—including a ferry, a locomotive, and a guided missile installation—the 75-year-old tank was by far the heaviest.

HOT STREAK → Seventy-four-year-old Dan DeCando, from Greenville, New Jersey, hit 37 holes-in-one in 2015, including aces on five nearly consecutive playing days at Darlington Golf Club in Mahwah. On December 10 and 11, he recorded holes-in-one, took his wife Christmas shopping on December 12, then continued his streak with aces on December 13, 14, and 15.

MAKESHIFT CRUTCHES → Li Juhong, a doctor in Wadian village in China's Chongqing Province, makes regular house calls to her 1,000 patients—even though she has no legs. She has taught herself to get around using her hands and two wooden stools for support, and she has worn out 24 stools in her 15 years as a doctor. She lost her legs at age four when she was run over by a truck but never let her condition destroy her dream of studying medicine.

VOLCANO SURFER → Without wearing any protective gear, American adventurer Alison Teal rode her surfboard right up to Kilauea Volcano in Hawaii as it erupted into the ocean on August 3, 2016. For a short time, she was able to swim within feet of the molten lava, which produces deadly fumes and is so hot it would cook a human body in seconds.

WEIGHTLIFTING GRANDMA → When she was 76, grandmother Shirley Webb, of East Alton, Illinois, struggled to get out of her chair and had to use a handrail to climb stairs, but after going to the gym for two years, she can now deadlift 237 lb (108 kg).

WAVE RUNNER → Lindsey Russell, from Oxford, England, ran 19.6 mi (31.5 km) in an inflatable ball floating on the Irish Sea. The BBC TV presenter spent almost 10 hours inside the huge ZORB ball, which was fitted with rudders to help her steer it and was attached to a 550-lb (250-kg) frame to make it more stable in the open sea.

ACTIVE BODYBUILDER → Retired dentist Charles Eugster is still an active bodybuilder at age 97. Dr. Eugster, who was born in London, England, but now lives in Zurich, Switzerland, did not start lifting weights until he was 87. He became a rowing champion in his nineties, and at age 95, he ran the indoor 200-meter sprint in just 55.48 seconds.

SEVEN HITS → Playing for the San Francisco Giants against the Miami Marlins on August 8, 2016, Brandon Crawford became the first major league baseball player in 41 years to get seven hits in a game. His hits came off six different pitchers and helped the Giants gain an 8-7 victory.

EXTRA DIGITS

➔ In China, a baby boy nicknamed Hong Hong was born with an incredible 31 fingers and toes, an extreme case of polydactylism. His mother, who also suffers from the condition, has 12 fingers and 12 toes, while the boy has 15 fingers and 16 toes. The condition affects about 1 in every 1,000 births, and the extra digits are usually surgically removed, but since the procedure is expensive, the family is currently consulting doctors and trying to raise the money.

GIANT TUMOR

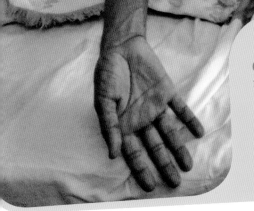

In October 2015, Gurmeet Singh underwent surgery to remove a 121-lb (55-kg) malignant tumor—the largest tumor in the history of medical science.

The 26-year-old was left bedridden for almost four years after a biopsy report confirmed the inflammation in his right thigh was cancerous. Doctors in New Delhi, India, had to amputate his leg to remove the growth, and amazingly, the tumor weighed close to 1.5 times Singh's body weight. After the surgery, he weighed just 81.6 lb (37 kg)! Singh is now able to walk with the aid of a walker, and doctors hope a prosthesis can be made for him soon.

WORLD TOURIST → Norwegian explorer Gunnar Garfors visited all 198 countries in the world by the age of 37. His first international trip was to Greece when he was just a year old, and the last country visited on his list was Cape Verde in 2013.

SLACKLINE PERIL → In April 2016, French balance athletes Nathan Paulin and Danny Menšík walked 3,346 ft (1,020 m) across a slackline suspended nearly 2,000 ft (600 m) above the ground between two mountain faces in Aiglun, France. The perilous crossing in windy conditions took Paulin 1 hour 15 minutes, and on a third attempt, Menšík followed in just 40 minutes.

HIPPO COLLECTOR → Becky Fusco, of Meriden, Connecticut, has collected more than 600 items of hippopotamus memorabilia—including salt and pepper shakers, ornaments, plush toys, a bottle of red wine with a picture of a hippo on the label, and a hippo-studded belt.

YOUNG HELPER → Despite being blind, Pepe "Dodong" Nelson earns money to support his family by climbing 60 coconut trees a day to harvest the fruit. He is helped by his five-year-old daughter, Jenny, who guides him to work every day and then leads him around the Philippine coconut plantation.

Nineteen-year-old Davion Teaheartt, of St. Petersburg, Florida, performed 59 back handsprings in a row.

CUP PYRAMID → A team of 22 students from Delhi, India, built a 22-ft-tall (6.7-m) pyramid using 57,000 plastic cups.

FROZEN CHESS → Russian ice swimmers played chess in frozen Lake Shartash, near Yekaterinburg, in December 2015, wearing only bathing suits. The players were submerged up to their chests in the water but said the freezing temperatures helped them focus quickly on the next move.

PERFECT BALANCE → Doug McManaman, of Amherst, Nova Scotia, Canada, can balance 31 hockey pucks in a stack on the back of his hand. He can also balance 33 hockey pucks on top of a pole, which is then balanced on his chin while he kneels, and he can balance a billiard ball atop a pole perched on his right ear for more than a minute while kneeling.

NO HANDS → Alexei Romanov, of Zelenodolsk, Russia, is an accomplished pianist despite being born without hands. He was inspired to play by listening to Mozart, Vivaldi, and other great composers, and when friends taught him how to read notes, he began entering music competitions—and winning.

people

187

HOFF WAS INSPIRED BY A VOYAGE THAT TOOK PLACE 120 YEARS AGO.

ATLANTERHAVS ROERNE
Kåre Rudjord

Harbo and Samuelson were featured in the very first Ripley's Believe It or Not! book!

ATLANTIC
ANTICS

➔ **Seventy-year-old Stein Hoff of Norway is the oldest person to have attempted to row across the Atlantic Ocean—a total of 3,000 mi (4,830 km) from New York to the Isles of Scilly—alone!**

The idea came to him after learning about fellow Norwegians Frank Harbo and George Samuelson who, in 1896, became the first people to row across an ocean. Completing their journey in just 55 days and in a small 18-ft (5.5-m) wooden rowboat named the Fox, the duo made the feat sound easy.

However, even with a 24-ft-long (7-m) vessel he christened the Fox II, plus modern navigational tools and a 90-day time limit, Hoff was unable to recreate the voyage—proving just how difficult the task truly is.

His hopes were dashed when, on day 84, winds became so strong that his boat rolled over multiple times and all four oars and the rudder were broken. Hoff sent out a distress signal and was soon rescued. The record for oldest person to row solo across the Atlantic remains held by his wife, Diana Hoff, who spent 113 days rowing from England to the Canary Islands and then across to South America at the age of 55.

A carrier vessel, the *Ludolf Oldendorff*, responded to Hoff's distress call.

Weeks of rowing left Hoff's hands covered in callouses.

Hoff was glad to be back on land with his wife, Diana, who successfully rowed solo across the Atlantic in 2000.

189

HAMMER HEAD

Ripley's
EXCLUSIVE

⊕ John Ferraro's skull is more than two times thicker than the average human's, and he uses it to hammer nails into wood, snap baseball bats in half, and bend steel bars!

Ferraro shocks scientists and amazes audiences with his ability to withstand incredible amounts of force to his head, with apparently no negative side effects. The average human skull is 7 mm (.28 in) thick— but an MRI scan revealed that Ferraro's is 16 mm (.63 in)! This biological advantage allows him to achieve feats like repeatedly head-butting nails into wooden planks encased in metal, with nothing but a thin piece of cloth between his forehead and the nail head.

Q *How did you first discover your amazing ability?*

A When I was about 13 years old, I got in a tussle with my younger brother and chased him outside. As he tried to escape, he ran into the house with me trailing him. He decided to avoid the potential older brother pummeling and shut the heavy oak front door as I was running toward the entrance of the house. As it began to close, I went headfirst through it— splitting and cracking the front door and yanking it off its hinges!

What are some of the craziest stunts you perform?

The most dangerous would be getting slammed by a jackhammer as it breaks a cinderblock on my head. Not only do I feel continuous impacts from the hammer, but the blade comes within a fraction of an inch from my skull. Having 16-lb (7.26-kg) bowling balls dropped on my head from heights of 10 to 15 ft (3 to 4.6 m) continuously is a testament to my resilience and strength. When there is only one thin patio block between the bowling ball and my skull, that brings the impact to a whole new level.

My motto has always been "It's mind over matter—if you're out of your mind, it doesn't matter!"

Does anyone else in your family have an extra-thick skull or unique abilities?

As far I know, I am unique and the only one that has double-thick bone density and strength. Although my daughters sometimes are very hardheaded in different ways!

Have you ever experienced any negative side effects from using your head as a hammer?

I have not suffered any ill effects like concussions, injuries, or broken bones over the years, which has amazed doctors, neurologists, and brain trauma experts. I even had my brained scanned and looked at by various brain trauma studies, and they found my brain is in perfect condition. The skin on my forehead has gotten tougher over the years.

What do you like to do in your free time?

Besides reading the latest publications from Ripley's Believe It or Not!, I love to perform and spend time with my family and friends. I am an avid collector of old time circus, vaudeville strongman, and professional wrestling memorabilia.

Do you train, and if so, how often?

I train instinctively and focus on surpassing the limits I achieved the training day before. It's all about knowing my body. How I heal, how I recuperate, and what level I will be able to go beyond the pain barrier is always a factor on how I will train that given day. I go in full throttle some days; other days it's time to back off. I was blessed with a genetic gift, as my skull is more than double the thickness of the average man. I pride myself on being a performer; I am always thinking of ways to show my headstrong abilities. One training day I may balance a 500-lb (226.8-kg) barbell on my bare head; another day I will head-butt and break hammers in half or bend coins against my head, and another day I will train on neck and full body conditioning.

These MRI scans compare the average human skull (left) to John "The Hammerhead" Ferraro's (right).

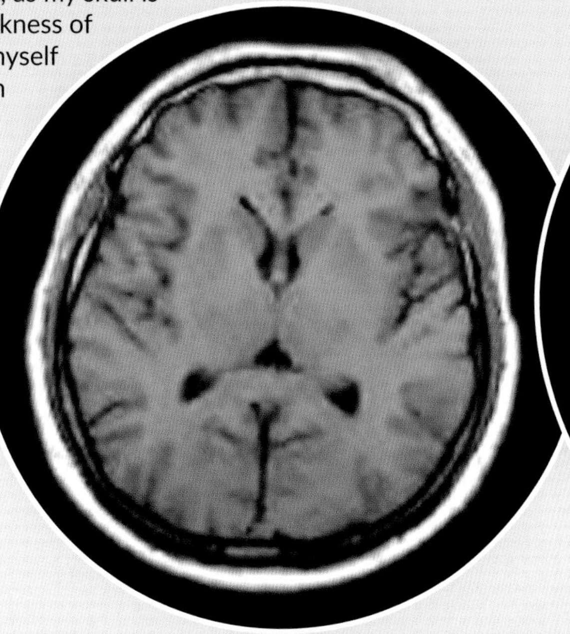

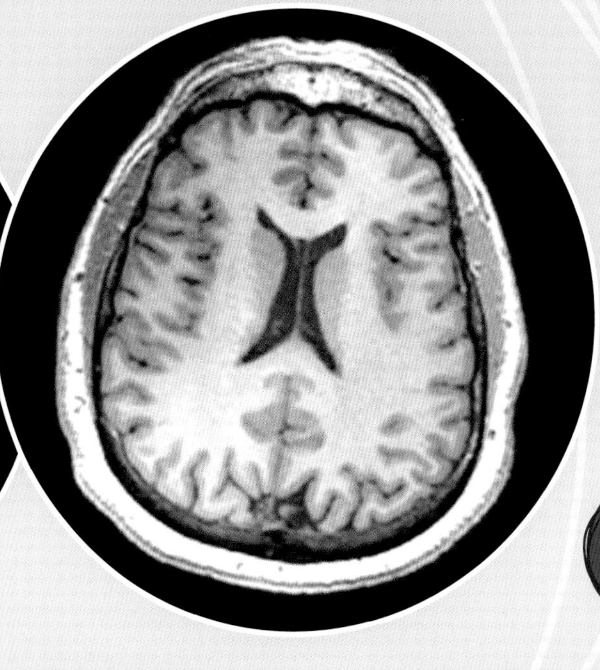

people

193

Chilly Chilies

→ Men and women brave the heat and confront the cold in a bizarre pepper-eating contest in Hangzhou, China.

The Feast of Fire and Ice competition requires participants to sit in a bucket of ice water while eating as many fiery-hot chili peppers as they can. The contrast in temperature is such a shocking sensation that many competitors have to drop out. The winner was able to down 62 peppers in just three minutes!

CAREFUL WALK →
Daredevil Josh Beaudoin, from Wasilla, Alaska, walked a slackline high above a pool containing live alligators at an alligator farm in Colorado. He did not wear a safety harness, and there was no room for error, especially when at one point an alligator came within 1 ft (30 cm) of his leg.

HIGH SUSPENSE → Doug Smode, from Calgary, Alberta, Canada, is able to suspend himself in midair by means of six metal hooks that are inserted through his face. Each hook is then attached to ropes that are tied to a thick tree branch. He can also pull a heavy bus with hooks inserted into the skin of his butt.

THROWN OVERBOARD → After the boat on which he was traveling struck a rock off Vancouver Island and threw him overboard, Kevin Strain, from Malcolm Island, British Columbia, Canada, survived the night by hanging on to a small crabbing float for more than two hours. With no life jacket, he managed to keep his head above water with the help of two empty metal containers and a crab float as a series of whirlpools threatened to drag him below the surface.

BICYCLE REPAIRMAN → Despite losing both legs and nine of his fingers in a horrific accident in 1993, Yue Jin, of Jilin City, China, has become a skilled bicycle repairman. He spent all of his savings to buy some repair tools and then went on to learn the art of fixing bicycles by using his one remaining finger and the palms of his hands.

DAY TRIP → Adam Leyton, from Leeds, England, visited 12 different European countries in 24 hours, using only public transportation in the form of trains, buses, and airplanes. He set off from Germany on May 25, 2016, and traveled through Luxembourg, France, Belgium, the Netherlands, Denmark, Sweden, Poland, the Czech Republic, Slovakia, and Hungary, before finally arriving in Austria on May 26. He had to run the final 2.5 mi (4 km) across the border into Austria to complete his challenge within the time limit.

ROOF SHOT → Tyler Toney shot a basketball from an incredible height of 533 ft (162.5 m) in 2016. The successful shot was performed from the roof of the Cotter Ranch Tower in Oklahoma City, Oklahoma, to the hoop way down on the ground below. Toney is one of five friends from Frisco, Texas—along with Cody Jones, Garrett Hilbert, and twins Coby and Cory Cotton—who are collectively known as sports entertainers Dude Perfect.

DESERT DRAMA → Ann Rodgers, a 72-year-old from Tucson, Arizona, survived for nine days and nights in the desert wilderness by drinking pond water and eating plants. She had been on her way to visit her grandchildren in Phoenix in March 2016 when she got lost and her vehicle ran out of fuel. She was unable to get a cell phone signal to summon rescuers and was only found after a search flight crew spotted a "help" sign that she had made with sticks.

ACTUAL SIZE!

HEAVYWEIGHT RUNNER → Although he weighs a mighty 545 lb (247 kg), 35-year-old Derek Mitchell, of Kansas City, Missouri, completed twenty-one 3.1-mi (5-km) races and two 6.2-mi (10-km) races in one year. His determination to get fit came after he was diagnosed with a noncancerous tumor on his pituitary gland, a condition that slows down his metabolism and made him obese.

BACKWARD MILE → On November 23, 2015, Aaron Yoder, the head track and field coach at Bethany College, Lindsborg, Kansas, ran 1 mi (1.6 km) backward in only 5 minutes 54 seconds. He undertook a rigorous training regimen to train the different muscles required to run backward rather than forward.

DESERT MARATHONS → Australian athlete Mina Guli ran seven desert marathons on seven different continents in seven weeks between February and March 2016. She completed grueling marathons in Spain's Tabernas Desert, the Arabian Desert in Jordan, the Antarctic Desert, Australia's Simpson Desert, the Richtersveld in South Africa, Chile's Atacama Desert, and the Mojave Desert in the United States.

ICE RACER → In February 2016, Russian driver Mikhail Aleshin drove a modified race car on solid ice at 141.7 mph (228 kmph) on frozen Lake Lovozero in the country's Murmansk region, located above the Arctic Circle.

WHEELCHAIR BACKPACKER → Since August 2014, Quan Peng has backpacked over 1,740 mi (2,800 km) the length and breadth of China in a wheelchair. He lost the use of his legs in 2004 when he underwent surgery to remove a tumor from his spine. The procedure damaged his nerves, permanently paralyzing his legs. Wheeling himself around, he sometimes covers as much as 37 mi (60 km) in a single day.

BODY STRENGTH → Chinese police officer Mao Weidong planked for 8 hours 1 minute and 1 second at a contest in Beijing, China, in May 2016—and then celebrated the achievement by doing push-ups. In planking, the body has to be kept in a straight line from head to toe with the weight placed on the forearms and toes.

MINI MARVEL → Seventeen-year-old Adam Reed made his high school's varsity football team despite standing just 4.5 ft (1.4 m) tall and weighing a mere 95 lb (43 kg). By contrast, Tedarrell Slaton, the biggest player on the team for the American Heritage School in Plantation, Florida, is 6.5 ft (2 m) tall and weighs 338 lb (153 kg)—more than three times heavier than Adam.

RIVER COMMUTE → For 15 years, 71-year-old Gabriel Horchler, a librarian from Maryland, rowed his way to work in downtown Washington, D. C. The idea came when he was stuck on his motorcycle in heavy traffic and thought about commuting to work instead on the Anacostia River, which runs parallel to the freeway. So every other working day, he cycled from his home to the river, rowed his 21-ft-long (6.4-m) fiberglass racing shell 5 mi (8 km) downriver, and then hopped onto another bike to take him to the Library of Congress. The entire journey took him about 90 minutes. He would then take the metro home, and the next day, he would reverse the routine by taking the metro to work and rowing back home.

BENDY BOY

→ Mohammed al-Sheikh, a 12-year-old Palestinian boy, has such a flexible body that he can eat with one leg wrapped backward around his head! Standing 4.5 ft (1.4 m) tall and weighing just 64 lb (29 kg), he can also walk while his legs are bent all the way behind his head, and perform handstands on the backs of galloping camels and horses.

BELIEVE IT DOUGH-NOT!

→ New Yorker Yasir Salem is not your average athlete. He's managed to combine two extremes: speed-eating and bicycle racing. He specializes in doughnut races, during which competitors stop in the middle of a race to eat as many doughnuts as they can, as every doughnut eaten shaves minutes off their final finish time. For the 2016 Donut Derby in Pennsylvania, Salem ate 55 doughnuts and biked 36 mi (41.8 km), leaving him with an adjusted finish time of -10 minutes!

STINGING COMPETITION

Championship winners, Pete Wellman and Naomi Harris, show how the painful plant leaves its eaters with a black-stained tongue.

→ While more famous eating competitions involve foods like hot dogs or chili, a pub in Dorset, England, instead holds the annual World Nettle Eating Championship!

Stinging nettle is a plant covered in hundreds of tiny, sharp hairs that contain skin-irritating chemicals. The contest started in 1997 when two farmers made a bet over who had the longest nettles, with the loser having to eat an entire stalk. Now dozens gather every year to see how many 2-ft-long (0.6-m) stalks they can devour within an hour. One competitor, the appropriately named Phil Thorne, ate 86 ft (26 m) to win the 2016 championship.

YOU'VE GOTTA BE YOLKING!

➡ Believe it or not, penguin egg yolks remain translucent when cooked! People of the Falkland Islands have been eating penguin eggs for centuries. They have a fishy taste and bright orange yolks. While the collection of rockhopper penguin eggs has been banned due to excessive harvesting, a limited number of gentoo penguin eggs can still be collected by those with the proper license.

DEADLY DIETS

Competitive eating is **DANGEROUS** and should only be done by professionals—these stories show how an eating contest can quickly turn into **TRAGEDY**.

k Miller died in 1906
.5 kg) of **LIMBURGER**
a bet with two friends.

Indigenous people of Canada and Alaska tell a legend of a man whose **STOMACH BURST** after he ate a large amount of dried hemlock bark and then drank water.

In 2007, Jennifer Strange of California died of **WATER POISONING** after she drank nearly 2 gal (7.5 l) of water in three hours without relieving herself.

d
Tunisia
EGGS in
experienced
died on the

While **SPEED-EATING** onigiri, or rice balls, in Japan in 2016, a man passed out and died three days later in the hospital.

Edward Archbold of Florida choked on **ROACH PARTS** and died in 2012 after eating 2 oz (60 g) of mealworms, 35 superworms, and dozens of discoid roaches.

people

197

Displaced Abdomen

Elias Woodford of Morrin, Alberta, Canada, told us the story of how he was reading a Ripley's book when he came across a 1940s cartoon of Anato Hayes displacing his entire abdomen. Elias said to himself, "I can do that!" and to prove it, he sent us this picture. The 13-year-old uses the muscles in his abdomen to move his organs to the back of his body, creating an unbelievable gap below his ribs!

⬆ **YOUR UPLOADS**

Believe It or Not!
by Ripley

ANATO HAYES
ANATOMICAL WONDER

DISPLACES HIS ENTIRE ABDOMEN

MARVEL OF MUSCULAR CONTROL

TRUCK LEAP ➜ Las Vegas-based Bryce Menzies jumped a distance of 379 ft (115 m)—more than the length of a football field—in his 900 brake horsepower, Pro 2 race truck in Santa Fe, New Mexico.

RIVER RACER ➜ Norwegian daredevil Morten Blien rode a snowmobile for 131.7 mi (212 km) on the surfaces of the Karasjok and Tana rivers in Finnmark, Norway. He used a conventional snowmobile designed for riding on snow at up to 90 mph (144 kmph) but stripped it back to make it light enough to speed along the water for more than four hours.

SUBWAY RACE ➜ Starting at Far Rockaway-Mott Avenue and finishing at Flushing-Main Street in Queens, lawyer Matthew Ahn traveled to all 469 New York City subway stations in 21 hours 28 minutes 14 seconds.

ELDERLY JUMPER ➜ Dilys Price, a retired schoolteacher from Cardiff, Wales, still goes skydiving at age 84. She only started skydiving when she was 54—because before that she was terrified of heights—but has since completed more than 1,100 jumps.

PIE CHAMPION ➜ At the 2016 Silver Slipper World Meat Pie Eating Championship in Bay St. Louis, Mississippi, Joey "Jaws" Chestnut, from San Jose, California, ate 23 six-ounce spicy meat pies in 10 minutes.

ESCAPE ARTIST ➜ Taryn Eason, from Springhill, Louisiana, can escape from a pair of locked police-grade handcuffs in just 30 seconds by dislocating her shoulders. She has Ehlers-Danlos syndrome, a rare genetic condition that enables her to bend and dislocate the joints in her body at will.

PASSED DOWN

➜ Brianna Worthy of Ridgeland, South Carolina, shares a unique birthmark with her grandmother, mother, and daughter, MilliAnna! They all have a bright white streak of hair at the center of their foreheads, caused by the harmless hereditary condition known as poliosis. MilliAnna and her family's matching streaks may go back even further than four generations, as the grandmother was adopted and never met her biological parents.

ITEMS TYLER CAN BALANCE INCLUDE A BAT, TENNIS RACKET, CRUTCH, IRONING BOARD, CHAIR, WHEELBARROW, LADDER, BIKE, PENCIL, SUNGLASSES, AND MORE!

RIPLEY'S EXCLUSIVE

→ **Tyler Scheuer, of Pennsylvania, can balance just about anything on his face, including a 10-ft (3-m) ladder!**

The 22-year-old is a graduate of Palm Beach Atlantic University and a professional halftime show performer, wowing his audiences with amazing feats of stability. Tyler discovered his unique talent when he was 11 years old and successfully balanced a bat on his nose while he was bored at baseball practice. After some experimenting and practice, he soon found out that if he can lift it, he can balance it!

Q *Is there a secret to how you do your tricks?*

A No secret; I really don't know how I balance stuff.

What part of your face do you find is the best spot for balancing large objects?

Easier items on the nose, but when I get heavier items, they go on my chin.

What's your favorite thing to balance?

Sunglasses, or babies sitting on chairs.

Have you ever gotten hurt while performing your stunts?

I've never gotten hurt, or dropped anything. Ever.

What's next on your list of things to balance?

Fire, chainsaws, animals.

Well BALANCED

NO CHEATING

To prevent cheating during a written exam, over 1,000 applicants for the Indian Army in the state of Bihar were ordered to strip to their underwear and take the test outdoors in February 2016.

DANNY'S WAY → Using an 85-ft-high (26-m), 256-ft-long (78-m) ramp that enabled him to hit speeds of 55 mph (88 kmph) on takeoff, professional skateboarder Danny Way launched himself into an air trick that peaked 25.5 ft (7.8 m)—about the height of a two-story house—above the ground near San Diego, California.

AGE GAP → The age difference between Denver Broncos's Peyton Manning (39) and Carolina Panthers's Cam Newton (26) in Super Bowl 50 was the largest between starting quarterbacks in Super Bowl history.

BIG BOUNCE → Martin Mienczakowski, from Bristol, England, bounced for a distance of 10 mi (16 km) around an athletics track on a hoppity hop bouncy ball.

TOUGH GIRL → At age 10, Kyleigh Bass, from Kansas City, Missouri, completed an unbelievable 2,110 consecutive sit-ups in 90 minutes. Although she suffered severe stomach pains partway through, she was inspired not to give up by her mother, Michelle Leer-Bass, who had recently battled through her first half-marathon race.

STICKER BALL → StickerGiant, of Longmont, Colorado, created a giant sticker ball that had an average circumference of 8.8 ft (2.7 m), weighed 231 lb (105 kg), and was made up of 171,466 stickers.

YOUR UPLOADS

Kitchen Couture

Novice seamstress Julie Mattes from Springfield, Ohio, created this colorful potholder dress completely from scratch! Julie sent Ripley's this picture of her wearing her creation. Amazingly, it took 10,980 loops to make all 305 potholders, and it took 11,070 nylon loops and 1½ years to complete the outfit.

SIDE-WHEEL DRIVE → In Chennai, India, Jagathish M. powered his three-wheeled tuk tuk up to 50 mph (80 kmph) before tilting it and driving it on two wheels for a distance of 1.37 mi (2.2 km).

FAMILY ADVENTURE → For their "Big Crazy Family Adventure," photographer Bruce Kirkby and his wife Christine Pitkanen took their two young sons Bodi and Taj on a 13,000-mi (20,900-km) journey from their home in Kimberley, British Columbia, Canada, halfway around the world to a remote Buddhist monastery in Ladakh, India, using any form of transport except airplanes. Instead they traveled by canoe, container ship, tuk tuk, riverboat, train, taxi, pony, and even elephant and yak.

10,000 DAYS → Lenworth "Kip" Williamson, of Saugus, Massachusetts, has run for more than 10,000 consecutive days. He achieved that landmark in 2016, 27 years after vowing to run every day for the rest of his life as long he was able. He goes out in all weather, running at least 3 mi (4.8 km) a day.

FOUL BALLS → On April 11, 2016, spectator Bill Dugan, of Roseville, Michigan, caught five foul balls in the first eight innings as the Detroit Tigers baseball team lost 7-4 to the Pittsburgh Pirates at Comerica Park, Detroit. Sitting behind home plate, he caught three pop-ups—all on the fly—and two ricochets that bounced off the press box. He gave all five to nearby children. The 39-year-old has caught more than 200 balls in his years as a Tigers fan, his previous best being four in a 2002 game against the Seattle Mariners.

ROBOT GOLFER → Eldrick the robot— named for Tiger Woods (whose real name is Eldrick)—hit a hole-in-one at the par-3 16th hole at TPC Scottsdale, Arizona, 19 years after Woods himself executed an ace on the same hole.

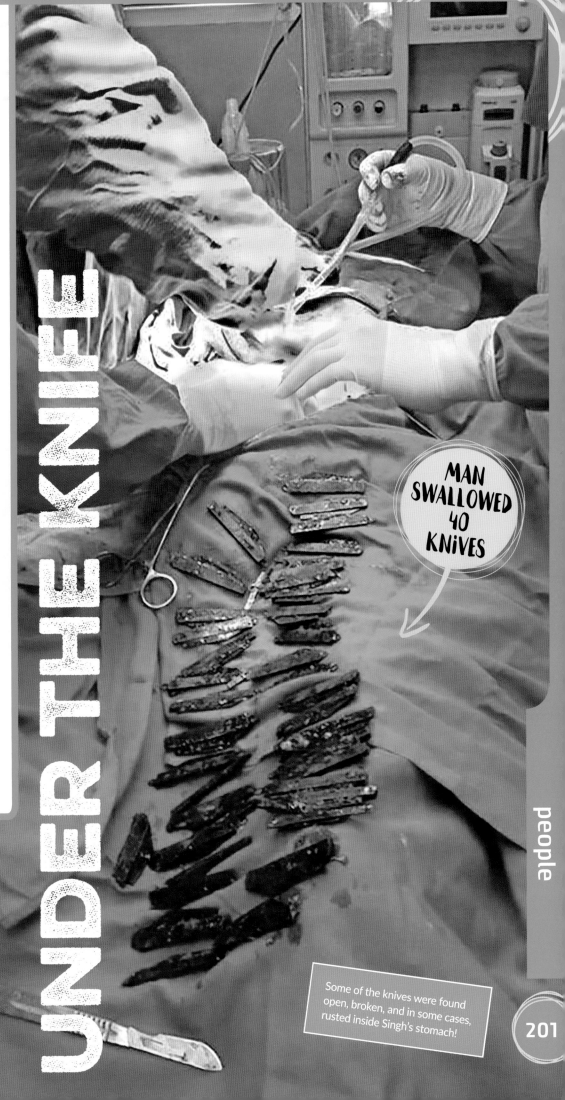

SENIOR GRADUATE → Shigemi Hirata, of Takamatsu, Japan, graduated from college in 2016—at age 96. Motivated by his interest in Japanese pottery, he enrolled in a ceramic arts course at Kyoto University of Art and Design at age 85 and received his bachelor's degree after taking 11 years to complete the required credits.

BUS PULL → Sixty-six-year-old Manjit Singh, of Leicester, England, pulled a double-decker bus weighing over 26,000 lb (11,800 kg) with his hair. He dragged the bus a distance of 50 ft (15.2 m) with just his tiny ponytail. Previously the strongman has pulled a single-decker bus 20 ft (6 m) with his ears and a double-decker bus 55 ft (17 m) with his teeth.

MARATHON GREETING → Juan Diaz de Leon and his friend Matt Holmes, both of Denver, Colorado, shook hands continuously for 43 hours 35 minutes in January 2016.

BULL RIDER → Greg Casteel, a barbershop owner from Aspen, Colorado, still rides bulls at age 55. Known as "Cowboy Greg," he has been hanging on determinedly to 1,500-lb (680-kg) to 2,200-lb (1,000-kg) bulls for over 40 years in one of the world's most dangerous sports. In that time, he has won eight championships, suffered 13 concussions, and broken countless ribs, a leg, a wrist more than once, and a thumb at least five times.

COLD FEET → Andrzej Novosiolov, from Kiev, Ukraine, has walked everywhere barefoot since February 2006—even in temperatures as low as –7°F (–21.6°C). When it gets colder than that, he runs to keep his feet from freezing.

⊕ A man in India swallowed 40 knives over the course of two months!

Mr. Singh experienced a strange compulsion to eat metal, leading him to consume foldable knives that are 7 in (17.8 cm) long when opened. Surgeons in Gurdaspur, India, spent five hours removing the foreign objects from the man's body, taking special care to not injure Singh as they pulled out the sharp blades.

UNDER THE KNIFE

MAN SWALLOWED 40 KNIVES

Some of the knives were found open, broken, and in some cases, rusted inside Singh's stomach!

people

201

BIKE BURNOUT → Riding a Victory Octane motorbike, Victory Stunt Team rider Joe Dryden completed a spectacular burnout of 2.2 mi (3.6 km) at Orlando Speed World, Florida, on March 2, 2016. He had hoped to go even farther around the small oval racetrack, but after seven laps his rear tire disintegrated, bringing the burnout to a smoky end.

CHILD GENIUS → At four years old, Sherwyn Sarabi, from Barnsley, England, recorded an IQ score of 160—the same as Albert Einstein and physicist Stephen Hawking.

CLAW MASTER → Using expert skill, Chen Zhitong has managed to grab 3,000 toys in six months on the claw machines at the Jianghu shopping mall in Xiamen, China. People gather around to watch him play, and the claw machine owners have even tried to persuade him to stop using their machines.

LIP BALMS → In just 21 months, Megan Baker, a student from East Sussex, England, collected more than 1,000 different lip balms, including ones from Egypt, New York, and Mauritius.

EXTREME EXTREMITY

⊙ **Five-year-old Vedant Joshi, of Gujarat, India, has a giant right foot measuring 11 in (27.9 cm) and weighing a whopping 12 lb (5.4 kg).**

Vedant suffers from an unknown disease, baffling hundreds of doctors from around the world. Despite his foot continuing to grow with his age and height, Vedant doesn't feel any pain and can walk and run.

Ripley's Exhibit
Cat. No. 54321
Human Hair Moths
Made entirely from human
hair, by Adrienne Antonson
Origin: United States
c. 2013

SHEAR EXHAUSTION → Ivan Scott, from County Donegal, Ireland, can shear an adult sheep in just 37.37 seconds. He has previously sheared 744 lambs in eight hours, which works out to just under 39 seconds per lamb in a tough endurance test.

TOY SOLDIERS → Jonathan Waters, an attorney from Macon, Georgia, has built up a collection of more than 5,000 toy soldiers. He began collecting them when he was five and now has military models from a wide range of American, European, and world wars, including figures depicting soldiers from medieval times.

KNUCKLE PUSHES → K. J. Joseph, the manager of a natural healing center in Munnar, Kerala, India, can complete 82 knuckle push-ups in one minute—about 1.35 push-ups per second.

SPEED SKATER → Czech-born extreme skateboarder Mischo Erban, from Vernon, British Columbia, Canada, reached a speed of nearly 60 mph (96 kmph) riding a customized electric longboard along an airport runway in Piran, Slovenia, in 2016.

PROLIFIC INVENTOR → Prolific Japanese inventor Yoshiro Nakamatsu has more than 3,500 patents to his name—over 1,000 more than Thomas Edison. Nakamatsu's imaginative designs include a pair of boots with springs to give extra bounce while running. His first invention—at age 14—was a kerosene pump, created after he saw his mother struggling to transfer soy sauce from a large container to a smaller one.

ENDURANCE QUEEN → Starting off in October 2015, 47-year-old endurance athlete Michelle Kakade, from Pune, India, completed the Indian Golden Quadrilateral Run of 3,731 mi (5,970 km) in 194 days. She ran about 22 mi (35 km) everyday, traveling through 56 towns and the cities of Mumbai, Delhi, Kolkata, and Chennai. The overall distance covered was equal to completing 142 full marathons.

MOTORCYCLE MISFORTUNE

Hamar Singh Rajput of India miraculously survived after being impaled through the neck by two iron rods. The 26-year-old lost control of his motorcycle and slammed into the back of a truck carrying construction materials, including 3-ft-long (1-m) iron rods. The impact of the crash caused the rods to go all the way through his body and out his back—it took doctors three hours to successfully remove them. Amazingly, Hamar never lost consciousness throughout the harrowing ordeal.

HAMAR THOUGHT HE "WAS GOING TO DIE ANY MOMENT."

203

Ripley's—Believe It or Not!®
www.ripleys.com/books

BLIND HIKER → Since losing his vision to a rare autoimmune disorder in 2006, Trevor Thomas, of Charlotte, North Carolina, has hiked around 20,000 mi (32,000 km) across the United States. Accompanied by his seeing-eye dog Tennille, he has also reached the 14,440-ft-high (4.402-m) summit of Mount Elbert in Colorado, the second highest mountain in the contiguous United States.

STEADY ROBOT → Xingzhe No. 1, a four-legged robot developed by a team led by Professor Li Qingdu from an information and communications college in China, walked 83 mi (134 km) around an athletics track in 54 hours without falling over—a total of 360,000 consecutive steps.

ANTLER ADDICT → James Phillips (a.k.a. Antler Man), from Three Forks, Montana, has found and collected more than 16,000 shed deer antlers. He has been collecting antlers for almost 60 years and in the 1980s sold 600 brown elk and 1,500 deer sheds to help put his three daughters through college.

BLINDFOLD SHOT → In Phoenix, Arizona, on November 12, 2015, the Harlem Globetrotters's Corey "Thunder" Law shot a basket from a distance of 69.5 ft (21.1 m)—while blindfolded.

BALANCING ACT → Nigerian athlete Harrison Chinedu walked for 6 hours 15 minutes in Lagos, covering a distance of 30 mi (48 km), while balancing a soccer ball on his head.

HIGH KICKS → Karate expert Pradip Timilisina, from Biratnagar, Nepal, can kick himself in the back of the head 60 times in a minute while standing up.

PUB CHALLENGE → Mags Thomson, from Livingston, Scotland, has visited almost 1,000 Wetherspoons pubs across the United Kingdom. Her quest to visit every Wetherspoons pub has taken her over 20 years. She began in 1994 and continued even after the death of her husband and companion Ian in 2010.

HELLO, MY NAME IS:

Known as **APTRONYMS**, these people's names are amusingly appropriate...

Usain **BOLT**: Lightning-fast Jamaican sprinter Bolt is regarded as the **FASTEST HUMAN** ever timed!

Marion **MOON**: Mother of *Apollo 11* lunar module pilot Buzz Aldrin, one of the first people to **WALK ON THE MOON!**

Bruno **FROMAGE**: Fromage was once the **"BIG CHEESE"** at Danone Dairy UK.

Scott **SPEED**: This American **RACECAR DRIVER** has a need for speed!

John **SHRAPNEL**: English actor Shrapnel once narrated a Science Channel documentary about the universe's biggest **EXPLOSIONS!**

William **WORDSWORTH**: As an 18th-century poet, Wordsworth helped spur the Romantic movement in **ENGLISH LITERATURE**.

MIGHTY WHIP → On July 20, 2016, in Fall Creek, Wisconsin, extreme whipcracker Adam Winrich cracked a whip that measured 238 ft (73 m) long. He managed to send a wave down the entire length of the manila rope whip, resulting in a crack right at the very tip.

PUZZLING HOBBY → Jodie Desbiens, of Windsor, Ontario, Canada, has completed more than 1,030 jigsaw puzzles. Her fascination started over 15 years ago when she bought a jigsaw featuring a picture of a tiger, and now every day she finishes at least one 1,000-piece puzzle before tackling a few smaller, 300-piece ones.

AMAZING MEMORY → Rebecca Sharrock, 25, of Brisbane, Australia, has highly superior autobiographical memory (or hyperthymesia), a very rare condition that means she can remember everything that has happened in her life since she was only 12 days old. With her incredible memory, she can also recite all seven *Harry Potter* books word for word.

SNOWBALL FIGHT → On January 31, 2016, more than 8,200 people gathered at Victoria Park in Saskatoon, Saskatchewan, Canada, to take part in a mass snowball fight.

SIX-DAY DIVE → In July 2016, Turkish scuba diver Cem Karabay remained underwater in the open sea off the coast of northern Cyprus for 142 hours 42 minutes 42 seconds—almost six days. While submerged, he downed food and liquids and even played backgammon.

TREE LIMBS

⊕ Abul Bajandar's arms and legs looked like they were turning into tree branches!

The Bangladeshi man is the third known case of an extremely rare skin disorder nicknamed the "tree man" disease. Bajandar first noticed the bark-like growths as a teenager and tried to remove them himself, but it proved too painful. Eventually the masses completely covered his hands and feet, making it impossible for him to feed himself or keep his job as a bicycle rickshaw puller. He has undergone surgeries to remove the growths and hopes to return to a normal life soon.

TWINNING WEDDING

➔ In November 2015, identical twin brothers Dinker and Dilraj Varikkassery married identical twin sisters Reena and Reema—in a ceremony involving twin priests, twin page boys, and twin flower girls! The wedding took place at Saint Xavier's Church in Thrissur, India, where all twin siblings even wore color-coordinated outfits. Unbelievably, the brothers had been searching for five years for twin sisters to marry, while the sisters had been searching for three years for suitable twin husbands.

SENIOR GYMNAST ➔ In 2016, Uzbekistan gymnast Oksana Chusovitina competed in her seventh Olympic Games, at age 41. The vault specialist won her first Olympic gold medal in 1992—almost five years before some of her rivals in Rio were even born.

EXTRA DIGITS ➔ Devendra Suthar, from Himmatnagar, India, has 28 fingers and toes. The carpenter has the rare condition polydactylism, giving him seven fingers on each hand and seven toes on each foot, although two of the toes are joined. He considers his extra digits to be lucky and has no intention of cutting them off.

After 16 surgeries, Bajandar may be the first person to be cured of this disease, provided the warts do not grow back.

HOSPITAL RESIDENT → Abdullah Kozan died in 2015 at age 70 after spending the last 47 years of his life in the hospital—even though he was not seriously ill. He was originally admitted to the hospital in Bursa, Turkey, in 1968 complaining of a headache, and after his treatment, staff allowed him to stay because he enjoyed living there and had nowhere else to go. In return, he helped out by delivering X-rays and medical documents.

LAST GAME → At his funeral wake, the corpse of Jomar Aguayo Collazo was dressed in a tracksuit, cap, and dark glasses and propped up at a table to play one last game of dominoes. He had been fatally shot in his mother's bar in Río Piedras, Puerto Rico, shortly before his 23rd birthday.

CAR ALLERGY → Geoffrey Evans, a doctor from Barnsley, South Yorkshire, England, found that he was allergic to his new $25,000 car and thus could only drive it for 40 minutes a week. He broke out in a rash whenever he sat behind the wheel of his new Audi because he was sensitive to the formaldehyde in the interior's plastics.

ZOMBIE HOUSE → For Halloween, Chris Walton and his family from Preston, England, spent $30,000 on special costumes and props from the United States to turn their house into a "Zombie Apocalypse" with 11 spooky rooms, including a blood-splattered bathroom, Dracula's lair, and an *Exorcist* room.

CHEWBACCA ARRESTED → A man dressed as Chewbacca from *Star Wars* was arrested in Odessa, Ukraine, while campaigning in support of Darth Vader, who was running for mayor in the city. He appeared in court in full Chewbacca costume after being unable to produce the necessary identification documents while driving Vader to the election.

ROYAL PASTA → His Royal Highness Emanuele Filiberto of Savoy, the grandson of Italy's last king, Umberto II, makes a living selling pasta from a food truck in Los Angeles. He has painted the truck in the colors of the House of Savoy and named it "Prince of Venice" after one of his titles. The House of Savoy ruled Italy from 1861 to 1946, when the country became a republic and Umberto was exiled after spending just one month on the throne.

TOO GENEROUS → A customer at a restaurant in Edgewater, Colorado, left a $1,000 tip for a $46 takeout order—but when he sobered up the next day, he returned and asked for the money back.

CHARGING BULL → A 2016 junior soccer game in Maryborough, Queensland, Australia, was interrupted when a bull invaded the field and charged the young players, sending them running for safety.

CANINE WIFE → When Mukesh Kerayi, a seven-year-old boy from the eastern Indian village of Manik Bazar, had a horoscope reading predicting that his first wife would die young, his superstitious family forced him to marry a female dog in a bid to minimize the potential tragedy. The dog wore a wedding dress for the ceremony, after which it was returned to the streets.

TREE PASSENGER → A woman was arrested for drunk driving after being seen driving through Roselle, Illinois, with a 15-ft-tall (4.6-m) tree embedded in the front grill of her car.

CARTOON CHARACTER → Pixee Fox, a Swedish model who lives in North Carolina, has spent $120,000 on over 15 surgeries to make herself look more like a living cartoon character—including having six ribs removed to shrink her waist to just 14 in (35 cm).

APOCALYPSE PLAN → Ian Coulthard, a window cleaner from Gateshead, England, has been hiding food in secret woodland locations for more than 10 years in preparation for an impending apocalypse.

MAKESHIFT MASK → A gunman robbed a Nashville, Tennessee, gas station using toilet paper as a mask. He entered the gas station, went into the bathroom, covered his face with toilet paper, and then demanded money from the clerk.

GLUED EYE → Katherine Gaydos, a mother-of-two from Lantana, Florida, accidentally glued her left eye shut for nine days after mistaking a tube of superglue for eye drops.

WRONG ANTHEM → Uruguay's soccer players were left looking puzzled before their 2016 Copa America game against Mexico in Glendale, Arizona, when the Chilean national anthem was played by mistake.

SPAM FAN → Mark Benson, from Liverpool, England, officially changed his middle name to "I Love Spam" in honor of his favorite food. He eats Spam for breakfast every day and is the proud owner of a Spam can suit and special Spam shoes.

PAN DRIVER → Police officers in Adelaide, Australia, arrested a 32-year-old man for using a frying pan to drive his car. He had removed the steering wheel and illegally replaced it with the cooking implement.

FIREFLY FOREST

> ➔ China's East Lake Peony Garden is home to 10,000 illuminating insects!

In an effort to protect the area's dwindling firefly population and promote breeding, this real-life enchanted forest is the world's first firefly-themed park! Believe it or not, firefly light is the most efficient light in the world—nearly half of the energy in the creature's chemical reaction is emitted as light!

MYSTERY FLAME

➡ There is a fire burning almost nonstop behind a waterfall in Orchard Park, New York! A small leak of natural gas makes the fire of Eternal Flame Falls possible and is thought to have been lit by Native Americans thousands of years ago. Although the 4- to 8-in (10- to 20-cm) flame can go out, the gas can be easily relit by anyone passing by with a lighter. Scientists are currently unsure how the gas is produced, as the rocks beneath the park are not hot enough to produce gas by known processes.

SUGAR SPREE ➡ A man was arrested for breaking into a restaurant in Sacramento, California, and sprinkling powdered sugar over his head and body.

DOZY JUDGE ➡ The trial in Muenster, Germany, of two men suspected of robbing a grocery store had to be stopped because one of the panel of five judges kept falling asleep during proceedings. The trial was restarted with a new judge.

Pet Funerals

➡ **Animatrans is the first funeral home in Belgium that caters only to pets.**

The company provides extravagant funerals, cremation, and lifelike taxidermy for beloved animals. While it may seem morbid, these services help many pet owners with the grieving process. The founder of Animatrans, Patrick Pendville, started the funeral home in 1995 as a compassionate alternative to standard animal disposal, which classifies dead pets as hazardous waste.

MARRIED ASHES → Grief-stricken Mr. Lai, from Hsinchu village, Taiwan, married the ashes of his dead girlfriend in a special ceremony, even dressing the urn in a wedding gown. He did so to demonstrate his commitment to her even after she was dead.

SPONGE LOVER → Emma Thompson, from North Tyneside, England, spends $10 a week on bath sponges—just so that she can eat them. She chews up to 20 sponges every day after first soaking them overnight in apple-flavored dishwashing liquid and then removing the scouring pad. She suffers from the condition pica, a disorder where people eat things with no nutritional value. She calls the foamy sponges her "guilty pleasure."

FAKE FRECKLES → Remi Brixton, of Los Angeles, California, has launched a cosmetic kit that allows people to add temporary fake freckles to their body. The kit comes with a set of 72 self-adhesive stencils and a rollerball containing a special skin-pigmenting formula. Users place the stencil where they want freckles and steer the rollerball over it to create lifelike freckles that can last for up to six weeks.

REFUSED PAROLE → Granted parole seven months before the end of his sentence, Maksat Yklasov instead demanded to stay in jail so that he could play in an important soccer match. Yklasov was captain of the soccer team at the prison in Taraz, Kazakhstan, and did not want to miss the big game.

DEAD FISH → Russian makeup artist Elya Bulochka used dead fish as facial accessories for a fashion shoot. She stuck dead angel fish, neon tetra, and other small fish to models' faces for a mermaid-themed photo session.

CLIFFHANGER PROPOSAL → Michael Banks scaled California's 600-ft-high (183-m) Morro Rock to propose to his girlfriend, who was watching via FaceTime video—but after she said yes, he got stuck on the way down and had to be rescued by helicopter.

CAT GUESTS → When animal lovers Louise Veronneau and Dominic Husson, from Montreal, Quebec, Canada, got married in 2016, their only guests were 1,000 cats. They chose for their wedding venue The Cat House on the Kings, a 12-acre plot near Fresno, California, that is surrounded by a cat-proof fence and is considered the largest cat sanctuary in the United States.

TOOTH EXTRACTION → Carl Schreiner, of Roseburg, Oregon, used a drone to pull out the wobbly first tooth of his five-year-old daughter Ariana. He tied one end of a piece of dental floss to the drone and the other end to the tooth, and when the quadcopter flew high into the sky, the loose tooth was extracted from her mouth.

SHOTGUN SALUTE → Following the death of Vietnam War veteran Walter "Jim" Hosey, of La Verkin, Utah, his family loaded 50 shotgun shells with his ashes and fired them off at the Southern Utah Shooting Sports Park in Hurricane.

BANANA RUSH → Police in Mumbai, India, force-fed a jewelry thief 40 bananas to retrieve the stolen gold chain that he had swallowed. The 25-year-old initially denied the theft, but an X-ray revealed that he had swallowed the chain in an attempt to conceal it. So police officers fed him bananas throughout the day until he passed it naturally. They then made him wash it and disinfect it.

HOLY CREDIT → The Nizhny Novgorod diocese of the Russian Orthodox Church was allowed to pay off an $11,500 debt to a construction company not with money but by promising to pray for the creditors' good health instead.

SLICE OF LIFE
→ In addition to funerals and taxidermy, the Animatrans funeral home for pets can also provide death masks for pet owners to display in their homes. The company creates a mold of the deceased animal's face in a long-lasting resin, resulting in a strikingly realistic recreation of its facial features.

1

December 11, 1895
Mary Lowry weds John Broadfield Warren. The dress was handmade in New York City for Lowry's high society wedding in Buffalo, New York. According to family lore, her waist measured just 18 in (45.7 cm)!

It's no surprise that every bride wants her wedding day to be special and her wedding dress to be perfect—but one family has worn the same perfect dress for over a century.

Ever since Mary Lowry first wore the Victorian-era satin silk gown for her nuptials in December 1895, her wedding dress has been worn by 10 more brides, starting with her own granddaughter. Lowry's dress was made in two pieces, with whalebone stays and a corset back, thereby allowing all the other brides to adjust the dress and wear it. Over time a tradition formed: the mother of whoever last wore the gown would be its keeper, until the next bride came along.

However, the 120-year-old dress almost didn't survive the ravages of time. Before 11th bride Abigail Kingston could wear the family heirloom for her wedding in October 2015, the gown had to be extensively restored due to the effects of aging—with Pennsylvania bridal designer Deborah LoPrestie and her team spending over 200 hours on the restoration. The gown now sits wrapped in muslin and stored in a cedar chest, ready for its 12th bride.

Yes to the DRESS

2

February 20, 1946
Jane Woodruff weds John Kearns. Lowry's granddaughter Jane started the dress tradition after her mother refused to wear it (she got married in the roaring '20s and wanted a flapper-style dress instead).

3

October 13, 1948
Virginia Woodruff weds Douglas MacConnell.

4

5

6

June 15, 1960
Sara Seiler weds
Duncan Ogden.

October 16, 1976
Laird MacConnell
weds
Timothy Hensler.

August 6, 1977
Leslie Woodruff weds
Richard T. Kingston Jr.
Leslie first saw the
gown at her Aunt
Sally's wedding in
1960 and thought
it was breathtaking,
telling her mother she
wanted to wear it.

7

8

11

October 17, 2015
Abby Kingston wears
the gown 120 years
after her great-great-
grandmother Mary.
She also wore her
great-grandmother's
ring and her
grandmother's locket.

June 2, 1986
Jane Ogden
weds James
Houston,
becoming the
eighth bride to
wear the dress.
The dress began
to be shortened
during the '80s.

October 30, 1982
Janet Kearns weds Mark Daigle.
Janet added lace to the dress to
conceal some of the damage to
the fabric over the years.

9

10

August 26, 1989
Virginia Kearns
weds
Charles Stinnett.

July 4, 1991
Ann Ogden weds
Robert Hausslien.

Heads Up!

⊙ **Nineteenth-century British army officer Major-General Horatio Gordon Robley collected preserved heads!**

The New Zealand Wars brought Robley to the island nation in the 1860s. While there, he developed a fascination with the Māori—New Zealand's indigenous people. In addition to being a soldier, Robley was also an artist and recorded much of his travels as sketches. He was particularly interested in Māori facial tattoos known as "moko," and using his artistic skill, he documented the markings and their meanings.

In his retirement, Robley began a collection of preserved Māori heads known as "mokomokai." Mokomokai were created by removing the brain and eyes, sealing every orifice, and then boiling, steaming, and drying the head before treating it with shark oil. The process preserved the facial tattoos that so intrigued Robley, who amassed a collection of 35 heads.

TODDLER CONVICTED → A military court in Egypt found Ahmed Mansour Qorany Sharara guilty of killing three people, participating in riots, and sabotaging public and private property—even though he was only 16 months old at the time. After the toddler was sentenced to life imprisonment, the authorities suddenly realized that they had convicted the wrong person and had meant to charge a teenager with a similar name.

CHICKEN SCENT KFC produced 3,000 bottles of Extra Crispy Sunscreen—a limited edition sunscreen that leaves the wearer smelling of crispy fried chicken.

HARDENED CRIMINAL → In March 2016, an 11-year-old boy took a cement mixer truck on a joyride and led police in Dodge County, Minnesota, on an hour-long chase at speeds of more than 70 mph (112 kmph).

DRONE WAXING David Freiheit, of Magog, Quebec, Canada, used a drone to wax his leg hair. He attached one end of a length of rope to the drone and the other end to a wax strip on his leg—and then launched the drone to yank away the strip and with it his leg hair.

SNOWMAN EXPLOSION

→ Every April in Zurich, Switzerland, a cotton wool snowman filled with firecrackers is set alight at exactly 6 p.m. during the traditional springtime festival called Sechseläuten (or Sechselaeuten). Named the Böögg (or Boeoegg), the snowman figure symbolizes the winter, and the burning of the effigy serves to drive out winter and herald the spring. It is said that the faster the snowman's head catches fire and explodes, the warmer the summer will be.

At the C1 Espresso Café in Christchurch, New Zealand, customers' meals are delivered to them via a pneumatic tube at speeds of 90 mph (144 kmph).

COUCH CAT → Rachel Barbee dropped off an old couch at a thrift store in Price, Utah, unaware that her beloved pet cat, Tiny One, was hiding inside it. The pair were reunited after surprised store staff took a picture of the cat and posted it on Facebook.

UNDERWATER WEDDING → Diving enthusiasts Justin and Crystal Reynolds got married underwater. The couple strapped on air tanks over their tuxedo and wedding gown and exchanged vows among whale sharks and manta rays in the 6.3-million-gal (28.6-million-l) tank at the Georgia Aquarium in Atlanta. They then shared their first dance underwater before surfacing for the reception.

Eighteen-year-old Devin Washington was hired by a Popeyes eatery in New Orleans, Louisiana, after helping to foil a robbery during his job interview.

EXPENSIVE TICKET → After being stopped by police in Queensland, Australia, for speeding in 2012, Mustafa Al Sharkarji was fined $180. Since then, he has spent more than $70,000 contesting the ticket.

NIGHT RIDE → In December 2015, the Stunt Freaks Team strapped on a few colorful LED lights and raced a motorbike and crosskart dune buggy in complete darkness on ice and snow. Shot in Imatra, Finland, this icy stunt took place in harsh subzero temperatures, which proved especially tough for the dune buggy, usually used to traverse sand dunes. The team waited six months for the right conditions before attempting the stunt, which saw them race side by side at night without headlights. The Finnish performers specialize in extreme motorsport videos, posting their death-defying feats on YouTube.

PROUD GRANDMA Carmen Baugh, of Raleigh, North Carolina, is so proud of her two grandchildren that she has covered almost every inch of her living room with hundreds of pictures of them, plastering photos on the walls, curtains, cushions, and even her own clothes. She had wallpaper specially made that features more than 30 different pictures of her grandchildren. She liked the design so much that she also used it for her soft furnishings and for a wearable shirt.

TOMATO ADDICTION Liam Pierce, of Gloucester, England, was addicted to tomatoes for 10 years. After choking on a pea at age two, he could not look at any vegetable without feeling sick and instead lived solely on a diet of tomato-based foods, including three bottles of ketchup a week. He developed a phobia about all non-tomato foods until he was finally cured by hypnosis.

DAS LIMO

With the help of 30 workers, Wahyu Pamungkas, a mechanic from Semarang, Indonesia, spent over a year building a Volkswagen Kombi van that is 25 ft (7.6 m) long and seats more than 20 people! Spending more than £20,000 ($26,500), he constructed his extra-long vehicle by joining together two existing vans and swapping the 1,500cc engine for a 2,000cc version.

MOBILE HOME For over two years, California sales manager Edward Mjelde has lived out of his Ford Escape SUV. By adjusting the seats, he is able to sleep lying down and stores all of his worldly possessions in the trunk. These include clothes, food, two miniature stoves, and a compact folding table and chair that form an outside work station. He showers at the gym, uses public washrooms, and when he parks near a Wi-Fi hotspot, he has the perfect outdoor office. Before adopting his new lifestyle, he walked 5,000 mi (8,047 km) across the United States from Delaware to California.

SAME SUIT To highlight the plight of female colleagues who often get criticized for their choice of clothes, Richard Stewart, the mayor of Coquitlam, British Columbia, Canada, wore the same dark blue suit to every council meeting for 15 months—and nobody noticed.

TURKEY AGAIN Jayne Winteringham, from Bristol, England, has eaten a Christmas dinner of roast turkey every day for more than 15 years—over 5,500 meals. In that time, she has eaten in excess of 82,000 brussels sprouts, but her festive diet has helped her stay the same weight of 134 lb (61 kg).

Gopher Museum

➤ Opening in 1996, the Torrington Gopher Hole Museum in Alberta, Canada, features dozens of stuffed gophers posed to depict the history and daily life of the town.

The rodents (actually Richardson's ground squirrels) are featured in around 50 tiny, elaborately painted dioramas—some dressed as fishermen, firefighters, a barber, a pastor, and even a bank robber!

ROUND AND ROUND ➔ On October 13, 2015, 64-year-old Oran Sands, from Carmel, Indiana, deliberately drove his car for 3 hours 34 minutes around a local roundabout. At the wheel of his 1987 Volkswagen Cabriolet, he traveled 65 mi (104 km), completing about 500 laps of the dog bone-shaped roundabout at 106th Street and Keystone Parkway. He came up with the idea after missing his turn on a roundabout on his way to work one day, forcing him to go all the way around again.

DRIFTED AWAY ➔ A man who stood on an 8-ft-long (2.4-m) piece of plywood in New York Harbor to watch the sun come up one morning in June 2016 ended up drifting helplessly for 2 mi (3.2 km) in choppy waters. Armaan Munglani, a visitor from London, England, had gone to the dock at the Newport Yacht Club and Marina in Jersey City, New Jersey, to wait for the sunrise, but his makeshift perch was swept away by the Hudson River current before he was finally rescued from the busy waterway near Governors Island more than two hours later.

NIGHT WALK ➔ Nineteen-year-old Taylor Gammel, of Arvada, Colorado, left home in a trance one night and wandered 9 mi (14 km) in tracksuit pants, a T-shirt, and socks—while sleepwalking. She eventually woke up three hours later, realized she was close to her uncle's house in the town of Westminster, and made her way there.

BUNGLING ROBBER ➔ A man who tried to rob a pharmacy in Beaver, West Virginia, foiled his attempt when he accidentally pepper-sprayed himself. He used the substance to incapacitate the pharmacy clerks but then walked into the cloud of spray himself.

BARNEY HEAD ➔ Firefighters in Trussville, Alabama, had to cut free a 15-year-old girl who had become stuck in a Barney the Dinosaur head. Darby Risner thought wearing the head might scare her friends at a sleepover, but it was she who became frightened when—despite tugging, twisting, and greasing with Vaseline—the head would not come off. She eventually had to go to a fire station—still wearing the head—where firefighters managed to end her 45-minute ordeal.

PERFECT RECIPE ➔ Steve Humphreys, a forensic scientist from Brisbane, Australia, ate chicken parmigiana at different restaurants in the city every week for a year in an attempt to discover the perfect recipe.

IDENTICAL COUPLE →
English artist and musician Genesis P-Orridge (born Neil Megson) has undergone extensive cosmetic surgery to make himself look exactly like his late wife, Lady Jaye. The transformation began in 2003 when the pair had matching breast implants. In addition to dressing identically, both went on to have eye and nose jobs, chin and cheek implants, lip plumping, and tattooed beauty marks—and the project has continued even after her death in 2007.

FREE BURGERS →
Melbourne, Australia-based fast food chain Mr. Burger offered customers free burgers for life if they legally changed their last name to Burger by July 31, 2016.

ANGRY CUSTOMER → A dissatisfied customer from St. John's, Newfoundland, Canada, called 911 in June 2016 to complain that there was not enough cheese on her pizza.

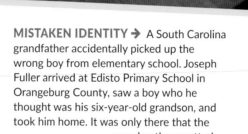

SPACE FLOWER
→ An orange zinnia blossomed aboard the International Space Station on January 16, 2016, becoming the first flower to sprout from NASA's veggie chamber. Perhaps astronauts can grow and snack on more than just lettuce and edible flowers in the future.

MISTAKEN IDENTITY → A South Carolina grandfather accidentally picked up the wrong boy from elementary school. Joseph Fuller arrived at Edisto Primary School in Orangeburg County, saw a boy who he thought was his six-year-old grandson, and took him home. It was only there that the grandmother spotted her husband's mistake, and he quickly returned the boy to school.

WORKPLACE PICTURES → Groom Au Phakphumphaisal and his bride Nattarin had their wedding pictures shot at their workplace—a gas station in Chachoengsao, Thailand. He wore a nice suit and she wore her bridal dress, but they continued serving customers.

STILL ALIVE → Madan-lal Kosla, an 83-year-old grandfather, opened a letter from Manchester City Council in England stating that he was no longer eligible for council tax support because he was dead. He then had to report to a job center with his passport to prove that he was still alive.

CHILI WEAPONS → Instead of using tear gas or plastic bullets, police officers in northern India aim to control unruly crowds by firing slingshots loaded with plastic balls filled with chili powder.

HAWAIIAN AIR →
Japanese company Seiren sold limited-edition underwear that had been hung for two days in fresh Hawaiian air, for $60 a pair. For its Hawaiian Breeze range, 100 pairs of boxer briefs were hung on a giant outdoor clothesline in Hawaii for 48 hours before being packaged individually in sealed glass containers.

PLANETARY PAPERWORK

→ After returning from the first moon landing, astronauts did not escape U.S. Customs and Immigration! Upon splashing down in the Pacific, the Apollo 11 crew—Buzz Aldrin, Neil Armstrong, and Michael Collins—had to declare that they brought back moon rocks and dust samples from their 1969 voyage.

MOON DISEASE TO BE DETERMINED!

PHONE HEADSTONES → A laser engraving company in Siberia, Russia, is offering iTombstones—gravestones carved from Ukrainian basalt to look like iPhones. Designed by Pavel Kalyuk, the $1,000 stones can even feature engravings of a selfie of the deceased.

ALMIGHTY JUDGMENT → David Shoshan, of Haifa, Israel, failed in his attempt to file a restraining order against God. He told the court that he was tired of God interfering in his life, but the judge called his request "delusional." Court documents noted that God did not appear at the hearing.

NAME BAN → A British court ruled in 2016 that a mother from Wales could not name her baby daughter Cyanide. The woman claimed that Cyanide is a "lovely, pretty name" with positive associations because it helped kill Nazi leader Adolf Hitler.

QUICK DIVORCE → A Saudi husband filed for divorce on his wedding night because he thought his new bride was spending too much time on her cell phone replying to congratulatory messages from friends.

SNOW TRIP → Steve and Kathleen Yarborough flew 1,630 mi (2,623 km) from Houston, Texas, to New York in January 2016 just to see some snow. The couple said they had never seen any snow in Texas, so when they heard about a blizzard in New York, they wanted to witness it firsthand.

A similar installation broke loose during the high winds of a typhoon in 2016—wreaking havoc as it rolled through traffic!

Moon Balloon

A massive, hydrogen-filled replica of the moon graced the streets of Nanjing, China, in celebration of the Mid-Autumn Festival.

Similar decorations can be found all throughout China during the fall season—traditional and moon-shaped lanterns, as well as giant inflatable rabbits, light up the country in honor of the many legends behind the Mid-Autumn Festival. On the 15th day of the eighth month of China's lunar calendar, Chinese families all over the world gather together to appreciate the full moon, eat sweet mooncakes, and enjoy each other's company.

The boys are carried around by their relatives during a procession, since their feet are not allowed to touch the ground for those three days.

PRINCELY MONKS

⊙ **Every spring, the Shan (or Tai Yai) people of northern Thailand and Myanmar hold an elaborate three-day ceremony called Poy Sang Lang to initiate boys between the ages of 7 and 14 as novice Buddhist monks.**

The boys have their heads and eyebrows shaved before being dressed in vibrant costumes and make-up, meant to symbolize Siddhartha Gautama, who was a prince before embarking on his path to enlightenment and eventually becoming the Buddha. On the third day, the boys are ordained, stripped of their princely adornments, and dressed in the simple saffron robes of a Buddhist monk. The extravagant rite of passage is believed to bring favor to the boys and families that participate.

BEAUTY CALIBRATOR ➔ In the 1930s, Hollywood cosmetics expert Max Factor (who coined the term "makeup") created a contraption to help him apply his own groundbreaking products to film industry elite—the "beauty micrometer." Despite looking like a medieval torture device, the metal mechanism precisely measured the contours of facial features so movie makeup could be applied to areas that needed to be corrected or enhanced.

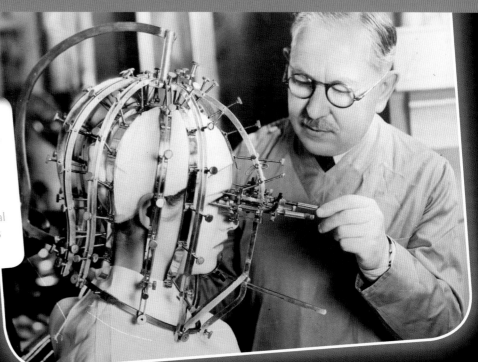

DIFFERENT DIRECTION ➔ More than 6,000 competitors from 28 countries take part in an annual running race up a steep, snowless ski jump hill in Titisee-Neustadt, Germany. Occasionally on all fours, the runners scramble up the same 460-ft (140-m) slope that ski jumpers usually hurtle down.

SOLO HONEYMOON ➔ Faizan Patel, from New Delhi, India, traveled around Europe on his honeymoon alone with a large photograph of his wife Sana after she realized a few days before the departure date that she had lost her passport. She persuaded him to go without her and to tweet her pictures of the adventure.

WASTED TIME ➔ Armed police officers laid siege to a house in Surrey, England, for 10 hours, only to find it was empty. More than 150 officers in riot gear with assault rifles waited patiently for the suspect they thought was inside to emerge, but when they finally stormed the house, they found nobody was home.

CHOPPER DENTIST ➔ Pilot Rick Rahim, of Great Falls, Virginia, used his helicopter to pull out his seven-year-old son Carson's loose tooth. A small thread was tied around the tooth and that was attached to a longer rope, which in turn was tied to the helicopter.

CHILD'S PLAY ➔ When a police car became stuck on a narrow path in Bamberg, Germany, while pursuing a moped that had run a traffic stop, one of the officers jumped on a child's 22-in-high (55-cm) bike, gave chase, and eventually arrested the suspect.

Frozen Car

⊙ Jason Yelen left his car in a parking lot overnight, only to find it completely encased in ice the next morning!

The parking lot was right next to Lake Erie in Hamburg, New York. On that particular night, extremely strong winds brought the water up from the lake and over the car, while freezing temperatures created an icy coating several inches thick. It was two days before Yelen was able to get his car out—a feat accomplished by four workers with shovels and 350 lb (160 kg) of deicer.

CARROT MAN ➡ When Anthony Di Lauro plucked this carrot out of his Wharton, New Jersey, garden in the summer of 2016, he was surprised to find it resembled a person with two arms and legs! His daughter Michele quickly snapped a photo and posted it to Instagram!

CHEESY NAME ➡ Meat-loving Simon Smith, of London, England, legally changed his name to Bacon Double Cheeseburger.

PILLOW TALK ➡ Since 2003, Lindsay Stamhuis, of Edmonton, Alberta, Canada, has kept a record of all the weird things her husband, Aidan Hailes, says in his sleep. She then texts him the manuscripts of what he has been talking about, ranging from giant bugs to Napoleon Bonaparte.

SLICED TONGUE ➡ Aarti Dubey, a 19-year-old college student in Reeva, Madhya Pradesh, India, sliced off her own tongue with a blade as an offering to the Hindu goddess Kali. She made the extreme sacrifice a day after dreaming that Kali was demanding her tongue in exchange for granting all her wishes. The girl fell unconscious immediately after the self-mutilation but later recovered after being treated by medics.

ILLEGAL CROSSING ➡ About 1,500 Americans who were taking part in the 2016 Port Huron Float Down on the St. Clair River washed up illegally in Canada. Strong winds on the river, which runs between Michigan and Ontario, blew the flotilla of inflatable rafts and inner tubes off course and toward the Canadian shore. Many were rescued from the water by the Canadian Coast Guard before being bussed to the U.S. border while a few tried to swim back to the United States.

DEATH DIVING ➡ In the Norwegian extreme sport of dødsing, or "death diving," daredevils jump from a 33-ft-high (10-m) board with their arms and legs spread out in an X formation and belly flop into the water. The aim is to hold the pose for as long as possible and then curl the body slightly at the very last second before hitting the water to avoid serious injury.

VOCAL POWER ➡ If you yelled for one year and seven months, you would produce enough sound energy to heat an eight-ounce cup of coffee.

CALF CAKE ➡ When Jamie Packard, of Maple Creek, Saskatchewan, Canada, asked her son Benz what kind of image he would like on his fourth birthday cake, the nature-loving boy said he didn't want a train or a football—he wanted one of a cow giving birth to a calf. Unfazed by the strange request, she used chocolate for the mother cow's backside, molded rice crispy squares into little hooves, and added cherry pie filling as the afterbirth.

DANGEROUS PROPOSAL ➡ Vidal Valladares stopped traffic on a busy freeway in Houston, Texas, by getting down on one knee and proposing to his girlfriend, Michelle Wycoff. He was subsequently charged with obstructing a roadway.

SOURTOE COCKTAIL

➡ Bold customers of the Downtown Hotel in Dawson City, Yukon, Canada, can consume the Sourtoe cocktail—a drink featuring a preserved human toe! The rules say the customer must touch the pickled toe with their lips while downing the drink. The 45-year-old tradition all started in 1973 when a preserved frostbitten toe was found in an old cabin. In 1980, a miner accidentally swallowed the first toe, but since then, more than 10 additional toes have been donated to the bar!

THE TOE

SKYDIVING PROMPOSAL → Eddie Staten, a student at Pomfret School, Connecticut, asked girlfriend Talia Gulino to the 2015 school prom while jumping out of an airplane.

COLANDER HEADGEAR → The Massachusetts Registry of Motor Vehicles allowed Lowell resident Lindsay Miller to wear a metal colander on her head in her driver's license photo after she said it was part of her religion. A committed Pastafarian, she belongs to the Church of the Flying Spaghetti Monster and says that wearing the strainer allows her to express her beliefs. The RMV does not permit head coverings on license photos unless it is for medical or religious reasons.

HORROR WEDDING → For their 2015 wedding venue, Melissa Cote and Tom Cowern chose the entrance to the haunted house at Spookyworld's Nightmare New England in Litchfield, New Hampshire, the attraction where they both work as actors. The groom wore black with a top hat, the bridesmaids wore black, the flower girl wore a skeleton costume, and the bride's father dressed as Beetlejuice, the spirit played by Michael Keaton in the 1988 movie of the same name.

FAKE FINGERS → For two decades, Yukako Fukushima has handcrafted hundreds of fake little fingers for Japan's reformed gangsters. Members of the infamous Japanese criminal organization, the yakuza, who have erred in some way traditionally self-amputate their little finger by way of apology to their gangland bosses, a ritual known as "yubitsume." The missing digit makes it difficult for them to reintegrate back into mainstream society, so Fukushima eases their transition from the underworld by supplying them with prosthetics.

CAT HANDBAG → Taxidermist Claire Third caused quite a purr when she listed Tom on New Zealand auction site Trade Me in September 2016. Tom is a cat—a cat she found as roadkill and then turned into a purse! Part of her "Glamourpuss Summer Collection," it took Claire more than 300 hours to craft this unique handbag.

ROBBERS FOILED → Two would-be bank robbers in Praia Grande, Brazil, wrapped themselves from head to toe in aluminum foil and crawled along the floor in an attempt to avoid the alarm's sensors, which can be activated by body heat. Although the alarm did not sound, their every move was captured on the bank's internal security cameras, and as soon as their images showed up on screen, the police were called.

PIXIE LOOK → Tattoo artist Grace Neutral, from London, England, has had her belly button surgically removed, her ears modified into a pointed shape, and her tongue forked— all to make her look like a pixie. She has also had purple ink injected into her eyeballs and has multiple scarification designs all over her face, which involves cutting off the top layer of skin in a pattern that then heals to leave a permanent scar.

DOLLYWOOD

PAGE-TURNER

➡️ It's easy to get lost in a good book, but getting trapped in one is another story! Squished in a Latin textbook published in 1684, this mouse now calls these covers his casket. It became his unlikely grave in the 19th century, when students at England's Salisbury Cathedral School turned their texts into a trap! The book—and mummified mouse—are now on display at the Cathedral Library.

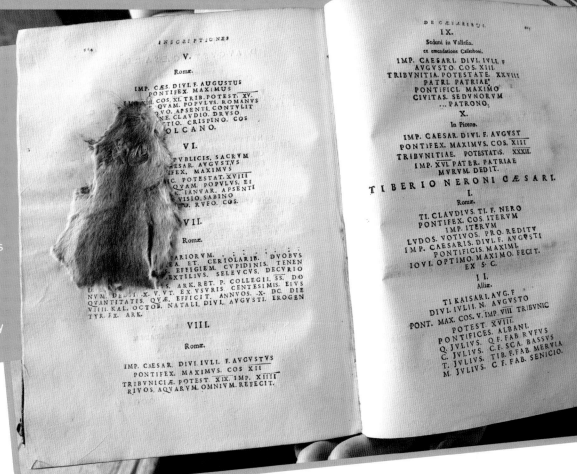

SMUGGLERS' HEARSE ➡️ When police officers in Khabarovsk, Russia, stopped a speeding hearse, they found 1,100 lb (500 kg) of smuggled caviar, worth $150,000, hidden under wreaths and inside the coffin. The driver claimed he was transporting a dead woman to a funeral home, but the officers noted that there was no corpse inside the vehicle.

SOUR TASTE ➡️ Ella Ginn, from Hastings, England, drinks two bottles of vinegar a week, which works out to 23 gal (105 l) a year. She has loved its acidic taste since childhood and regularly sips it from a wine glass. Her cravings are so strong that she has to keep sachets of vinegar in her handbag.

BURIED ALIVE ➡️ People in Moscow, Russia, can pay $50 to dig their own graves and be buried alive in a coffin in the hope that it will cure their fear of dying.

MARIO PROPOSAL ➡️ Video game enthusiast Shane Birkinbine, of Bentonville, Arkansas, proposed to his girlfriend Pam Edwards by creating a custom level on Nintendo's *Super Mario Maker* and spelling out the message "Pam Will You Marry Me" in blocks.

IRON STOMACH ➡️ Ten-year-old Brady Westphal, of Oklahoma City, Oklahoma, was thought to be suffering from a stomach flu until X-rays revealed the cause of his discomfort was that he had swallowed eight potentially deadly magnets.

LEGO LEG ➡️ After having his left leg amputated, Marc Cronin, from the West Midlands, England, while waiting for a new prosthetic limb to be fitted, built a replacement leg using his daughter's toy building bricks. The LEGO leg was strong enough to bear his standing weight, but he was not able to walk on it.

➡️ **Englishwoman Roz Edwards owns 20,000 mannequins, including replications of pregnant women, animals, and children.**

The entrepreneur buys unwanted dummies, repairs them, and then sells and rents them out of her "Mannakin" warehouse in Fulbeck, Lincolnshire, England. The piles and piles of fake bodies have earned the location the nickname "Dollywood." Some of her customers include popular shows like *The X Factor* and *Top Gear*, as well as singers Lady Gaga and Mika, who have featured the models in their music videos.

The average mannequin costs more than $700!

CHAIN HANG

→ These brave men appear to have no worries about hanging hundreds of feet in the air with little to no safety equipment. The fearless workers hold onto chains suspended from a crane as they labor to complete a skyscraper. In the 1920s, there were a lot fewer rules concerning worker safety during the construction of such towering buildings. In fact, during the early 20th century, there was a saying that for every one million dollars spent on a skyscraper, one worker would die.

Skyscrapers in the 1920s reached upwards of almost 800 ft (244 m)!

FLYING FISH → A baseball game in Japan between the Hanshin Tigers and the Tokyo Yakult Swallows was halted in the sixth inning when a dead fish landed on the field. Video footage of the incident revealed that the fish had fallen from the sky, presumably dropped by a passing bird.

HOME TO ROOST → Dozens of live chickens packed in crates fell off a moving truck as it turned a corner in Melbourne, Australia, and landed in the parking lot of a KFC restaurant!

COPYCAT CRIME → In 2016, German crime writer Frank Wündsch carried out a bank robbery in Leipzig that was exactly the same as one staged by the hero of his 2008 novel *Beer, Money and Tomatoes*. In the book, the robber fled with the money on a bicycle and changed his clothes behind an oak tree. The novelist also hopped on a bicycle with his $45,000 haul, but was arrested before he could reach his change of clothes—which were hidden behind an oak tree.

GETAWAY FOILED → A man who robbed two businesses in North Pole, Alaska, was unable to make his getaway because he had locked his keys in his car. So, using his own name, he called a taxi company who subsequently passed his details on to the police.

OPERA PRACTICE → Responding to reports of terrifying screams coming from a house in Amsterdam, the Netherlands, police officers kicked in the door and found an opera singer practicing loudly while wearing headphones.

CONFUSED TOURIST → A Chinese tourist who lost his wallet in Stuttgart, Germany, signed the wrong paperwork and ended up being placed in a refugee home. Instead of going to the police to file a stolen goods report, he somehow ended up at a different authority that presented him with an application for asylum. It was only when a translator from a Chinese restaurant was summoned that it became clear that the man had no desire to seek asylum, but merely wanted to complete his vacation by traveling on to France and Italy.

GIGANTIC CUBE → Tony Fisher, of Ipswich, England, has assembled a 220-lb (100-kg), 5-ft-tall (1.5-m) Rubik's Cube. It took him 156 hours to build and two days to solve.

LIVING DEAD → A couple staged their own funeral while they were still alive because they had no children to do it for them when they were dead. Dragan Maric, 61, and his 65-year-old wife Dragica arranged and attended their mock funeral in Pojezdina, Bosnia-Herzegovina, so that they could celebrate their lives with 200 friends and family.

DEADLY BAGPIPES → A 61-year-old British man died because he played the bagpipes every day. Doctors discovered that the mystery lung inflammation that eventually killed the otherwise healthy nonsmoker was caused by the fungi and yeast living inside his bagpipes. Every time he played the pipes, he inhaled the spores.

WILD AFRICAN CHEETAH!

CHEETAH GIRL → American silent film star Phyllis Gordon had a pet cheetah that she would leash and walk around town! The big cat was flown in to Britain from Kenya and can be seen here accompanying Gordon on a 1939 shopping trip in London. Exotic pets were extremely popular among the wealthy at this point in history. In fact, earlier in her life, Gordon also owned a small marmoset monkey that she would dress in sweaters and carry in her purse.

THE ISOLATOR

→ Block out all distractions with The Isolator—a 1920s mask that makes it impossible to focus on anything other than what's in front of you.

People have had trouble concentrating long before the invention of cell phones and computers. In 1925, science fiction pioneer Hugo Gernsbeck offered up a solution in the form of The Isolator—a noise-canceling mask with horizontal eye slits that allowed users to read just one line of text at a time. The helmet was connected to a tank of oxygen via a short tube to ensure the wearer had enough air beneath the thick layers of cork, wood, cotton, and felt.

Gernsbeck, pictured here, also developed "teleyeglasses," which allow the wearer to watch TV on tiny screens just inches from his or her eyes.

ICE ICE BABY → Arguably not the safest invention for babies was this sling created in 1937 by Wembley Monarchs ice hockey player Jack Milford. The athlete made the carrying device so his baby could join him and his wife while ice-skating. Thankfully, the carrier never caught on, as a stumble or fall by either parent would have meant certain danger for the suspended child.

Ripley's—
EXCLUSIVE

DRAGON LADY

⊙ **Eva Tiamat Baphomet Medusa, otherwise known as the Dragon Lady, has undergone extreme body modification in order to transform into a dragon.**

A former banker now living in Texas, Tiamat has had her nose and ears removed, her tongue bifurcated (split), her eyes stained green, almost all her teeth extracted, and horns implanted on her head. The 56-year-old also has extensive tattoos that resemble reptilian scales covering her face and body.

> "I was born again to my reptilian parents, which are the western diamondback rattlesnakes."

Q *How long have you been involved in extreme body modification?*

A It's taken 22 years so far for me to reach the point where I am now, and I have a personal goal to complete my transformation by the year 2025. My transformation involves body modifications from across the board: tattoos, piercings, extreme mods, and I'm working on a full-body western diamondback rattlesnake tattoo.

Have you kept any body parts that have been removed?

Yes, when I had my nose and my ears removed, I did keep parts of my body. They're stashed away in little jars at home. Little souvenirs.

Do you feel any of your senses are impaired by the modifications?

My sense of hearing has heightened, as well as my sense of smell. People really can't talk behind my back anymore because I can hear them. My sense of smell has also heightened because my nostrils are much closer to my sinuses. There's a price

to pay for beauty, and one thing is that I pretty much always have a runny nose, and I blow my nose about 50 or 60 times a day. I eat hot peppers every day, so that keeps my sinuses clear, and it keeps me from getting a stuffy nose.

Since having so many teeth removed, what does your diet consist of? Do you have any restrictions or anything you miss eating?

Basically, I don't chew my food; I gum it. I can't eat certain things anymore, such as nuts, and hard things, like hard chips. Even hard bread hurts my gums too much to eat. But my gums have become strong since I had my teeth removed. Since all my chewing teeth are gone, over the years, my gums got a little tougher. I also eat bugs.

What kind of reactions do you get when you are out in public?

When I first started my transformation, people were shocked and they were scared. One person tried to perform an exorcism on me on the city bus in Houston. But that's more of the negative. Surprisingly, most people are really receptive, warm, and very kind.

What has been the most painful or difficult body modification so far?

Honestly, my tongue bifurcation. Generally, tongue bifurcations are really not that big of a deal.

But mine was actually mutilated by a person who was misrepresenting himself as a body modification artist. Thankfully, it healed fine. I have a little bit of a lisp, but I like that; it's a little change that I welcome.

We read one of your Twitter posts from a while back, about when you ate some stinkbugs that were eating your plant. Do you ever eat bugs not as revenge?

Yes, I had a little garden where I planted zucchinis. I woke up one morning and all my plants were dead. I discovered that they were infested by stinkbugs. I was so angry that I gathered all those stinkbugs, and I fried them up in a little bit of butter and I ate them. As revenge. They ate my food, so I ate them.

I eat other bugs not out of revenge. I love bugs, and it's part of my diet (entomophagy) as a dragon. I think it's a great source of protein, and for the most part they're free. I eat all kinds of bugs. Cicadas are at the top of my list. Crickets taste like almonds. June bugs taste like buttered popcorn. The little wood lice we call roly-polies are crustaceans and members of the shrimp family, so they taste just like shrimp.

BODY MODIFICATIONS

HORNS:
"Last year, I had six additional horns added. My goal is to either have 15 or 18 horns total on my head."

NOSE:
"I also had my nose modified. Originally, my nose modification was inspired by Lord Voldemort from *Harry Potter*, but I went one step beyond that, creating my own unique look and my own unique nose, which is my dragon nose."

TONGUE:
"I got my tongue bifurcated in 2014."

EYES:
"I had the whites of my eyes, the sclera, stained permanently by injecting tattoo ink under the surface."

EARS:
"In 2015, I had both ears removed, which I call 'the double Van Gogh.'"

TEETH:
"I'm in the process of having most of my teeth removed. When I am done with my teeth, basically, my mouth will mirror as close as possible the mouth of a rattlesnake—two fangs at the top and a couple of small teeth at the bottom."

LOVES TO EAT BUGS!

TOOTH RING → California couple Lucas Unger and Carlee Leifkes got engaged on Halloween 2015—and instead of a diamond, his engagement ring to her featured one of his old wisdom teeth. Unger's father had kept his son's wisdom teeth following an operation to remove them when he was a boy, and the tooth was then made into a ring by a Los Angeles jeweler.

FAMILY FEUD → Taking his grudges to the grave, 64-year-old Hubert Martini wrote his own obituary notice—that was published in a German newspaper after his death—in which he banned his five siblings and their families from attending his funeral.

ROAD TRIP → A woman took the dead body of her 78-year-old husband on a traveling wake, driving for days through Alaska with his corpse inside an aluminum casket in her truck bed. She broke her journey to stop at canneries for fresh ice to keep him cold.

FATHER'S MEMORY → Erden Eruc, of Seattle, Washington, and Louis Bird, from Swindon, England, rowed 2,400 mi (3,840 km) from Northern California to Hawaii in just 54 days in 2016, averaging 44 mi (70 km) a day and completing about one million oar strokes. Bird's father completed the first solo rowing trip from San Francisco to Australia 30 years ago but disappeared in a later Pacific crossing.

BIRD RAGE → Responding to reports of a disturbance at a home in Brighton, Ontario, Canada, police officers discovered a man having a heated argument with his pet parrot.

CHIMNEY DEATH → A suspected burglar who attempted to enter a home in Huron, California, through the chimney was killed after the homeowner, not knowing he was there, lit a fire. The man had climbed into the chimney while the owner was away but then became stuck.

SALVATION MOUNTAIN

A thick paint job helps keep the mountain standing and protects it from sand and wind.

NUMBER PHOBIA → Massimo Cellino, the Italian owner of English soccer club Leeds United, is so superstitious about the number 17 that he had all seats with that number removed from his former club Cagliari's ground and replaced with 16B. No Leeds player is allowed to wear the number 17 shirt.

Completely remote, Salvation Mountain is located in an area called Slab City—a decommissioned Marine Corps base known as "the last free place on Earth"—where there are no laws, no power lines, and no running water, giving the area a strange, postapocalyptic feel.

IN THE MIDDLE OF NOWHERE!

→ Salvation Mountain, near Niland, California, is America's craziest peak. Made from hay bales and adobe, topped with a giant cross, it is 150 ft (45 m) wide and rises three stories high above the desert!

The late mechanic turned folk artist Leonard Knight began building Salvation Mountain with anything he could get his hands on in 1985, after his hot air balloon crashed in the desert. Over the years he defied government attempts to demolish it, and even lived at its foot in an old truck without electricity or water.

OVER 100,000 GALLONS OF PAINT!

CEREAL ADDICT → Phillip Patrick, from Worcester, England, is addicted to breakfast cereal—and eats nothing else for every meal of the day. He eats 13 bowls of cereal a day, goes through six boxes a week, and has eaten more than 14,000 bowls of cereal in the past three years.

INSULTED PRESIDENT → Turkish truck driver Ali Dinç sued his wife Gülcan in 2016 for apparently insulting the country's President Erdoğan and for daring to change the TV channel when the politician came on. She responded to her husband's actions by filing for divorce.

TONGUE TIED → Tim Pppppppppprice, of Leicester, England, legally changed the spelling of his name to deter telemarketers.

SUN GAZERS → Some women in Hong Kong stare at the sun to lose weight. They gaze at it for up to 45 minutes in the belief that its energy will replace the need for food and therefore reduce their appetite.

POLL POSITION → Sheldon Bergson legally changed his name to Above Znoneofthe so that he appeared last of 10 candidates on the ballot for the 2016 Whitby-Oshawa by-election in Ontario, Canada. Sadly for him, the public did not heed his plea to vote for "none of the above," and he did not win the election.

LUCKY NUMBER → Philadelphia Eagles quarterback Sam Bradford is so superstitious that he only eats things in threes on game days, including three after-dinner mints and three pieces of fruit.

DUMPSTER DRAMA → A man and a woman who fell asleep in a dumpster outside a convenience store in Tampa, Florida, had to be rescued after they were emptied into the back of a garbage truck. They were saved from being crushed after screaming loudly and banging on the sides of the truck.

BUBBLE CRAVING → While pregnant with her son Indie, Zoe Eastman, from Liverpool, England, took three bubble baths a day to satisfy her constant craving to eat bubbles.

231

Samurai WOMEN

➔ The history and legends of the Japanese *bushi*, or samurai, have long fascinated the world, yet history still overlooks the fierce female samurai who also followed the samurai code of honor, discipline, and morality known as *bushido*— "the way of the warrior."

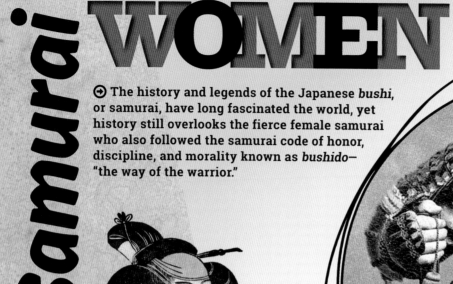

The onna-bugeisha were female warriors, members of the elevated samurai class in feudal Japan. Much like their male counterparts, young girls were trained in martial arts and the use of specific weapons, as it was their responsibility to protect their household, family, and honor during times of war. While the men were expected to fight on the battlefield on the offense and taught to wield the traditional samurai sword (katana), the women were expected to defend towns and strongholds and taught to wield the naginata and kaiken.

This defensive role evolved over many centuries. Before the modern ideal of the male samurai warrior, Japanese history was dominated by powerful female samurais, highly educated in science, mathematics, and literature. Most important, onna-bugeisha fought alongside men. While there are no records of women being recruited to serve in armies, recent archaeological evidence confirms their wider involvement in battle. Thirty percent of skulls found in three separate ancient battlefields were those of women, meaning an incredible one-third of the battle force were women. Despite their extensive involvement and sacrifice throughout history, honor and glory were reserved for male soldiers only—until now.

In the center of this woodblock print, Empress Jingū steps foot on Korean shores while her followers look on.

EMPRESS JINGŪ

➡ Empress Jingū (c. 169–269 AD) was a legendary onna-bugeisha who is said to have personally organized and led an invasion of Korea in 200 AD, after her husband Emperor Chūai, the 14th emperor of Japan, was slain in battle. According to legend, she miraculously led a Japanese conquest of Korea without shedding a drop of blood. Despite controversies surrounding her existence and accomplishments, in 1881, Empress Jingū became the first woman to be featured on a Japanese banknote.

NAGINATA ➡ The naginata—a cross between a sword and a spear, with a curved blade rather than a straight one—was ideal for female fighters; what mattered most was skill and speed. An iconic weapon, the naginata allowed female warriors to engage an opponent without being as close as they would be fighting with a sword. During the Edo Period (1603–1867), the naginata became a symbol of the social status of women of the samurai class.

MODERN MARTIAL ARTS TRAINING

→ During the Edo Period, many schools focusing on the use of the naginata were created and began to be increasingly associated with women. These schools are still common today, and naginata fighting is still practiced as a sport in Japan as well as around the world.

KAIKEN → When girls from samurai families reached womanhood, they were given a kaiken, or a dagger, which she could carry on her person at all times. The kaiken was a double-edged blade that would be used for self-defense in small, confined spaces. However, the most important purpose of the kaiken was to assist in *seppuku*, ritual suicide done to achieve an honorable death.

NAKANO TAKEKO

→ Becoming a master of martial arts when she was just 16, Nakano Takeko's skill and intelligence helped her become the commander of the new fighting force of onna-bugeishas during the Boshin War. This independent army, named the Women's Army, joined the male Aizu clan samurais in the Battle of Aizu in 1868. Takeko led a charge against Imperial forces and their modern firearms, and her ferocity during the fight made her a prime target—she was shot in the heart. Before her last breath, she asked her sister to cut off her head so that it would not be taken as a prize for the Imperial Army. Her head was buried next to a temple under a pine tree, and today a monument stands next to the temple to honor her. The Boshin War marked both the end of the age of the female warrior and the 1,000-year samurai era.

TOMOE GOZEN

⊙ The story of Tomoe Gozen takes place during the Genpei War (1180–85). Described as a beautiful woman with incredible archery and horse-riding skills, Tomoe Gozen was a formidable warrior and devoted servant of the Minamoto clan, often being sent out to lead the military charge. During the losing Battle of Awazu on February 21, 1184, Tomoe's commander ordered her to escape, but she refused and instead rode into the enemy forces, flung herself on their strongest warrior, unhorsed and then decapitated him. An inspiration and symbol of the strength of female samurai warriors, Tomoe Gozen is unique, as she is the only female warrior who is described in detail in the ancient Japanese samurai war tales.

Legendary onna-bugeisha Tomoe Gozen brandishes her naginata during the Battle of Awazu.

GRASSHOPPER TACOS

➜ Eating protein-filled bugs is more prevalent these days, so grasshopper tacos might be a delicious alternative to the usual variety. A traditionally Mexican cuisine, *chapulines* are dried grasshoppers smothered in mild chili powder and lime juice and fried to perfection. With their crunchy texture, they can be eaten on their own or as a filling in a taco—just take your pick.

GROWING GHOSTS ➜

Deep in the redwood forests of the Pacific Northwest, a genetic mutation has stumped scientists for years. Known as "ghosts of the forest," albino redwood trees are stark white in contrast to the evergreen branches they stand next to. Growing from bases of the region's giant redwoods, these smaller sprouts are now thought to be a kind of parasite, helping filter pollution.

TOP DOG ➜
In August 2016, Duke, a nine-year-old Great Pyrenees dog, was elected mayor of Cormorant, Minnesota, for the third year in a row.

DRANK URINE ➜
Angry at not being allowed to use the toilet at a store in Kaohsiung, South Taiwan, a woman peed in a cup on the counter and then drank it.

TAPED HOUSE ➜
When asked to watch over his parents' house for a few days, prankster Jonathan Harchick covered their home in Pittsburgh, Pennsylvania, in more than 1,000 rolls—equaling 60 mi (96 km)—of clear tape.

KIDNEY PLEA ➜
Desperate for a kidney transplant, Linda Deming, of Pownal, Maine, posted signs along the side of a road and advertised from her car. She received at least 50 offers from would-be donors, eventually finding a perfect match in Amber McIntyre, a married mother-of-four from Kenduskeag, Maine, and the surgery went ahead in 2016.

COIN CLUE ➜
Daniel Allan Thomas, from Port Talbot, South Wales, was jailed for two years for breaking into a post office after he tried to buy a used car with £1,000 ($1,500) in stolen coins that had been part of his haul.

DOZY THIEF ➜
A man who broke into several vehicles at a business in Harrodsburg, Kentucky, was found asleep in the driver's seat of one of the cars with his mask still over his face.

NAILED IT ➜
An orangutan in North Sumatra, Indonesia, recently got a manicure worthy of going ape over and not just because of the fabulous color he is now sporting! The endangered ape had just successfully undergone surgery and a staff member of the Sumatran Orangutan Conservation Programme painted his nails to help distract him.

CAMERA CREATURES

HiDDEN CAMERA!

➔ **An English media company captures wild animals on film by using hyper-realistic remote control creatures fitted with hidden cameras!**

John Downer Productions has built a variety of "Spy Creatures" for nature documentaries on animals such as lions and penguins. For a movie on dolphins, they employed the use of a spy sea turtle, nautilus, clam, tuna, and even a dolphin that can swim at speeds of up to 15 mph (24 kmph)! Wild animals are more likely to interact with the spy devices than with unfamiliar humans, giving viewers a one-of-a-kind glimpse into the animal's natural behavior.

TOSSED ALLIGATOR ➔ Joshua James was sentenced to a year of probation and fined $500 for tossing a live, 4-ft-long (1.2-m) alligator through the window of a drive-thru Wendy's in Royal Palm Beach, Florida. He said he found the gator by the side of the road and had intended to play a prank on a friend at the restaurant. No one was hurt by the alligator, which was captured and released into a nearby pond.

RIVAL OBITUARIES ➔
On August 5, 2016, *The Press of Atlantic City* newspaper carried two obituaries, one on top of the other, for the same man—Leroy Bill Black, of Egg Harbor Township, New Jersey— one saying he was survived by his wife, and the other saying he was survived by his girlfriend. The funeral home said the two women had different ideas about how the notice should read.

A peek inside the life-size robotic sea turtle Spy Creature!

TWEET VICTORY

⊕ **Believe it or not, bird-singing contests are common in Thailand, with thousands of spectators enjoying weekly and annual competitions.**

The birds are placed in ornate bamboo cages, and when they're ready to sing, the cages are hoisted onto raised hooks. Judges listen carefully to each bird, awarding points based on their melody, pitch, number of chirps, clarity, stamina, cadence, and volume. The birds are also under time constraints: a tiny bowl is floated in water, and when it begins to sink, time is up. The largest events see more than 1,000 birds compete, and prizes for the birds' owners include trophies and money.

SEEING DRAGONS → For the first 52 years of her life, a Dutch woman suffered from a rare condition where the human faces she saw metamorphosed into those of dragons. Initially she perceived actual human faces, but after a few minutes they would turn black and grow long, pointy ears and a protruding snout, displaying huge, vivid eyes and reptile-like skin. She was diagnosed as having prosopometamorphopsia, a psychiatric disorder that causes faces to appear distorted. Doctors gave her medication that eventually stopped the hallucinations.

ANATOMICAL UNIFORM → For their important 2016 play-off games, Spanish Third Division soccer team Club Deportivo Palencia Balompié wore flesh-colored jerseys and shorts that replicated the human anatomy and an "inside-out" design representing various bones and muscles in the body. The look must have unsettled their three opponents because CD Palencia beat them all to win promotion to Division Two.

DIFFERENT TIME → In October 2015, dreading the prospect of long, dark winter evenings, retirees Jim and Barbara Casey, from Cumbria, England, decided not to put their clocks back one hour in line with Greenwich Mean Time. Although staying on British Summer Time (Daylight Saving Time) left them out of sync with the rest of the United Kingdom for five months, they say that living an hour ahead helped them avoid traffic jams, shop at the supermarket when it was almost deserted, and get the best seats at restaurants.

DEAD MAN WALKING → A Chinese villager who was thought to have died in 2012, after which his family attended his supposed funeral, suddenly returned alive in December 2015. Ma Jixiang had gone missing from his home in Hunan Province in 2009, and a police report and subsequent DNA tests on his virtually unrecognizable body concluded that he had been killed in a road accident three years later. The corpse was cremated, but the family realized they had buried the wrong ashes when he unexpectedly returned home.

TOO GASSY → Adam Lindin Ljungkvist, a defender with Swedish soccer team Pershagen SK, was given a red card and sent off in a 2016 match against Järna SK's reserve team after referee Dany Kako deemed that the player's flatulence was "deliberate provocation" and "unsportsmanlike behavior." Ljungkvist claimed that he simply had a bad stomach.

GOLD FENDER

➲ An anonymous artist turned an eyesore into art in Melbourne, Australia, with nothing more than some gold spray paint! A Toyota Camry was left bent up and undriveable after someone crashed it into a tree and left it there, keys still in the ignition. Weeks passed and the car remained, prompting some creative individual to glam it up overnight, much to the delight of residents and art aficionados nearby.

SHORT RACE ➔ Kenyan athlete Julius Njogu was disqualified from the 2015 Nairobi International Marathon after it was discovered that he had only run about 0.5 mi (0.8 km) of the 26-mi (42-km) race. He had crossed the finish line in second place, earning himself a $6,300 prize, but race officials became suspicious when they noticed that he was not even sweating. The race director had not seen Njogu at all during the race and concluded that he had hidden among the crowd before joining in for the final stretch.

SKIN LIGHTS ➔ Tim Cannon, of Pittsburgh, Pennsylvania, has LED lights implanted under the skin of his hand. His Northstar v1.0 chip, which he himself created and which is about the size of a large coin, features a ring of red LED lights that glow when a magnet comes close to the sensor. These can light up tattoos from beneath the skin, emulating the bioluminescence of jellies and other deep-sea creatures.

PASTA FRIENDS ➔ When alarmed neighbors called police in Rome, Italy, to deal with the loud cries of a 94-year-old man and his 89-year-old wife, officers found the couple suffering from loneliness and cooked two plates of pasta for the elderly couple, who had been married for nearly 70 years.

LOST LEG ➔ Mark Warner, of Green Bay, Wisconsin, lost his prosthetic leg while on a fishing trip on Range Line Lake in Wabeno—but it was returned to him a month later after two canoeists paddling 3 mi (4.8 km) away spotted it sticking out of a beaver dam.

DUMP TRUCK ➔ Nick Huckson, a plumber from Sault Ste. Marie, Ontario, Canada, has had the driver's side of his truck painted so that it looks like the driver is sitting on the toilet. When a photo of his designer truck was posted on Facebook, it went viral and has led to a boom in Hudson's business.

LIVING VAMPIRE ➔ A 25-year-old man in Blackburn, Lancashire, England, has been living as a vampire for over 13 years. He has legally changed his name to Darkness Vlad Tepes (in honor of the real-life inspiration for Bram Stoker's Count Dracula), he sleeps in a custom-made wooden coffin, and regularly drinks cow and pig blood as well as a human blood substitute.

MAKES SCENTS ➔ The Demeter Fragrance Library of Great Neck, New York, sells more than 300 perfumes in scents such as Dirt, Frozen Pond, Curry, Lobster, Earthworm, Mildew, Pizza, Swimming Pool, and Funeral Home.

SPELLING LESSON ➔ Workmen sent to paint new yellow safety markings on the road outside a top-performing private girls' school in Cornwall, England, struggled with their spelling and ended up painting SHCHOOL in large letters on the street.

COFFEE URN ➲ At his funeral in Casale Corte Cerro, Italy, in 2016, Renato Bialetti's ashes were buried in a large replica of the famous octagonal, aluminum Moka coffee pot which his father Alfonso invented and of which 330 million have been sold worldwide.

→ Grandmother Meenakshi Raghavan, from southern India, has been practicing the martial art Kalaripayattu for 68 years—and counting.

She began learning the art at seven years old, and now at 74 years old, she teaches 150 pupils in the town of Vatakara, as well as performs up to 60 shows a year. Kalaripayattu (sometimes shortened to Kalari) is a dance-like form of self-defense, using swords, daggers, spears, and sticks. Meenakshi is especially proud to teach and empower young girls to be self-sufficient, confident, and, not to mention, deadly.

FIGHTING GRANDMA

DUMB CROOKS → Two people who robbed a house in Clarksville, Tennessee, of PlayStation equipment and then tried to pawn the stolen goods were unaware that it was the pawn shop owner's house that they had burgled. Edward Dial immediately recognized the items and notified the police, resulting in the pair's arrest.

BIBLE EMOJI → An iBook titled *Bible Emoji: Scripture 4 Millennials* retells all 66 books of the Bible using emojis in place of key words.

WELL-ROUNDED → Paul D'Ambrosio of Brighton, Massachusetts, has acquired 1,101 diplomas in varied areas, ranging from marital arts to criminal investigation and ordination as a minister!

EGGS-ERCISE → "Real Bill" Kathan, of Vermont, can do push-ups while balancing on raw eggs. While visiting Ripley's headquarters in November 2015, he did push-ups while balancing his entire body on three eggs—one under each hand and one under his toes. After that he did 16 one-armed push-ups with an egg under his hand and 11 push-ups with an egg beneath each hand while balancing an egg on a spoon in his mouth!

SWAN RIDE → When the town of Katy, Texas, was hit by 20 in (50 cm) of rain in a single day on April 18, 2016, dedicated midwife Cathy Allen Rude succeeded in reaching her place of work at the Katy Birth Center by riding a large inflatable swan through the flooded streets.

↑ **YOUR UPLOADS**

Two-Nosed Rat

Jennifer Clark from Ontario, Canada, submitted this photo of her pet Hogley, a rat born with two noses and a short round head. With "double the snoots and twice the cutes," as Hogley's Facebook page says, the beloved pet unfortunately died, spawning fan art and well-wishes from her social media followers.

PUSHBALL

⊙ **Moses Crane, of Massachusetts, invented the sport of pushball in 1894 after years of hating football.**

Football wasn't always fun to watch. Before the days of high-definition cameras and instant replay, the small ball was difficult for spectators to see and follow during the game. To solve this problem, Crane invented a sport with a ball so big it was simply impossible to miss. A regulation-sized pushball was 6 ft (1.8 m) in diameter, filled with air, and weighed between 50 and 100 lb (23 and 45 kg). The object of the game was to—surprise—push the ball to your opponent's side of the field, where an H-shaped goal was located. Sadly, pushball eventually faded into sports history as the novelty wore off and people realized just how ridiculous it was.

DAILY PIZZA → To raise money for autism, Kyle Feeney, from Mamaroneck, New York, ate pizza every single day for a whole year—and then celebrated the achievement by having a pizza tattooed on his butt.

BRICK SNACK → When she was pregnant with son Rylee, Jenny Mason, from Liverpool, England, developed a craving for eating bricks, mortar, sand, and dirt. She used to scrape the walls of her house for something to crunch on and would buy soil from a garden center to eat out of a bowl.

ROBOT ESCAPES → A robot named Promobot IR77 escaped from a laboratory in Perm, Russia, in June 2016 and then caused a traffic jam when its battery ran out in the middle of the street. The humanoid robot, which has been fitted with artificial intelligence that enables it to learn from its experiences and surroundings, escaped after an engineer forgot to shut the gate in the laboratory's testing grounds. However, when it made another bid for freedom a week later, scientists considered dismantling it.

FORGOT WIFE → Flying off on vacation, 80-year-old Londoner Maurice Hunter accidentally left his wife Carolyn at the airport in England and only realized she was not on the plane when he landed in Spain. He went to the toilet at Stansted Airport just before their flight and then boarded the plane, assuming that she had gone on ahead. Once on board, he even waved at a woman whom he mistook for his wife of 47 years.

FINGER LICKIN' → Kentucky Fried Chicken in Hong Kong launched chicken-flavored nail polish in 2016. The "finger lickin' good" product came in two colors—beige (original flavor) and red (hot and spicy).

SILENT CHEERS → Elanora Heights Public School, an elementary school in Sydney, Australia, has banned clapping at school assemblies to respect students who are sensitive to noise. Instead children are encouraged to express their appreciation by silently punching the air and making excited faces.

Genuine 6 in (15.2 cm) Mexican tarantula spider.

Ripley's Exhibit
Cat. No. 171813

Spiderweb Dress
By Robert Bernard de Leon

Origin: Orlando, Florida

MORGUE HORROR → A man who was declared dead after drinking too much vodka at a party in the Khansanky region of Russia suddenly woke up to find himself in the freezer at the local morgue surrounded by dead bodies. Alerted by his cries for help, doctors rescued him from freezing to death, whereupon he went straight back to the party.

STRANGERS RECRUITED → When it became apparent that nobody was expected to show up at the funeral of 83-year-old former music teacher Francine Stein in Orangetown, New York, an appeal was sent out on Facebook for 30 strangers to attend. Even though they had never met her, the volunteers paid their respects, acted as pallbearers, and helped bury her.

At some point, pushball was played on horses and even in cars!

FROZEN OUT → While playing baseball for the Toronto Blue Jays, Rickey Henderson once fell asleep on an ice pack that he was wearing for an ankle injury and later missed three games because of frostbite.

BRADY SUPPORT → To show its support for New England Patriots quarterback Tom Brady during the 2015 "Deflategate" scandal, Foxborough Country Club, Massachusetts, changed all 18 of the flags on its golf course to number 12—Brady's uniform number.

FAKE FUNERAL → Sixty-six-year-old Zhang Deyang of Rizhao, China, paid over $2,500 to stage his own mock funeral in February 2016 just to see how many people would turn up. With no wife or children, he was worried that nobody would care for him in the afterlife.

CEMETERY CONNECTION → In 2016, the authorities in Moscow, Russia, began offering free Wi-Fi at the city's three main cemeteries. Their aim is to encourage more visitors to Moscow's historic burial grounds, where many famous Russians were laid to rest.

SIX-MONTH SANDWICH → Andy George, from Minneapolis, Minnesota, spent six months and $1,500 assembling a sandwich from scratch. Growing and preparing every single ingredient, his tasks included killing a chicken with his bare hands, baking his own bread, making cheese and butter, growing cucumbers, and collecting sea salt from ocean water.

THIEF TRAPPED → A 31-year-old man had to call 911 for help after becoming trapped in the trunk of a car that he was attempting to steal. He had attempted to access the car in Missoula, Montana, via the unlocked trunk but did not realize that the vehicle had an automatic trunk closure mechanism. He was only freed after officers were able to obtain a key from the owner.

PATIENT SUITOR → Alexander Pieter Cirk, a 41-year-old Dutchman, waited for 10 days at Changsha Huanghua International Airport in Hunan Province, China, having flown there to meet a woman he had befriended online. Even when she failed to turn up, he refused to leave until he was eventually taken to a hospital, suffering from exhaustion.

HIDE-AND-SEEK → An adult hide-and-seek contest takes place each year in Consonno, Italy. Teams of five compete in the two-day World Nascondino Championship where the hunted try to hide from a search team made up of football and rugby players before reaching a target placed in the middle of an open field.

The labyrinth's French lavender peaks in the springtime and blooms throughout the summer!

LAVENDER LABYRINTH

➔ **Cherry Point Farm's fragrant lavender labyrinth is so big that it can be seen on Google Earth!**

Owner Barbara Bull of Shelby, Michigan, began designing the labyrinth in 2001. With the help of artist and architect Conrad Heiderer, she mapped out a fragrant flower footpath with an herb garden at the center.

It takes about an hour to reach the garden, but don't worry, you won't get lost and have to survive on the apple, peach, and cherry trees throughout. Unlike mazes, labyrinths are continuous winding paths!

INDEX

Page numbers in *italic* refer to stories with images

Ripley's Believe It or Not!

www.ripleys.com/books

ACKNOWLEDGMENTS

Cover © Markus Gann/Shutterstock.com, © Andriy_A/Shutterstock.com; **4** (c) Ken Scicluna via Getty Images, (b) Pictures - Coyote Peterson, Photo Credit - Mark Laivins, Company Credit - Brave Wilderness; **5** (tl) Valeriano Fatica - Fruit Carver, www.valerianofatica.com/youtube = Valeriano Fatica, Facebook Page = Valeriano Fatica, Instagram = Valeriano Fatica, (cr) REUTERS/Chris Helgren, (b) Stunt Freaks Team/Barcroft Cars; **10** (tr) Jeff Cremer/@JCremerPhoto, (bl) MADAREE TOHLALA/AFP/Getty Images; **11** (t, bl) VCG/VCG via Getty Images; **12–13** (dp) Ravikanth Kurma/Rex Shutterstock; **14–15** (dp) REUTERS/Tyrone Siu; **17** (tl, bl) ASSOCIATED PRESS, (cr, br) VCG/VCG via Getty Images; **18** (t, b) Caters News; **19** (tr) Fox Photos via Getty Images; **20** (tl) Public Domain {{PD-US}} Library of Congress Prints and Photographs Division Washington, D.C. 20540 USA http://memory.loc.gov/master/pnp/pga/01700/01789u.tif, (tr) Mary Evans Picture Library/Alamy Stock Photo, (cr) Martyn Goddard via Getty Images, (bl) f 1.2/Alamy Stock Photo, (bc) Public Domain {{PD-US}} Library of Congress Prints and Photographs Division Washington, D.C. 20540 USA http://lcweb2.loc.gov/master/pnp/habshaer/ne/ne0100/ne0103/color/218333cu.tif; **21** (tl) Pictorial Press Ltd/Alamy Stock Photo, (tr) Adwo/Alamy Stock Photo, (cr) AF archive/Alamy Stock Photo, (br) KRITINA LEE KNIEF via Getty Images; **22** (t) Alex Treadway via Getty Images, (b) VCG via Getty Images; **23** (b) VCG via Getty Images; **24** (b) MICHELLE LYNN FRITZ/ CATERS NEWS; **25** (sp) Birds Collection, Department of Vertebrate Zoology National Museum of Natural History, Smithsonian Institution Photo by Chip Clark, 1992; **26–27** Paul Koudounaris; **28** (t) Jonathan Goldberg/Alamy Stock Photo; **29** (r, c) MARIO LAPORTA/AFP/Getty Images; **30** (b) TOBIAS FRIEDRICH/CATERS NEWS; **31** (tr, b) VCG/VCG via Getty Images, (cl) Shao ying - Imaginechina; **33** (b) Håvard Kjøntvedt, Norwegian Environment Agency; **38** (b) Alan Band/Fox Photos/Getty Images, (t) Bettmann/Contributor via Getty Images; **39** (tl) Keystone-France\Gamma-Rapho via Getty Images, (br) Ed Brown/Alamy Stock Photo, (c) Steve Vidler/Alamy Stock Photo, (bl) Carolyn Clarke/Alamy Stock Photo, (t) JH Kuva/Alamy Stock Photo, (b) Lainey Morse; **40** MARK RALSTON/AFP/Getty Images; **42** (tr) Lexus UK/Barcroft Cars, (b) @ fflava/Instagram; **43** (t) Lexus UK/Barcroft Cars, (bl) © Psammophile, Wikimedia Commons // CC-BY-SA 3.0, (br) © Geomr, Wikimedia Commons // CC-BY-SA 3.0.; **44** (tl) Schumin Web Photo Licensing, (r) KENA BETANCUR/AFP/Getty Images, (bc) Stuart Dee via Getty Images; **44–45** (bkg) © Phongphan/Shutterstock.com; **45** (tl) Bettmann/Contributor via Getty Images, (r) Bettmann/Contributor via Getty Images; **46** (tr, bl) Faisal Magray/Cover Asia Press; **47** (t) VCG/VCG via Getty Images; **48** (tc) Ravikanth Kurma/Rex Shutterstock, (b) Fish caught by Ed Grant while fishing on the WANNA DO III. Photo taken by Doug Corbit; **49** (t) Ravikanth Kurma/Rex Shutterstock; **50** (cl, b) © wdeon/Shutterstock.com; **51** (tl) Fox Photos/Getty Images, (tr) Topical Press Agency/Getty Images, (cl, b) IJF BURNS UNIT/CATERS NEWS; **52–23** Hypnox Photography, Wittypixel Photography, Isometric Studios, Matthew Russell Boman, Colin Gray, Cody Augustine, Ren Murray; **54–55** (dp) Bill Bachman/Alamy Stock Photo; **56** (bl) Timothy Allen via Getty Images; **56–57** (dp) Timothy Allen via Getty Images; **58** (t) John Crowe/Alamy Stock Photo, (tc) Popperfoto/Getty Images, (b) REUTERS/Dinuka Liyanawatte; **59** Scott Beahan Shutterly Perfect Portraiture; **60** Catedral de Sal de Zipaquirá S. A SEM.; **61** REUTERS/Ahmad Masood; **62** (bl) Hemis/Alamy Stock Photo, (br) Kevin Frayer/Getty Images; **62–63** (bkg) Kevin Frayer/Getty Images; **63** (bl, br) Kevin Frayer/Getty Images; **64** (t) VINCENZO PINTO/AFP/Getty Images; **65** (tc) © National Geographic Creative/Alamy Stock Photo, (tr) © Neil Setchfield/Alamy Stock Photo, (b) © siete_vidas/Shutterstock.com; **66** (t) VCG/Getty Images, (br) VCG/VCG via Getty Images; **67** (b) © Jim Epler from San Diego, USA, Wikimedia Commons // CC-BY 2.0.; **68** (tl) © Lena Krasovska, Wikimedia Commons // CC-BY-SA 3.0, (tr) Pyotr Sivkov\TASS via Getty Images, (b) Courtesy of U.S. Department of Energy; **69** (t) © Alexander Blecher, blecher.info, Wikimedia Commons // CC-BY-SA 4.0.; **70** (l) VCG/VCG via Getty Images; **70–71** VCG/VCG via Getty Images; **72–73** (dp) Koichi Kamoshida/Getty Images; **73** (tr) ASSOCIATED PRESS; **74** (tl, cl, bl) Trevor Williams/Getty Images; **75** (tr, b) Richard Ellis/Getty Images; **76** (bkg, br, bl) STUART WALKER/Alamy Stock Photo; **77** Photos by Gregory Halili; **78** (t) Junko Kimura/Getty Images, (bl, br) © SWNS.com; **79** (tr) REUTERS/Sergio Perez, (b) ASSOCIATED PRESS; **80** (b) JTB MEDIA CREATION, Inc./Alamy Stock Photo; **80–81** (bkg) Martchan/Alamy Stock Photo; **81** (b) Martchan/Alamy Stock Photo; **82** (tl, bl) Atid Kiattisaksiri/LightRocket via Getty Images; **83** (t, cr) RINO SGORBANI/CATERS NEWS; **84** REUTERS/Stringer; **85** (t) WENN; **86** (bl, br) Elizabeth Harper/Barcroft Media; **86–87** (bkg) Elizabeth Harper/Barcroft Media; **87** (bl) Elizabeth Harper/Barcroft Media; **88** (cr, bl) Suzy Bennett/Alamy Stock Photo, (tl) Bill Bachman/Alamy Stock Photo; **89** (tr, c) The Asahi Shimbun via Getty Images, (bl) Arco Images GmbH/Alamy Stock Photo, (br) Cameron Davidson via Getty Images; **90** (tr) Ken Scicluna via Getty Images; **90–91** (dp) ASSOCIATED PRESS; **92–93** (dp) FLPA/Alamy Stock Photo; **94** (t) Oliver Bunic/Bloomberg via Getty Images, (bl) DANNY GOODDING/ CATERS NEWS; **95** Mike Dexter/Barcroft Media; **96–97** (b) Laurentiu Garofeanu/Barcroft; **97** (tr) Laurentiu Garofeanu/Barcroft; **98–99** Sumaya Hisham/Corbis via Getty Images; **100** (tr) ANAS HAMDANI/CATERS NEWS, (b) ECO SUPARMAN/CATERS NEWS; **101** (tr) Transcendental Graphics/Getty Images, (c) Mark Rucker/Transcendental Graphics, Getty Images, (bl) Joe Pepler/REX/Shutterstock; **102–103** © Yoji Okata/Nature Production/Minden Pictures; **104** (tl) Sijori Images/Barcroft India via Getty Images, (tr) REUTERS/Sukree Sukplang, (bl) YASUYOSHI CHIBA/AFP/Getty Images; **105** (bl) Photographer: Dikathola Kedikilwe, Project affiliations: UNSW, Taronga Conservation Society Australia and Botswana Predator Conservation Trust, (br) Photographer: Ben Yexley, Project affiliations: UNSW, Taronga Conservation Society Australia and Botswana Predator Conservation Trust; **106** (t) BRYAN SNYDER/ CATERS NEWS, (b) FLPA/Alamy Stock Photo; **107** Frans Lemmens via Getty Images; **108** (bl) © MYN/John Tiddy/NPL/Minden Pictures, (br) The Asahi Shimbun via Getty Images; **109** Abhimanyu singh Rajvi/Barcroft Media; **110** (tr) MyLoupe/UIG via Getty Images, (c) Whitney Hayward/Portland Press Herald via Getty Images, (b) Scott Ramsay/Barcroft Media; **111** (tl) CHARLIE LYNAM/CATERS NEWS, (tr) Jeremy Durkin/REX/Shutterstock, (c) ADRIAN WARREN/ARDEA/CATERS NEWS, (cr) MIKEY JONES/CATERS NEWS, (b) ASSOCIATED PRESS; **112** (bl) AFP/Getty Images/Kenting National Park Headquarters; **113** (t) Duncan McMorrin/Barcroft Images, (br) Caters News/ Gabriela Franzoi Dri; **114** (t) Courtesy of Janice Savage, (b) © Zachary Culpin/Solent News & Photo Agency; **115** (t) Andrew Mason/Solent News/REX/Shutterstock, (b) ASSOCIATED PRESS; **116–117** VCG/VCG via Getty Images; **117** (tr) David Jones/PA Archive/Press Association Images; **118** (br) Barcroft USA/Getty Images; **119** (tl) Merlin D. Tuttle/Science Source, (br) frans lemmens/Alamy Stock Photo; **120** (tr) Xu xiangdong - Imaginechina, (bl) VENICE BEACH FREAKSHOW/CATERS; **121** (tl) © Yamamoto Noriaki/Nature Production/Minden Pictures, (tr) © Malcolm Schuyl/FLPA/Minden Pictures; **122** (bc) Sinar Sakti Images/Barcroft Media; **122–123** (t) Fabrizio Proietto/Alamy Stock Photo; **123** (b) Pictures - Coyote Peterson, Photo Credit - Mark Laivins, Company Credit - Brave Wilderness; **124** (t) CATERS NEWS, (bl) RuaridhConnellan/Barcroft Media; **125** MATHEW WALLACE/CATERS NEWS; **126** (tl) Jeff Cremer/@JCremerPhoto, (br) CATERS NEWS; **127** ASSOCIATED PRESS; **128** (tr) © Pete Oxford/Minden Pictures; **129** (t) © Pete Oxford/Minden Pictures, (bl) TOM MOSES/MERCURY PRESS; **130** (tl) Jeremy Durkin/REX/Shutterstock, (bc) Terry O'Neill/Getty Images, (bl) Kevin Mazur/WireImage; **131** (sp, br) 28 LAB/CATERS NEWS; **132–133** (dp) Aflo Co. Ltd./Alamy Stock Photo; **134** (b) © Britt Reints, Flickr Creative Commons // CC-BY 2.0, (cl) © Dan Soto, Wikimedia Commons // CC-BY-SA 3.0.; **135** (tl) Photos 12/Alamy Stock Photo, (tr) Tanto Yensen/Solent News/REX/Shutterstock; **136** (tl) Frank Augstein/AP/REX/Shutterstock, (b) TORU YAMANAKA/AFP/Getty Images; **136–137** (tc) Frank Augstein/AP/REX/Shutterstock; **137** (tr) Frank Augstein/AP/REX/Shutterstock, (b) Westend61 GmbH/Alamy Stock Photo; **138** (l) dinotomic (Instagram) atomiccircus (Facebook); **139** (tr) B Christopher/Alamy Stock Photo, (c) EPA European Pressphoto Agency b.v./Alamy Stock Photo, (br) REUTERS/Kim Kyung-Hoon; **140** (t) Historic Collection/Alamy Stock Photo, (b) All Photos - Sculpture + Concept Joseph Reginella; **141** (sp) Noah Scalin (NoahScalin.com); **142–143** Valeriano Fatica - Fruit Carver, www.valerianofatica.com YouTube = Valeriano Fatica, Facebook Page = Valeriano Fatica, Instagram = Valeriano Fatica; **144** (bl) Jessica Siskin/ @mister_krisp; **145** (b) Navid Baraty; **146** (tl) Akio Kon/Bloomberg via Getty Images, (tc) Courtesy of John Coniglio, (c) Carissa Grall of Rogue Siren Studios, (bl) CATERS NEWS, (br) © Penny Stamp; **147** (tr) REUTERS/Alamy Stock Photo, (c) Aflo Co. Ltd./Alamy Stock Photo, (bl) Aflo Co. Ltd./Alamy Stock Photo; **148** (tl) Matt Cardy/Getty Images; **149** (c) Joe Kohen/WireImage, (bl) Yana Paskova/Getty Images, (br) Taylor Hill/Getty Images; **150** Brad Lawrence of the company Black Light Visuals (BLVisuals); **151** (t) MARIA CALLS/AFP/Getty Images, (b) Collection Christophel/Alamy Stock Photo; **152** (t) ASSOCIATED PRESS, (bl) Supplied by WENN.com; **153** (tl) ASSOCIATED PRESS, (tr) Associated Press, (b) ALTON TOWERS PRESS OFFICE/CATERS NEWS; **154** (tr) Dan Leeth/Alamy Stock Photo; **154–155** Sabrina Sieck, thanks to John Preble of the Abita Mystery House, (bkg) Philip Scalia/Alamy Stock Photo; **156** (b) JIJI PRESS/AFP/Getty Images, (t) Images courtesy of Twelve South; **157** (t, cl) VLADIMIR MULDER/CATERS NEWS, (br) Ribs & Burgers, @ribsandburgers; **158–159** © 2015 Andy Davies/HR Giger Museum; **160** (t) REUTERS/Toru Hanai; **161** VCG/VCG via Getty Images; **162** (tr) Frazer Harrison/Getty Images New York for Fashion Week: The Shows, (cl) Philip Wolmuth/Alamy Stock Photo, (cb) VOLODYMYR SHUVAYEV/AFP/Getty Images; **163** Evan Wondolowski (www.theartofe.com); **164** (tl) ASSOCIATED PRESS, (br) Chien-Chu Lee/Rex Shutterstock; **165** (tr) Maitree Siriboon in association with Thaillywood Artist Residency; **166** (tc, c) WENN; **167** (tr) DIMITAR DILKOFF,NIKOLAY DOYCHINOV/AFP/Getty Images; **168** (tc) Courtesy of Paqui Chips, (bl) VCG/VCG via Getty Images; **169** (t, tr) © Crawley New/ SWNS.com, (b) Li Fuhua/VCG via Getty Images, (br) VCG/VCG via Getty Images; **170-171** (dp) MIKOLAJ MIKOLAJCZJK/BARTOSZ OSTALOWSKI/CATERS NEWS; **172–173** Courtesy of RocketNews24; **174** Imaginechina; **175** (tr) Diana Lepe Spezzia, (b) Annika Elisabeth Luis, Facebook.com/elisabethluiseannika; **176** Public Domain {{PD-US}} Powelson, 58 State St, Rochester, NY; **177** Public Domain {{PD-US}} Beinecke Rare Book and Manuscript Library; **178** (t) MANJUNATH KIRAN/AFP/Getty Images, (b) VCG/VCG via Getty Images; **179** CATERS NEWS; **182** (tl) CATERS NEWS, (b) FREDERIC J. BROWN/AFP/Getty Images; **183** (sp) Cover Asia Press/Faisal Magray; **185** (sp) Public Domain {{PD-US}} Library of Congress Prints and Photographs Division Washington, D.C. 20540 USA http://hdl.loc.gov/loc.pnp/pp.print, (bl) Public Domain {{PD-US}} Jessie Tarbox Beals, (br) Public Domain {{PD-US}} The South Carolina Library, University of South Carolina, Colimbia, S.C. in The Pygmy in the Zoo; **186** (b) Zhou Min/VCG via Getty Images; **187** (t) CATERS NEWS; **188** (tl) Gibsons of Scilly, (tr, br) Courtesy of Stein Hoff, (bl) Photo by Roland Gavrilov; **188–189** (bkg) Courtesy of Stein Hoff; **189** (tl) Elisabeth Hoff, (tr, br) Courtesy of Stein Hoff; **190** MIKOLAJ MIKOLAJCZJK/BARTOSZ OSTALOWSKI/CATERS NEWS; **191** (tr, c) Mustafa Najafizada/ Cover Asia Press, (br) ASSOCIATED PRESS; **192** (c, cr, b) CATERS; **193** (tl, tr) CATERS, (b) John Ferraro; **194** (t) VCG/VCG via Getty Images; **195** (b) MAHMUD HAMS/AFP/Getty Images; **196** (tl) CATERS NEWS, (tr) Ruaridh Connellan/Barcroft USA, (b) REUTERS/Chris Helgren; **197** (tr, c) Donald Morrison; **198** (bl) BRIANNA WORTHY/CATERS NEWS; **200** (t) STRDEL/AFP/Getty Images, (b) Courtesy of Julie Mattes; **201** (r) Dinesh Dubey/Barcroft Media; **202** (tr, b) Shariq Allaqaband/ Cover Asia Press; **203** (br) CATERS NEWS; **204–205** (b) Sony Ramany/NurPhoto/REX/Shutterstock; **205** (tr) ANIL MADHAVAN/COVER ASIA PRESS, (bl) SAM JAHAN/AFP/Getty Images; **206** (dp) Claudio Sieber/Barcroft Media; **208–209** (dp) Kei Nomiyama/Barcroft Media; **210** (t) Gregory Pleau/www.gregorypleau.com via Getty Images, (b) REUTERS/Yves Herman; **211** (cl, bl) REUTERS/Yves Herman; **212–213** Leslie Woodruff Kingston; **214** (t) © Wikimedia Commons // CC-BY 4.0, Wellcome Library, London. Wellcome Images images@wellcome.ac.uk http://wellcomeimages.org Horatio Robley, seated with his collection of severed heads 1895 Published: 1895, (b) Stunt Freaks Team/Barcroft Cars; **215** (tl) epa european pressphoto agency b.v./Alamy Stock Photo, (tr) REUTERS/Alamy Stock Photo, (br) Stunt Freaks Team/Barcroft Cars; **216** (b) WF Sihardian/Barcroft Media; **216–217** (t) Raymond Walsh (www.manonthelam.com); **218** (t) Public Domain {{PD-US}} NASA, (b) Public Domain {{PD-US}} NASA/U.S. Customs and Border Patrol (retrieved from space.com); **219** (tr) Xinhua, (b) Imaginechina; **220** (t, b) Claudio Sieber/Barcroft Media; **221** (sp) Claudio Sieber/Barcroft Media; **222** (t) General Photographic Agency/Getty Images, (b) John Normile/Getty Images; **223** (tl) Anthony Di Lauro, (bl) Chester Voyage/Alamy Stock Photo, (br) Chester Voyage/Alamy Stock Photo; **224** (tc) Fairfax Media NZ/The Press, (bl) © Tom Maddick/Newsteam/SWNS Group; 224–225 (c) © Tom Maddick/Newsteam/SWNS Group; **225** (tr) Matt Cardy/Getty Images, (br) © Tom Maddick/Newsteam/SWNS Group; **226** (tl) Topical Press Agency/Getty Images, (br) B C Parade/Getty Images; **227** (t) Bettmann/Contributor via Getty Images, (cl) Alfred Eisenstaedt/The LIFE Picture Collection/Getty Images, (br) L. C. Buckley/Fox Photos/Getty Images; **230** (br) © Public Domain {{PD-US}} The Jon B. Lovelace Collection of California Photographs in Carol M. Highsmith's America Project, Library of Congress, Prints and Photographs Division; **230–231** (dp) © taylorandayumi, Wikimedia Commons // CC-BY 2.0; **231** (tr) © Tricia Savino, Wikimedia Commons // CC-BY-SA 4.0; **232** (tr) Universal History Archive/UIG via Getty Images, (l) Public Domain CC0 1.0 Universal (CC0 1.0): Purchase, Joseph Pulitzer Bequest, 1918; **233** (t) Public Domain {{PD-US}} 1880 Yoshitoshi painting, (tr) © PHGCOM, Wikimedia Commons // CC-BY-SA 3.0. Source: Own work, photographed at Japan Currency Museum, (bl) World History Archive/Alamy Stock Photo, (br) Chronicle/Alamy Stock Photo; **234** (tl) © age fotostock/Alamy Stock Photo, (bl) © Samuraiantiqueworld, Wikimedia Commons // CC-BY-SA 3.0, (br) JTB Photo/UIG via Getty Images; **235** (tr) Public Domain {{PD-US}} Bequest of Robert S. Shaull, 1990. Artist:; Toyohara Chikanobu (1838–1912), (b) Public Domain {{PD-US}} artsanddesignsjapan.com. Artist: Toyohara Chikanobu (1838–1912).; **236** (tl) © Cole Shatto, Wikimedia Commons // CC-BY-SA 3.0, (tr) JORGE UZON/AFP/Getty Images, (cr) OMAR TORRES/AFP/Getty Images, (bl) Ulet Ifansasti/Getty Images; **237** (t, br) © John Downer Productions ; **238** (bl) MADAREE TOHLALA/AFP/Getty Images; **238–239** (dp) MADAREE TOHLALA/AFP/Getty Images; **240** (tl) Kim Goodwin, (bl) ASSOCIATED PRESS; **241** (tl, tr) Jimmy George/Barcroft Media; **242** (tr) © Public Domain {{PD-US}} Photographs of Frank R. Snyder Collection, Miami University Archives, Oxford, Ohio, (b) Gerhard Riebicke/ullstein bild via Getty Images; **243** (bl) Bettmann/Contributor via Getty Images; **244–245** (dp) Cherry Point Farm; **Master Graphics** Exhibit Tags: © Oil and Gas Photographer/Shutterstock.com, © Elovich/Shutterstock.com; **Infographics** Icons made by Freepick, MadebyOliver, and Gregor Cresnor from www.flaticon.com; Created by Freepik; icons8.com

Key: t = top, b = bottom, c = center, l = left, r = right, sp = single page, dp = double page, bkg = background

All other photos are from Ripley Entertainment Inc. Every attempt has been made to acknowledge correctly and contact copyright holders and we apologize in advance for any unintentional errors or omissions, which will be corrected in future editions.

CONNECT WITH RIPLEY'S ONLINE OR IN PERSON

31 ZANY LOCATIONS

There are 31 incredible Ripley's Believe It or Not! Odditoriums all around the world, where you can experience our strange and spectacular collection and shatter your senses again and again!

Amsterdam THE NETHERLANDS
Atlantic City NEW JERSEY
Baltimore MARYLAND
Blackpool ENGLAND
Branson MISSOURI
Cavendish P.E.I., CANADA
Copenhagen DENMARK
Gatlinburg TENNESSEE
Genting Highlands MALAYSIA
Grand Prairie TEXAS
Guadalajara MEXICO
Hollywood CALIFORNIA
Jeju Island KOREA
Key West FLORIDA
London ENGLAND
Mexico City MEXICO
Myrtle Beach SOUTH CAROLINA
New York City NEW YORK
Newport OREGON
Niagara Falls ONTARIO, CANADA
Ocean City MARYLAND
Orlando FLORIDA
Panama City Beach FLORIDA
Pattaya THAILAND
San Antonio TEXAS
San Francisco CALIFORNIA
St. Augustine FLORIDA
Surfers Paradise AUSTRALIA
Veracruz MEXICO
Williamsburg VIRGINIA
Wisconsin Dells WISCONSIN

Stop by our website daily for new stories, photos, contests, and more! **WWW.RIPLEYS.COM**

Don't forget to connect with us on social media for a daily dose of the weird and the wonderful.

/RipleysBelieveItOrNot @Ripleys youtube.com/Ripleys @RipleysOdditorium

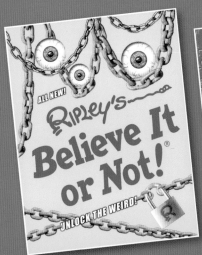

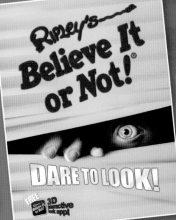

ABC's and 123's

Share some silliness and fun as little ones learn their ABC's and 123's. Filled with wacky, wonderful characters and sweet illustrations, they'll enjoy counting and saying their alphabet again and again!

FUN FACTS & SILLY STORIES

Filled with wacky stories and colorful images of crazy animals, incredible talents, amazing people, and goofy events, readers will have a hard time putting these books down!

THE MANE EVENT!

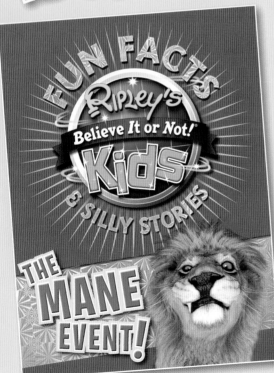

Featuring brand new Believe It or Not! stories, puzzles, and games, Ripley's fans are guaranteed to giggle and gasp their way through *Fun Facts & Silly Stories: The Mane Event!* Other titles in this series: *The Big One!, One Zany Day!,* and *Odd Around the World!*